T0275886

Preserving the Promise

Preserving the Promise
Improving the Culture of Biotech Investment

Scott Dessain, MD, PhD
Associate Professor
Lankenau Institute for Medical Research
Wynnewood, PA, USA

Scott E. Fishman, MA
President
Ethos LifeScience Advisors
Doylestown, PA, USA

ELSEVIER

AMSTERDAM • BOSTON • HEIDELBERG • LONDON
NEW YORK • OXFORD • PARIS • SAN DIEGO
SAN FRANCISCO • SINGAPORE • SYDNEY • TOKYO

Academic Press is an imprint of Elsevier

Academic Press is an imprint of Elsevier
125 London Wall, London EC2Y 5AS, United Kingdom
525 B Street, Suite 1800, San Diego, CA 92101-4495, United States
50 Hampshire Street, 5th Floor, Cambridge, MA 02139, United States
The Boulevard, Langford Lane, Kidlington, Oxford OX5 1GB, United Kingdom

British Library Cataloguing-in-Publication Data
A catalogue record for this book is available from the British Library

Library of Congress Cataloging-in-Publication Data
A catalog record for this book is available from the Library of Congress

ISBN: 978-0-12-809216-3

For Information on all Academic Press publications
visit our website at https://www.elsevier.com

Working together
to grow libraries in
developing countries

www.elsevier.com • www.bookaid.org

Publisher: Mica Haley
Acquisition Editor: Kristine Jones
Editorial Project Manager: Molly McLaughlin
Production Project Manager: Edward Taylor
Designer: Victoria Pearson

Typeset by MPS Limited, Chennai, India

Contents

Translation Gap 2
Good Innovation Is Not Always a Good Investment

Translation Gap 3
Technology Transfer Wastes Money and Innovation

Epilogue

Preface

We'd like one hundred thousand dollars.

That is where the events leading to this book started, nine years ago. We didn't know each other at the time, but had been introduced by a business development guy who knew one of us was a potential investor and the other had a biotech start-up that needed money.

The transaction never happened, for a variety of reasons: the ask was too high, one of us wanted to be involved in managing the company and the other just wanted a check, the technology didn't have a target yet—and yes, we almost forgot, the stock market had experienced the worst crash since 1929 just the day before.

Fast-forward 4 years to a panel discussion called the Entrepreneur's On Ramp, when we found ourselves together again at the speaker's table. We're both interested in medicine, and we think new product development should be in service to patients, with finance the byproduct rather than the primary driver. We were both frustrated with seeing lousy, worthless (except in a financial sense) ideas get funded, and critical, transformative, life-saving ones get shelved for want of funding.

So we decided to write a book about it.

There are lots of books about "smart" investing. There are self-affirming autobiographies of people who have done really well providing capital for growing companies. And there are books about the arcane technical details of the deal. But no one has really deconstructed the early-stage, pre-venture capital commercialization process, to find out why so many good technologies can't get the support they need to reach the clinic. Nor has there been a thorough examination of all the friction in the system: why it's so difficult to get stuff out of the university, why entrepreneurs have to spend a huge amount of their time chasing the next round of funding instead of on development, why at any given time biotech is either the *belle du jour* or the scary witch everyone runs away from, why a toxic mix of macroeconomics and investor peccadillos determine whether you and I are going to get cured of cancer in 20 years, and why Angels have passively bought into the venture capital premise that if you throw enough stuff at the wall some of it will stick.

These are some of the difficult questions we've wrestled with and tried to answer with this book. We believe in the intrinsic value of innovation, particularly as it relates to healthcare, and our arguments proceed from that basis. Big dreams should have the opportunity to be realized. The process should be infused with as much adventure as pain. There are good reasons Angels invest in ultra-high-risk propositions like biotechnology, that transcend simple calculations of return on investment. It all comes down to the idea that solving the mysteries of why our bodies malfunction is a worthwhile thing to do.

We're sure some of our ideas will be challenged. Capable investors will point to past successes as evidence that the system works, and understate the influence of being in the right place at the right time. The few technology transfer offices that are enjoying the fruits of enormous payoffs will say that all is well in the world of moving technology from the lab to the clinic. Founders with billion dollar enterprises will explain how it's just a matter of being unremittingly clever and capable. That's all true, but to pluck a concept from the political world, these are really the one-percenters. Most investors in therapeutics companies lose their shirts. Most technology transfer offices struggle with restrictive annual budgets and balky faculty, chasing upfront payments and counting the number of executed deals to prove their value to the university. Most founders end up disappointed after a grueling, painful experience, in a development and financing landscape that has come to be known as the Valley of Death because so many innovations die trying to cross it.

It doesn't have to be this way. There are better ways to make decisions, to align interests, and to find common cause in the mutually compelling goals of making people better and making lots of money. The expression "doing well by doing good" comes to mind, and there's a lot more to it than a rationalization for accumulating wealth. It's really what this book reaches for. Is it the stars? Maybe, if you're the one whose illness gets cured a couple of decades from now because something didn't get shelved for the wrong reasons. More likely, it's advancing the possibility of everyone in early-stage biotech development doing better, in an environment that's more realistic, more satisfying, and financially and societally more productive. We understand it's not possible to get there with grandiose prescriptions for doing the "right" thing. We're all motivated by self-interest and more amenable to change when there's something in it for us, and we've tried to explain what that something is.

So we've maintained the vision that prompted our book in the first place, but pulled and tugged and looked under the carpet to figure out why things aren't working better than they are and to come up with realistic prescriptions for better outcomes—that also happen to be fulfilling for those involved. We invite you to share our journey over these pages, and present *Preserving the Promise* as a hopeful step in stimulating an important discussion.

Scott Fishman and Scott Dessain

Acknowledgments

Scott Dessain:

I would like to share my gratitude for George Prendergast, for encouraging this project while I should have been writing grants and papers; to Immunome founders Greg Licholai and George Hobbs, for initiating me in the world of biotech and providing guidance over the years; to the Immunome investors and team who shared their wisdom and experience over the years, especially Barbara Schilberg, Marie Lindner, Michael Widlitz, Tim Pelura, Joan Lau, Jane Hollingsworth, Shawn Bridy, Kate Shay, Richard Pigossi, Jonathon Lawrie, Phil Wagenheim, Michael Rapoport (Rapp), and especially Wistar Morris, who also motivated me by giving me a copy of his own book about investing; to Todd Lincoln, who introduced me to Scott Fishman and the first investors to support Immunome; to my friends and advisors during my Whitehead Institute years, including Bob Weinberg, Tom Ittelson, Aaron Schwartz, Pat Granahan, and Cindy Bayley; to Don Drakeman, Steven Ries, Martina Molsbergen, Christine Cavalier and Michael Zasloff for wisdom and inspiration; to the individuals who gave their time for interviews, whether we used their stories or not; to the Planet Money podcast; and to my gentle canine writing companions, Buddy and Mikey. Mostly, I would like to thank my family, Tracey, Carly, and Jena for their love and support, and my late mother, Leslie Dessain, who strongly encouraged this project from the beginning.

Scott Fishman:

This book reflects a lifetime filled with professional guidance and friend-ships. I am thankful most recently, for insight and advice on topics in the book, from Dora Mitchell, Michael Hagy, Greg Harriman, Heather Steinman, Oye Olukotun, David Zuzga, Davood Tashayyod, Jenn Hartt, and Pitou Devgon. For their friendship and wisdom over the years, my heartfelt appreciation goes to Janna Walsh, Beverly Reid, Dick Beltramini, Therese Flaherty, Laura La Rosa, Mary Ann Sarao, and Andrew Aprill. I am obliged for sage advice to many of those already acknowledged by my coauthor, and to colleagues too numerous to mention at Research by Design, the University of Pennsylvania, Philadelphia University, and Robin Hood Ventures. I've learned much of what is really important in life from Pearl Roth, who knows a thing or two after 93 years and is the finest role model I can imagine. My special thanks go to Mark Dimor, a lifelong friend who has always been my honest guide to keeping the world in perspective. Love and thanks to my wife Kate Fishman, who has been my vital sounding board for ideas and language, and a tireless cheerleader despite (or because of) my eccentricities. And last but never least, bottomless thanks to my children Katie and Sarah, who make all things worthwhile.

· We both want to thank the outstanding editorial team at Academic Press/ Elsevier: Kristine M. Jones, who first saw the promise in the book; Molly M. McLaughlin and Edward Taylor, who provided thoughtful and responsive project management; Melissa Read, for the uncelebrated task of copy editing; and Ofelia Chernock, for her expertise with book design and marketing strategy.

Innovation Meets
the Translation Gap

Chapter 1

Stop the Madness and Cure Something

You and thousands of runners have just finished a Mother's Day 10K road race to support breast cancer research. You do so expecting that the money you've raised will ultimately lead to new treatments, for the benefit of people you love. And that is undoubtedly the intent of most fundraising efforts, and a reasonable expectation for the outcome. How, then, would you feel if we told you that the science supported by those funds, before it ever gets a shot at helping anybody, will need to enter a so-called "Valley of Death" (VoD) from which it is highly unlikely to emerge in the form of a new drug? What if we added that the likelihood of success is only tangentially a function of whether or not the science has tremendous promise for a cure? Or that the decisions around whether promising science makes it out of the VoD are made mostly by investors whose interest in financial return generally trumps the clinical implications, and for whom the discovery is simply one hand in a high-stakes gamble? Would you be worried about whether you had made a difference, or disappointed, scratching your head that all of that scientific effort might not help anyone ... because of a *financial* objective? That seems probable. We share those frustrations, and set out a case here for making things better.

We are accustomed to a life dizzy with innovation, so we expect that raising money for a cure will make a difference. We believe in the mythology of the scientist, the immense power of the human mind to understand the smallest details of our genetic makeup, to wipe out an infectious disease, to engineer a magic bullet for our cancers, to figure out what has gone wrong with our bodies and make it better.

And the money we raise does go to the right places initially, to support the work of the scientists and physicians at our universities and nonprofit research institutes. The beating heart of the process, perpetually sought after yet rarely achieved, is a "eureka" moment. Teams of scientists find the reward for years of work in a unitary discovery: one true fact about nature, previously unknown, that suddenly crystallizes dozens of questions about a disease into a clear path to the clinic. Breaking nature's code is an intricate process, driven by curiosity,

Preserving the Promise. DOI: http://dx.doi.org/10.1016/B978-0-12-809216-3.00001-4

informed by intuition and made real by brute force. The aphorism is true that "Nature doesn't give up her secrets easily."

We can cite a number of examples, probably familiar, where scientific breakthroughs translated into medicine that changed the world. One: the discovery that the poliomyelitis virus could be inactivated in a way that would make it safe to give to healthy children, but still induce a lifelong immunity to the virus. Eradication of the scourge of polio from industrialized society was rapidly achieved, and eradication of the virus from the planet may be in its final stages. Two: the discovery that during a heart attack, clots that form in the small blood vessels in the heart can be dissolved with a bacterial protein, clearing the channels for blood to return and preventing irreversible destruction of the heart muscle. Another: the discovery that AIDS is caused by a retrovirus, unlocking the identification of proteins that can be inhibited by a cocktail of anti-retroviral drugs for a lifetime. And more recently: the discovery that an immune cell can be programmed to kill tumor cells, so that a T cell could be taken from the blood of a young girl with leukemia, genetically modified, and given back, where it beat her cancer into a complete remission. The modern drug development paradigm rests squarely on the ability to capitalize on scientific discovery, to channel the "Eureka" moment into a life-saving product.

Yet, these discoveries are usually a long way from being able to help patients. It is one thing to shrink a tumor in a mouse, it is another to translate that finding into a cure for human patients. Robert Weinberg and his colleagues first published the discovery of the HER2/neu protein, an important target for breast cancer therapy, in 1982, and the discovery that cancer cells in mice could be killed with a monoclonal antibody that binds HER2/neu in 1986. Yet it wasn't until 12 years later, in 1998, that the drug targeting it, trastuzumab, was approved for use in breast cancer patients.

Another problem is that many seminal discoveries are *platforms*, new methods of finding something that could be a cure, that aren't realized yet. They are literally hundreds of millions of dollars and years of work away from making a difference. Most of this work of converting a platform to a therapeutic cannot be done within the usual venue of discovery, a university lab. Academics are rewarded for the *basic science* of revealing nature's secrets, not for the risky process of making a drug and testing it in patients. Public grants often support basic science but preclude commercial development, and funding is simply not available at the level required for noncommercial entities to make and market their own drugs. Thus, technologies need to exit the academic environment to begin clinical development.

At some point in their development, promising discoveries may be acquired by large pharmaceutical and biotechnology companies, which envelop them in enormous drug development ecosystems that push them toward the clinic. There's a lot of noise about this, particularly of late, as biotech assets have been purchased from early stage companies at fairly staggering prices. This is the end game for most start-ups and the early investors who fund them. But, it's almost always a long road to get to this kind of exit. The capacity and range of pharma interests is focused by economic rather than medical imperatives, and most of these discoveries have to make it on their own for a very long time, nurtured by a start-up that must continually seek additional investment. The most financially promising, and/or maybe those championed by the most influential and well-connected scientists, find support from venture capital, and consume tens of millions of dollars evolving the discovery into something that has enough scientific and clinical support to interest a big biotech or Big Pharma buyer.

The vast majority of discoveries, even some of those that make the headlines, do not leave the university with a silver spoon in their mouths. Shepherded by their founders, separated from their university homes, they enter the VoD. The purpose of the process that has come to be known as the VoD is to connect an invention with the requisite resources to move it along the development path. The process for how those resources are gathered and used, or misused, in nurturing these discoveries is the focus of this book.

We define the beginning of the VoD as the moment a provisional patent is filed for a discovery by a university, and the end as when the intellectual property identified in that patent has become a realized invention, an animal-tested molecule that can be submitted to the US Food and Drug Administration (FDA) for approval of testing in humans. At that point, money is much easier to come by and the technology will live or die on the basis of its merits: is it safe, does it work, does it produce outcomes better than existing alternatives, and most of all, is it a clinical proposition with the potential to generate substantial marketplace value?

A typical biotech start-up in the VoD is a semicohesive band that includes an inventor, an entrepreneur, and early advocates and financial supporters. There is a struggle to raise money to achieve scientific milestones. Scientific success enables additional money to be raised, which supports more discovery, in a leap-frog game of alternating scientific and financial risk. The most treacherous part of the VoD is the earliest, inhabited by companies that have reached their inception as commercial entities, but have yet to generate venture capital or pharma support. They may be funded by public money, such as grants from the National Institutes of Health, but these are often limited in scope and almost always hard to come by. The most important supporters of these early companies in the VoD are often Angel Investors, individuals with capital to deploy either individually or in groups. Angel investing is a high-risk proposition, sometimes capricious in its interests, and susceptible to investment fads and macroeconomic shifts. There are simply not enough of these people or groups to support all the potentially worthwhile discoveries in the VoD, and there is a formal and unforgiving winnowing process that inevitably results in the death of worthwhile innovations and, for reasons of financial rather than clinical potential, the progression of worthless ones.

The conventional mechanisms for investing in technology and new companies are incompatible, fundamentally, with the optimal means for financing early stage technologies and bringing them to the clinic. When biotechnology began in the 1980s and surged into the 1990s, money was flowing freely and inefficiencies in the business model could be easily rationalized since the output-to-input ratio appeared to reflect a limitless upward trend line. Unfortunately, since the economy tanked in 2008, the investors and strategic partners all abrogated their responsibilities for nurturing technologies to the false promise of de-risking and operational efficiency. Everyone adopted a silo mentality, and much of the capital—the wind in the sails of development—either disappeared from the system or became much more difficult to access.

There's been another surge and (likely) bust cycle in the interim. The fundamental problems of financially-, rather than clinically driven, development, and the mismatch of available capital to potential opportunities persist. The result is that most biomedical innovations will never survive the journey from the laboratory bench to the patient bedside. The process for early stage financing and development, which has never worked very efficiently, is now worse than it has ever been, even as slashed pharmaceutical industry research investment has made it even more important that these early technologies survive. Biomedical science has yielded transformational discoveries: the complete human genome sequence, RNA interference, genome editing with CRISPR-Cas9, and the fields of genomics and proteomics, as well as enhanced tools for adapting the natural healing processes of stem cells and the immune system. What if these discoveries were to die in the VoD?

The problem implicit in this is what we call the *Translation Gap*, three systemic pitfalls that doom most of what we produce:

1. *Universities don't make what companies need.* Science is produced to a different standard than is needed for commercialization. Its emphasis is on innovation rather than the rigorous validation and proof-of-concept needed for uptake by investors and pharma. Patenting early technologies forces them into the VoD before they are ready to support the commercialization process.
2. *Good innovation is not always a good investment.* The value of a discovery as an investment does not correlate with its level of innovation or clinical value. Many of our best technologies die because they don't make sense as an investment to Angel and other early investors.
3. *Technology transfer wastes money and innovation.* The process of transferring technologies from non-profit research institutions to the for-profit VoD is poorly conceived and inconsistent. Confusion over conflict-of-interest policies, costly licensing practices, and difficulties collaborating after licenses have been executed all impose a substantial financial burden on the system that is essentially a tax on innovation. Time wasted by administrative process harms patients and reduces Return on Investment (ROI).

We considered whether our definition of the Translation Gap should include the fact that the system can only support a limited number of drugs, far fewer than the possibilities created by our university researchers, and that our lack of investment in them is wasted opportunity. This is certainly the case, but simply saying that the system needs more money is uncreative and likely doomed to fail, because without fixing the Translation Gap, much of the increased money would be wasted anyway. The challenge is to look within the Translation Gap to find solutions that can be implemented through better efficiency, collaboration, and synergistic activities. Understanding how the Translation Gap operates, and what frequently goes wrong, reveals solutions that will produce better results for everyone involved, from inventors, to universities, entrepreneurs, doctors, patients, and even to Wall Street.

Chapter 2

Into the Valley of Death

Nobody is fully auditing the entire scope of start-up activity in the Valley of Death (VoD), but it's clearly extensive. Companies arrive there by something of a funnel, which for universities is mediated by Technology Transfer Officers. The Association of University Technology Managers (AUTM) is a nonprofit organization of these professionals, who essentially act as conduits between scientists/inventors and commercialization initiatives in the VoD. A recent AUTM survey of technology transfer by academic institutions reported 914 companies started in FY 2014, up from 818 started in FY 2013, and a total of 4688 start-ups in operation at the end of the year [1], reflecting a continuing upward trend [2]. Brady Hugett, the Business Editor at the industry journal *Nature Biotechnology*, surveyed top institutions and estimated that roughly 63% of academic start-ups are in the life sciences [3]. This would translate to about 1091 new biotechnology start-ups in the 2013–14 period for just the 191 institutions that responded to the AUTM survey (of 302 queried).

Perhaps a more comprehensive view is held by Dr. Jeffrey Sohl, who has directed the Center for Venture Research (CVR) at University of New Hampshire for over 20 years. The CVR was founded by Dr. William Wetzel, the first person to use the term "Angel" to describe investors in early stage companies. The 2014 CVR report estimated that 7780 biotechnology ventures received Angel funding in 2013 [4]. This is a substantial underestimate according to Dr. Sohl, as only 29% of the Angels and Angel groups responded to his request for information: "Nobody has [a clear sense] about what is going on. I'm sure we're way under" [5].

Each of these ventures carries the creativity, aspirations, and labor of academic scientists, and most ride on a discovery powerful enough to find advocates to carry it toward, if not into, the VoD. But what do they face?

In the 1990s through the early 2000s, the best of these companies could have had a reasonable chance of coming into the VoD with the support of Venture Capital firms (VCs), which amass large funds of institutional money that they invest in early stage companies. In biotechnology, these funds are typically used to create a lead drug and test it in patients. VCs get their money back when the company they

Preserving the Promise. DOI: http://dx.doi.org/10.1016/B978-0-12-809216-3.00002-6

9

support is acquired by a pharmaceutical company (Big Pharma) or sells shares on the stock market in an Initial Public Offering (IPO). Many of the early investments made by VCs in the heady early years of biotechnology did not pay off, and the economic crash in 2008 sent investors running for shelter—and rather definitively in directions other than healthcare. Biotechnology VC activity has seen a dramatic upsurge in the past 24–36 months, but that's the tail end of development efforts that started a decade or more ago, not the result of an improved VoD.

Don Drakeman is a cofounder and former CEO of Medarex, a monoclonal antibody (mAb) company that was sold to Bristol Myers Squibb in 2009 for $2.1 billion. Under Drakeman's leadership, Medarex created the breakthrough immunotherapy drug for melanoma, called ipilimumab, which was launched in 2011 and had 1-year sales of $706 million, as well as nivolumab, the ground-breaking immunomodulator drug which, at the time of writing, has received Food and Drug Administration (FDA) approval for treatment of melanoma, non small cell lung cancer, and kidney cancer. He joined the top-tier international VC firm, Advent Venture Partners a year before the biotechnology bust in 2008. According to Drakeman, "about one-third of the VCs left in the crash of 2008 and money for biotech investment became a dry well" [6]. He observed that in the 3 years after the crash his firm had looked at 1000 investments. "Only 100 were junk. 900 were deals that all made good arguments." Advent funded three of these deals. Drakeman said that most of the other big firms he was familiar with were funding at about the same rate. Between 2009 and 2013, only 495 start-up/seed-stage companies received VC funding in all of the biosciences [7]. The number and dollar volume of VC investments in the life sciences has surged in the most recent period, which we'll look at more closely in later chapters, but the structure and particularly the timing of these investments—later rather than earlier in the development cycle—and investors' expectations and timeline for return, remain heavily stacked against early stage companies.

According to data from PricewaterhouseCoopers and the National Venture Capital Association, 2015 was an historic year for VC funding in biotech sector, with over $7.4 billion invested [8]. This sounds great, until you get a bit more granular about the funding of start-ups seeking to cross from early Angel financing into the VC space. The increase in money invested did not budge the rate of start-up support by VCs, which remained near its 15 year average; rather, it increased the amount of funding for each start-up, which ranged 2–3 times higher than the historic average.

Even these positive trends are not likely to be permanent, and early signals suggest that the supply of money for biotech investing may be contracting, even as the investment business model changes. Bruce Booth of the early stage-focused Atlas Venture (blogging as Life Sci VC) and many other sources reported the markets got jittery in the third quarter of 2015, with crossover investors pulling back from biotech syndicates. This resulted in a drop of nearly $700 million (−32%) invested in the fourth quarter of 2015, compared to the second and third quarters of the same year, which corresponded to a contraction in the biotech IPO market. Booth further describes four likely shifts that he sees changing the VC model, but not necessarily in ways that are likely to increase the opportunities for VoD companies to achieve VC support [9]:

- A decline in the evaluation of traditional VC funding pitches, in favor of proactive, early collaboration with early stage prospects: "A more frequent path today is for a venture firm, working with a talented pool of entre- preneurs-in-residence, to scan through great science or technological con- cepts that emerge out of academia and to push forward to form a company around it."
- Less syndication in favor of individual venture firms pursuing greater auton- omy in governance and decision making, and higher returns: "Cutting back on syndication helps solve for the Venture Capital Math Problem. If you only own 15–20% of your exits, getting to an attractive 3× + overall fund return is very difficult."
- Greater focus on the science versus modeling markets: "Most of our deals are drug discovery or preclinical at the time we make our initial investment decisions. No drug discovery stage start-up needs to have a market model for what its sales forecast will be in the distant future; instead they need to have a credible thesis for how they will address an important medical issue in a transformative way, differentiated from other approaches, and a path for progressively de-risking that opportunity."
- Less focus on formal business plans and more on hands-on business build- ing: "That might be very helpful in tech deals, but it's just not as valuable in R&D-driven early stage therapeutics companies, where the specific scien- tific and clinical hypotheses are the more appropriate focus."

These observations are from the perspective of one player in an increas- ingly narrow group of VCs who focus on very-early stage biotechnology. In that respect, their concerns and challenges are not distinctly different from those faced by Angel-funded university spinouts. These early stage VCs are relying less on the narratives from entrepreneurs, in favor of their own experience and intuition, and backing their selections with Series A rounds large enough to match their own expectation of the marketplace, while relieving the company of the need to immediately go out and raise more money. And the effect isn't to increase the number of start-ups that can get funding; Booth also notes that "start-up formation remains as constrained as ever" and hasn't really deviated from the 15 year average; "the universe of innovative VC-backed biotech com- panies is very tight."

What is true for the majority of VCs—aversion to early stage biotech risk— is also true for Angels. Investment rates by Angel groups in biotech, in fact in anything health-care other than a recent flurry of interest in health IT, have also moved to a risk-averse stance. This has been given a modest and probably transient boost by the flurry of high-profile biotech acquisitions and IPOs, but the formula and probability of success haven't fundamentally changed for the sector. A prominent East Coast Angel Investing Group reviewed its investment pitch statistics of the preceding year. Of all the submissions made, only 22% were given an opportunity to present, and 13% were considered worthy enough for the group to undertake the due diligence process to determine the quality of the investment [10]. Fewer than one in five of the companies that participated in due diligence were funded, so only 2.3% of the submissions received money from the group.

A more favorable success ratio comes from funding for small businesses by the National Institutes of Health (NIH). Through the Small Business Innovation Research and Small Business Technology Transfer grants programs, the NIH funded 16.3% of the grant applications it received in 2013, providing over $300 million in support of 862 grants [11]. The numbers for 2014 were even better: almost $400 million went to support 1154 grants, at a success rate of 21.2%. But the majority of these are small, Phase I grants, limited to a total of $150,000 and intended to provide support for 6–12 months—much less than is needed to run a development-stage company. And in the grant cycle, the time from submission to funding can stretch to 9 months or more. So start-ups cannot escape the need to ask private investors for money.

Money in, of course, doesn't reflect the output of the VoD, and perhaps a better way to estimate rates of success in the VoD is to look at how many university inventions actually make it to the clinic. Of 41 new drug entities (NDEs) approved by the FDA in 2014, only four originated in university start-up companies [12]. Olaparib, an ovarian cancer drug, was invented by Kudos, which was started by Steve Jackson of the Wellcome Trust Sanger Institute. Peramivir, an influenza drug, came out of by BioCryst Pharma, founded on the basis of discoveries made by Dr. Charles E. Bugg at the University of Alabama and Dr. John A. Montgomery of the Southern Research Institute. Tavaborole, a toenail fungus treatment, was developed by Anacor, which captured technology pioneered by Dr. Lucy Shapiro at Stanford University and Dr. Stephen Benkovic at Pennsylvania State University. BioMarin's drug elosulfase alfa was approved for the rare disease Mucopolysaccharidosis Type IVA. BioMarin is atypical as it has remained independent while assembling a panel of five drugs based on technology from academic labs.

If we combine these four with the two additional drugs that were licensed from academia—miltefosine (Knight Pharma, from the University of Gottingen) and belinostat (Spectrum Pharmaceuticals, from the University of Glasgow)—the interdependence between the academic research enterprise and the drug industry is clear (6/41, $\approx$15%). Yet, with hundreds of new companies started each year, no doubt thousands since the commercial biotechnology surge in the early 1990s, it's evident that the aggregate number of new drugs is a fraction of the potential yield from universities and research institutes.

It is a long and tortuous process to transform an idea into a drug, and the duration isn't mediated by the excitement of the discovery or its prospective clinical value. (The exception is that the regulatory requirements may be reduced and the time abbreviated for an orphan drug and/or condition for which there is no other treatment.) The story of Human Genome Sciences (HGS) is illustrative of the time and cost involved [13]. HGS was founded in 1992, at the beginning of the era of high-throughput DNA sequencing which enabled rapid identification of genetic code. HGS was the collaboration of genomics pioneer Craig Venter and Harvard professor and biotechnology giant William Haseltine. The company exploited the newly minted techniques for sequencing DNA to identify which portions of the human genome were associated with human diseases. The founding of HGS was supercharged by a $120 million deal with SmithKline Beecham (now GlaxoSmithKline). Building on the excitement of isolating an estimated 20,000 previously undescribed human genes, HGS had an IPO just one year after its founding and eventually reached a market capitalization of over $8.5 billion.

By 1995, HGS had its first drug candidate in the clinic, a growth factor called repifermin, with the potential to treat a variety of conditions: venous ulcers (chronic wounds resulting from poor blood flow), Crohn's disease (an inflammatory disease of the bowel), and chemotherapy-induced mucositis (breakdown of the tissues in the mouth). Three years later, HGS initiated another clinical study of a drug created from their platform efforts, mirostipen, for treatment of chemotherapy-induced neutropenia. By 2009—17 years after founding—HGS had leveraged their innovation and biotech muscle to introduce 21 new biologically targeted molecules into clinical testing. Yet, only three of these ever made it to the clinic: ABthrax (raxibacumab), a mAb antidote for anthrax toxin (bought by the US Strategic National Stockpile), Benlysta (belimumab) a mAb treatment for systemic lupus erythematosis, and albiglutide, a diabetes medication approved following the GSK purchase.

At the time the company was sold to GSK for $3.6 billion, it had spent $2.7 billion on Research and Development, a substantial proportion of the $3.9 billion that the company had raised. If you had put money into the company, depending on the timing of your investment, you might consider HGS to be a success or a failure. But in the final analysis, some of the best minds in science, working on the cutting edge of genomics for 20 years, and spending billions of dollars on R&D, resulted in 3 products from 21 "shots on goal." A start-up company trying to progress a new molecule with a few hundred thousand dollars in Angel money has a very long way to go.

Time and distance to approval are significant impediments to funding for companies engaged in development of therapeutics. Diagnostics or medical devices may also face these problems, albeit on a smaller scale. Even a company with a device or diagnostic or molecule that has already demonstrated efficacy in an animal model, an early step in development, faces considerable and protracted uncertainty in the VoD. The impact of this on progression and availability of new treatments in particular categories cannot be overstated.

Consider antibiotics, for example, Drugs in this category would seem to offer a relatively straightforward path to the clinic based on unmet need and practical ability to assess both efficacy and toxicity. If a developmental compound cures an infection without killing a mouse, it might do the same in humans. Infectious organisms express a variety of distinct proteins that can be aggressively targeted by drugs, which should make them attractive development targets. Yet the level of big pharma development activity in this area has nearly evaporated (compared to the past), because the relationship between risk and return in today's market is less advantageous than for other categories.

The decrease in antibiotic development activity is partly because antibiotics need to be given in relatively large doses, increasing the potential for harmful side effects such as allergic reactions or kidney damage. Recent attempts at introducing new drugs for septicemia (bacterial infection of the blood), for example, have had disappointing results [14]. A bigger reason is that infections are discrete events, and the industry that decides which drug programs it will ultimately acquire from VoD companies is more interested in chronic recurrent treatments that provide an ongoing income stream. This is the concept of "lifetime customer value," and it's dramatically higher for chronic diseases. The result? Substantial cutbacks in antibiotic discovery by Big Pharma—this, despite a rapid and frightening increase in organisms resistant to existing antibiotics, so-called "superbugs" such as *Clostridium difficile*, Carbapenem-resistant Enterobacteriaceae and Methicillin-resistant *Staphylococcus aureus* (MRSA) [15]. Because start-ups pursuing antibiotics may be less attractive to big pharma partners, they are less attractive prospects to investors in VoD companies.

A stark example of this calculus is Merck's purchase of Cubist. The Lexington, MA-based organization was one of a limited number of companies involved in antibiotic research [16]. In the excitement following its June 2014 FDA approval for tedizolid, an antibacterial drug effective against MRSA, Cubist declared a goal of producing four new antibiotics by 2020 and committed to spending $400 million to R&D in the following year alone. Cubist was a good match for Merck, a company that had committed minimal internal R&D resources to antibiotics over the preceding decade and wanted to build a pipeline in the category. But, in March 2015, just 3 months after it purchased Cubist, Merck fired 128 researchers who were involved in new antibiotic discovery. That same week, AstraZeneca announced that it was spinning out its Infection iMed, an early stage antiinfectives R&D group with a novel small molecule in Phase II testing for gonorrhea, and cutting an estimated 95 jobs because it hadn't been able to find a buyer for the unit. [17]. If major companies consider the field to be too high risk or too low in long-term return, this has to give pause to any start-up company contemplating preclinical development of an antibiotic.

The problem isn't limited to categories with a high risk-to-return ratio. In complex diseases, such as cancer, rheumatoid arthritis, and Alzheimer's disease, the drugs need to bind human proteins that do not have significant differences between the diseased tissue and the normal tissue. To achieve biological specificity that can tell the difference between a diseased cell and a healthy one is the core problem in biotechnology, one that requires a deep understanding of etiology, and what needs to be adjusted to make things right. There is a profusion of ongoing development work in these areas, despite what would appear on the surface to be a lower probability of technical success. The reason, as we'll explore elsewhere, is that investment decisions tend to prioritize programs that could yield the greatest return, and discount ones that may have a higher probability of success but smaller financial prospects. In this calculation, investment in drugs for chronic illnesses win based on extraordinary pricing strategies and the fact that patients with chronic illnesses need to be treated for a lifetime.

The industry's solution to the disparity in lifetime value between a drug that cures a disease with a short treatment course and one that needs to be taken chronically is to apply value-based pricing, especially to the former. (Value here being the cost of treatment by a new mechanism vs. the current standard of care, and their respective financial impact on outcomes.) This is how we arrive at nine different pills for hepatitis C, the most recent of which are undeniably transformative but can cost up to $94,000 for a course of therapy. We should be thankful that these drugs were developed in an environment that would otherwise discourage their progress. But it's easy to see the financial calculus affecting decision making at the earliest stage, determining as a matter of investment whether or not a particular program should be pursued. The analysis will always be made: the number of patients multiplied by the number of doses and the price of each dose, with lifetime customer value largely determined by the number of years of patent protection left after approval. If the projected annual revenue is less than some company threshold for development—the proverbial billion-dollar "blockbuster"—an important clinical discovery may never have a chance.

The potential impact of this is *failure to find a cure*, and it may be especially catastrophic for smaller groups of patients if value-based pricing doesn't address the financial gap. Let's consider a particularly susceptible population, children aged 0–14 years of age with brain and other central nervous system tumors. There are ~3500 new such diagnoses annually in the United States [18]. Our best efforts, which use a combination of surgery, multiple courses of chemotherapy, and radiation, have enabled a 5-year survival rate that exceeds 70%, but these tumors are still the most common cause of pediatric cancer death in the United States. Assume success in clinical trials of an hypothetical new treatment. If each of these children were to receive six doses of a drug, a company's annual revenue target (the magical $1 billion) would demand that each dose be priced at $55,000 for a total lifetime customer value of $330,000. Current drug pricing models could make this possible—but let's say there's an analogous drug that can be used in tens or hundreds of thousands of adult patients. Which one will receive development funding, translating into an acquisition of a VoD company that invented the drug?

Drugs that treat adults in addition to children simply have a better chance of reaching the clinic. "Practically the only way you can get a preapproval drug tested for pediatric cancer is to piggyback on an adult trial," according to Dr. Theodore S. Johnson, a pediatric glioblastoma researcher at the Georgia Regents University Cancer Center [19]. Another related factor that threatens development of drugs for smaller populations like pediatrics is the short period of patent protection. There are so few patients that a clinical trial for a rare childhood disease may take 10 years or more, and competition for patients from a limited cohort to enroll in trials is fierce [20]. Patent protection that forestalls the introduction of generics only lasts 20 years from the date of filing. If a large chunk of this time is used for preclinical development, and more than half is required for the clinical trial, the potential IRR (internal rate of return) on the project is compromised.

Advocates for pediatric disease research are well aware of this calculation, and are making forceful efforts to increase NIH and other support for pediatric-specific research. As blogger Vashni Nilon wrote, after losing her eighth-grade daughter to glioblastoma, "The thing that keeps me up at night is wondering if there is a test tube on a shelf somewhere that contains the cure" [21].

NDEs for pediatric diseases are extremely rare. Only one modern biotechnology drug has been approved exclusively for pediatric cancer, ever, and this was in 2015 [22]. Unituxin (dinutuximab) provided clear overall survival benefits for children with aggressive neuroblastomas who received intensive chemotherapy, radiation therapy, and bone marrow transplantation. Unituxin is a mAb that binds to a lipid complex that is specific to the surface of neuroectodermal cells (the disialoganglioside GD2). The discovery of Unituxin has its roots in academia, when Dr. Nai-Kong V. Cheung, currently head of the neuroblastoma program in the Memorial Sloan Kettering Cancer Center's Department of Pediatrics in New York, created the antibodies that defined the GD2 antigen [23]. In a stunning demonstration of the slow pace of pediatric cancer research, Dr. Cheung first published these seminal results over 30 years ago [24].

Of course, the decision about whether to pursue treatments for any of the 7000 rare diseases that affect adults and children is also subject to these same financially relevant but clinically agnostic calculations [25]. It is impossible to understand the processes that determine the success of a technology in the VoD without realizing that hundreds of millions of dollars of institutional capital will eventually need to be raised for a drug to be successful. Whether a technology has the chance to survive the VoD and make it to the clinic has everything to do with whether it supports a clinical and financial pathway that will net billions of dollars in revenue. If the investment proposition doesn't appear able to achieve an expansive revenue target, a drug candidate is not likely to find traction among institutional investors and therefore make its way to acquisition by big pharma. The prospect is daunting for even the most committed and courageous early stage investors.

The VoD was so named because companies and technologies die in it. It is an imperfect vehicle for advancing drugs from the university to the clinic, with incentives stacked against solutions for many of our most pressing medical needs. It is also a poor environment for virtually everyone participating in it: the inventors, the IP holders, the entrepreneurs, the investors, and those whose livelihood depends on the successful transition of a drug to a marketed therapeutic.

This book is about the Translation Gap, which makes the VoD so lethal, and what we need to do to change it. The VoD is packed with great discoveries that could dramatically change how we treat illnesses and are the product of both unprecedented technological advances and a massive global basic research effort. It's also characterized by a profoundly low tolerance for risk in therapeutics, biotech and medical devices, which directly translates into less appetite for healthcare innovation. (Health IT, a current darling of many investors, is the exception.) Participating in the VoD is inherently a gamble, but it shouldn't be a blind one, and it shouldn't be a process that stifles innovation or ignores important medical needs because they don't fit a conventional investment model; quite the opposite.

Our analysis reveals that the Translation Gap fundamentally relates to resources, how they are raised, deployed … and wasted. In this book, we will explore the structure of the VoD, the activities of those who participate, and how resources flow into and within the VoD ecosystem. We will explore how the VoD is an independent market for capital rather than medicine, and how the competitive forces within this market often destroy the very technologies the investments are supposed to support. We will build on these understandings to explain how the cost-efficiency of the VoD can be improved, thus improving its ability to be a rational investment of both money and time, and enabling the system to better succeed in its ultimate goal of creating value that includes but also transcends financial results.

REFERENCES

[1] Association of University Technology Managers. AUTM licensing activity survey: *FY2014*; 2015.

[2] Association of University Technology Managers. AUTM licensing activity survey: *FY2013*; 2014.

[3] Huggett B. Top US universities, institutes for life sciences in 2014. Nat Biotechnol 2015;33(11):1131. Available from http://dx.doi.org/10.1038/nbt.3394.

[4] Sohl J. The Angel investor market in 2013: a return to seed investing. Center for Venture Research, April 30, 2014.

[5] Interview with the authors, February 26, 2015.

[6] Interview with author Dessain, September 9, 2013.

[7] Battelle and Biotechnology Industry Organization. *Battelle/BIO State Bioscience Jobs, Investments and Innovation 2014*. June, 2014.

[8] PricewaterhouseCoopers and the National Venture Capital Association. MoneyTree™ Report—Q4 2015/full year 2015 Summary. <www.pwcmoneytree.com>; 2015.

[9] Booth B. LifeSciVC. Biotech venture data: disappearing crossovers, and few but well-*funded startups*. 8 February, 2016.

[10] Personal communication with author Dessain. December, 2014.

[11] National Institutes of Health. NIH small business innovation research (SBIR) and small business technology transfer (STTR) grants: applications, awards, success rates and total funding by phase fiscal years 2005–2015. <https://report.nih.gov/success_rates/>; [accessed 08.02.16].

[12] US Food and Drug Administration. Novel new drugs summary. <www.fda.gov/Drugs/DevelopmentApprovalProcess/DrugInnovation/ucm429247.htm>; 2014 [accessed 08.02.16].

[13] McNamee LM, Ledley FD. Assessing the history and value of Human Genome Sciences. J Commer Biotechnol 2013;19(4):3–10. Available from http://dx.doi.org/10.5912/jcb.619.

[14] McKenna M. Researchers struggle to develop new treatment for sepsis. Sci Am 2013;308(4).

[15] Hirschler B. Big pharma: Few new antibiotics in the works. *Chicago Tribune*, March 13, 2013. http://articles.chicagotribune.com/2013-03-19/health/ct-met-antibiotics-pipeline-20130319_1_drug-resistant-tuberculosis-resistant-bacteria-ketek; 2013.

[16] Carroll J. UPDATED: Merck to shutter Cubist unit in May, axing most of the 128 R&D staffers. FierceBiotech 2015 March 6, 2015. www.fiercebiotech.com/story/merck-shutter-cubist-site-may-axing-128-staffers/2015-03-06.

[17] Newsham J. Two Boston biotechs cutting 200 jobs. *Boston Globe*, March 7, 2015. <http://www.bostonglobe.com/business/2015/03/07/eight-things-you-may-have-missed-friday-from-world-business/7pJAPuRUEy5NzJww0AN3bM/story.html>; [accessed 26.05.15].

[18] Ostrom QT, de Blank PM, Kruchko C, Petersen CM, Liao P, Finlay JL, et al. Alex's lemonade stand foundation infant and childhood primary brain and central nervous system tumors diagnosed in the United States in 2007–2011. Neuro Oncology 2015;16(Suppl. 10):x1–x36.

[19] Personal communication with author Dessain, April 5, 2015.

[20] Boklan J. Little patients, losing patience: pediatric cancer drug development. Mol Cancer Ther 2006;5(8):1905–8.

[21] Nilon V. The giant cluster**** that is cancer treatment. Grief is the New Black 2015 March 17, 2015. http://griefisthenewblack.wordpress.com/2015/03/17/the-giant-cluster-that-is-cancer-treatment/.

[22] US Food and Drug Administration. FDA approves first therapy for high-risk neuroblastoma. FDA News Release, March 10, 2015. <www.fda.gov/NewsEvents/Newsroom/PressAnnouncements/ucm437460.htm>; 2015.

[23] An Interview with Nai-Kong V. Cheung <http://www.mskcc.org/pediatrics/childhood/neuroblastoma/interview-nai-kong-v-cheung>.

[24] Cheung NK, Saarinen UM, Neely JE, Landmeier B, Donovan D, Coccia PF. Monoclonal antibodies to a glycolipid antigen on human neuroblastoma cells. Cancer Res 1985;45(6):2642–9.

[25] Rare Disease Foundation. About us. <www.rarediseasefoundation.org/about>; [accessed 31.03.15].

Chapter 3

Clinical Promise ≠ Investment Practice

I truly believe I am working with the breakthrough treatment of the century [1].

When Dr. David Horn first learned about IMT504, he felt he had a winner. IMT504 is an oligonucleotide, a molecule structurally related to DNA, which has powerful stimulatory effects on multiple components of the immune system. His optimism is understandable, since the molecule has shown promise against infectious and other diseases [2,3].

Dr. Horn is an energetic 59-year-old physician, clinical researcher, and entrepreneur. Board certified in Internal Medicine and Infectious Diseases, he has held senior clinical research positions at Merck and Bristol-Myers Squibb and has over 30 years experience in drug development and clinical trials. He first learned about IMT504 while engaged as a consultant, performing due diligence on the molecule for a group of investors. What impressed him most was the effectiveness of IMT504 in many animal models and the safety of the molecule in animal and human toxicity tests.

In 2011, he quit his medical practice, licensed the IP and founded Mid-Atlantic Biotechnology (MABT). This was a risky move, but, as he explained, "I like clinical medicine but one needs to immerse oneself as a clinical physician or work in industry. The industry route and forming a corporation was and is necessary to raise money to do anything."

MABT's business model is opportunistic, trying to follow up on the many potential uses of IMT504 demonstrated in animal models. As an immune stimulator, it amplifies and broadens the immune response to influenza vaccines (a phenomenon called epitope spreading), which increases the ability of one strain of influenza vaccine to induce an immune response against a different strain [4]. This could enable existing vaccines to better protect against new influenza strains, which mutate from existing strains and can be hard to anticipate. The vaccine produced for the 2014–15 influenza season had a vaccine efficacy (VE) rate of only 19% against Influenza A viruses [3]. Dr. Horn proposes that

Preserving the Promise. DOI: http://dx.doi.org/10.1016/B978-0-12-809216-3.00003-8

19

influenza vaccines incorporating IMT504 will provide better VE against new or mutated influenza strains: "I'm pretty sure we can make a universal flu vaccine. Probably the most important thing in the world is to prevent a pandemic influenza, and I think we have the technology to do it."

He is exploring other applications, including treatment of *Pseudomonas* infections in Cystic Fibrosis patients, and has received an orphan drug designation for use of the molecule in rabies virus exposure. Surprisingly, IMT504 may also be helpful for Type I diabetes, as suggested by regeneration of pancreatic islet cells in a rat model of diabetes, and an orphan drug application is pending for this indication as well [5]. Last but not least, the immune-stimulating effects of IMT504 may have an anti-cancer effect, as suggested by the experience others have had with similar molecules. Cancer Immunotherapy was named the "Breakthrough of the Year" by *Science Magazine* in 2013 [6], and MABT is pursuing proof of concept data in animal and human models. "I think we may be sitting on the best cancer therapy that exists. I'd love to be able to prove it, or disprove it."

In spite of all this, Horn notes that raising money has been difficult. "It's painful, incredibly, incredibly painful. The science should be the most complex part of it, but it's not." The reasons are twofold: the prospect of voracious equity demands from institutional investors and a time-consuming need to instill the company's passion in skeptical early stage investors. He has avoided venture capital firms (VCs) for his early work in order to retain as much equity as possible and has been frustrated with Angel fundraising. "We wasted a lot of time with Angels who do not understand what we are doing. To understand what we are talking about you have to be really educated. It's a huge divide—everybody says they are going to cure cancer, so what is so special about you?"

As a result he's funded most of the company by himself, using his savings and consulting income. MABT does not have its own laboratory, so Dr. Horn has leveraged his increasing data set to build collaborations with the National Institutes of Health and academic laboratories, and that has continued to move his project toward the clinic. But he needs to attract an investor or clinical partner who can fund the necessary clinical trials.

> *Time is ticking. The world is just so screwed up. I haven't advanced it as far and fast as I want to, but I'm in the game, and I can be in the game for a lot longer before I can say it is a success or failure. All of the ingredients are there. I haven't made a fatal mistake…that's my greatest accomplishment so far.*

There's admittedly a choice being made in the story above, to consciously steer away from potential sources of funding that the founder feels would compromise his progress. We relate the story for a broader purpose, to address the impact of funding imperatives on scientific and clinical progress.

Rather than companies failing in the market, our thesis is that companies are set up to fail, and often do, because there's a failure in the market that invests in biotechnology. If we're looking at revenue-stage companies, we talk about their performance in generating revenue from customers. But performance among prerevenue companies like those in the Valley of Death (VoD) is a different matter. They aren't selling anything yet to physicians or health systems or patients. They're selling themselves as an investment instrument to financiers. If these companies fail in the VoD, *it's because they are being failed by the market for biotechnology investments.*

We are referring here to the market for capital to support product discovery and development, as distinguished from the commercially- and clinically driven demand for new medicines and devices. The journey through the VoD is difficult by design, as it is reasonable and prudent to filter the wheat from the chaff. But it is rendered impassable for many companies by an environment that abhors risk and migrates to short-term return. Instead of sorting the most promising candidates from the standpoint of clinical value, it is a financially driven winnowing mechanism that filters out short-term risk instead of ferreting out long-term value.

The capital markets operate by unsentimental principles. The requirement for success is the availability of capital, and the primary cause of failure in the VoD is a lack of capital. The process of acquiring capital has narrowed from a difficult but navigable task to an impulsive and often arbitrary one.

Think about the following for a minute. An early stage company has not started making money, is still navigating the treacherous path of product development, is still subject to the political vagaries and practical dysfunction of regulatory authorities, and still has to prove clinical safety and superiority in complicated and expensive clinical trials before it can even try to file for approval. Even if it does manage to do all those things, it finally, immutably faces the merciless landscape of competition and reimbursement.

Nothing is certain or predictable in the early stages of biotech discovery and development. And yet any discovery needs to have an apparent financial value to investors in order to attract financing. *So this thing, this early stage company, is somehow "valued" by financial investors, at each round of investment, at an amount that reflects a chain of what-ifs.* The size of the number for a prerevenue company is a multiple of the money already invested, has a relation to commercial sales and profit potential that is strained to incredulity, and is, in the absence of revenue, infinity times current sales.

More than almost any other investment, the value of a biotechnology company is unknowable, especially in preclinical stages, and depends mostly on what somebody will pay for the company and whether they think they can eventually sell it to someone else for a higher price. Because of the amount of money involved, and the absolute dependence on Angel and Venture Capital investment, the economics of biotechnology financing are subject to global economic bubble–bust cycles that, as with many macroeconomic forces, have very little to do with the value of what the companies are trying to accomplish.

The first biotechnology bust was collateral damage at the end of the "dotcom" bubble in 2000. In the 30 months between May 2000 and October 2002, the NASDAQ stock exchange dropped by 78%, subtracting $4.2 trillion in market value from the economy [7]. The NASDAQ biotechnology index, which had been experiencing a bubble of its own, lost more than half of its value. As with all market bubbles, this was reactive, the end result of overindulgent allocation of easy money to marginal ideas. Much of the run-up in valuations was fueled by a massive market-driven increase in the availability of private and institutional capital, which in turn fed on speculation about how sequencing the human genome would create the ultimate platform for drug discovery.

It didn't help investor appetite for biotech when, in 2001, the Food and Drug Administration (FDA) rejected Imclone's Biologics Licensing Application for its new cancer drug Erbitux (cetuximab), which crushed Imclone's stock price [8], spilled over to perceived prospects in other biotech investments, and reinforced a growing sense at the time that the human genomics revolution was going to be harder to convert into drugs than had been expected. Even without any specific bad news, the market capitalization of Human Genome Sciences dropped to $1.1 billion from a previous high of over $8.5 billion.

It was almost as bad in 2008, when the subprime mortgage crisis crushed retirement funds, home values, and investment assets, causing combined financial losses in the United States of $8.3 trillion and triggering the longest recession since the Great Depression [9]. The valuations of existing public biotechnology companies were relatively unchanged, but interest in new companies faded as a few utterly miserable biotech development outcomes sucked all the optimism out of the room. One example: DeCode Genetics, a Reykjavík, Iceland-based company that leveraged studies of the relatively homogeneous Icelandic population to identify genes associated with common diseases. Led by its founder, Kári Stefánsson, DeCODE produced a mountain of spectacular insights about how inheritance contributed to the development of diseases as diverse as diabetes, schizophrenia, heart disease, and cancer. But its investors could hardly have been happy. By the end of 2006, the company had booked operating losses of $535 million [10]. From a peak market capitalization of $463 million in 2004, DeCODE's stock price completely crashed in 2008 [10]. Declaring bankruptcy, the company sold its assets, presumably at a fire-sale price since only one investor group bid on the sale [11]. (DeCODE continued to innovate, and was eventually acquired by AMGEN for $145 million [12].)

Another example: the Seattle-based company Targeted Genetics (TGEN) was an early pioneer in gene therapy. They planned to cure disease by introducing genes into patient cells using adeno-associated virus, an especially safe vector method. They acquired technologies that had originated in academic institutions, including the Fred Hutchinson Cancer Research Center in Seattle, the University of Pennsylvania in Philadelphia, and Children's Hospital in Columbus. TGEN ran into trouble when a young mother died after her second injection of an experimental arthritis drug in 2007. Her death was reminiscent of the 1999 death of Jesse Gelsinger, a young man treated at the University of Pennsylvania for a metabolic disorder, because both patients had received experimental gene therapy for a nonfatal disease. The catastrophe was profiled in a highly critical article in the *Washington Post* [13].

The FDA soon ruled that the young mother had died of an infection that was unrelated to the experimental treatment. The damage had been done, however: investors lost their interest in gene therapy, even though the trial was soon restarted and the treatment was eventually shown to be safe [14]. By the end of 2008, the company had run through $315 million, founder and CEO H. Stewart Parker had resigned, and TGEN was at risk of bankruptcy [15]. To stay afloat, the company abandoned its gene therapy ambitions, sold its manufacturing capability, folded itself into an antibiotic company, and moved to London [16,17].

The failures of these companies weren't isolated events, and they helped fuel risk aversion among biotech investors already reeling from the global financial crisis. The result was the near-extinction of biotech initial public offerings (IPOs) as a potential exit strategy for at least 5 years. In 2007, globally, there were 51 biotechnology IPOs that raised an average of $58 million [18]. The year 2008 saw only one biotechnology IPO, and that raised only $22 million. The burden of financing early stage biotech ventures thus fell entirely on either outside investors, or on big companies willing to make an early bet on the technology. Big Pharma retreated largely into sponsored research agreements or license options with limited upfront payments. VCs almost en masse shifted to a late entry strategy. And shell-shocked by turmoil in the markets, early stage investors retreated to other categories or entirely to the sidelines. Nascent biotech companies and other healthcare start-ups, like other organizations throughout the economy, were left in a cash crunch, chasing a diminishing pool of funding sources. By the end of 2008, when a substantial percentage of even public companies had less than one year's worth of cash, that same metric applied to half of all biotech firms with a market capitalization under $250 million [19].

A diminished pool of available funds from IPOs and strategic partners "trickled down" to heightened caution and a virtual refusal to participate in very early stage funding on the part of investors deploying institutional capital, including VCs. The confluence of less capital with heightened sensitivity to risk meant fewer ventures funded, and this contraction profoundly affected the progress of innovative biotechnologies. Between September 2008 and May 2009, more than 35 US companies halted development of drugs for significant unmet medical needs, even though they had shown encouraging results in clinical testing [20].

Another macroeconomic issue worth mentioning is the effect of the 2008 stock market crash on disposable income and therefore availability of private (vs institutional) capital. Constraints on liquidity, real or perceived, will always impact private funding for early stage companies. Because high net worth individual investors saw their assets shrink in the recession, there was less money available from "friends and family" the historical first source of funding for new ideas, and from Angel investors. Compared with the prior year, 2008 saw a 26% retraction in the total dollar value of Angel investments in all fields, a retreat that continued through 2009 [21]. This reflected a decrease in average deal size, as the numbers of Angels, companies, and investments were essentially unchanged.

Comfort with spending "disposable income" isn't just an issue of whether to buy a Bentley or a yacht. Because early stage investing has everything to do with psychological ratios of risk and return, the question of whether to put money to work on inherently high-risk early stage investments is influenced by confidence in the economy. In general, people are more likely to act to avoid loss than to seek return, and a drop in ready assets makes it easy to feel uncomfortably at risk. The version of belt tightening that occurs at this level is a diminished appetite for ideas, even exciting or important ones, that carry an unacceptably high probability of loss.

The biotech IPO market recovered beginning in 2013 and hit an all time high in 2014, with 63 deals netting a total of $4.9 billion [22]. Similar to the prior biotech investment booms, this rapid expansion was driven by macroeconomic factors in addition to genuine and well-deserved enthusiasm for progress in the industry [23]. Six years of nominal interest rates and marginal returns from other fixed income investments caused institutional investors to seek greater yields elsewhere. As Geoffrey K. Watson, an economist at TD Asset Management in Toronto, Canada, notes, this fueled "a boom in equity financing by institutional investors looking for opportunities to get a little more yield, because they weren't getting it from the Treasuries" [23]. Non-VC investors were jumping on the same bandwagon, as the annualized rate of money invested in biotech in 2014 was almost $12 billion above the amount raised by VCs.

From the perspective of academic spinouts in the VoD, it is important to note that this biotech "boom" is investment in late-stage projects. According to Michael Greeley, General Partner at the early stage-centric Foundation Medical Partners VC firm and blogger at "On the Flying Bridge", later-stage rounds captured 72% of the dollars invested in the first quarter of 2015 [24].

As we write this, in early 2016, there is tremendous uncertainty around change in the pharmaceutical/biotech industry. Biotech IPOs have rapidly tapered off and mergers and acquisitions activity is being pushed back, as extreme drug pricing practices have attracted legislative attention (see chapter: Getting to Australia), world markets are in turmoil, crude oil prices recently hit a 12-year low, and the NASDAQ biotech index is down 40% from its high in June–August 2015. Macroeconomic conditions affect the interest and ability of Angel investors to support early biotechnology, and the boom–bust cycles of biotech investing over the past 20 years have encouraged a model that shunts capital away from early stage, high-risk ventures.

We are left with a "Catch-22" that is likely to continue for the foreseeable future: The serious money is available only to purchase late-stage assets that have already cleared many costly development hurdles. There is not enough money left in the system to propel more than a relative handful of (serendipitously) funded start-up "research projects" through the early stages of development.

In summary, it should be increasingly clear from the impact of external economic events that an enormous number of entities continue to vie for an increasingly unreliable pool of capital. The macro effect, as we have seen, is not unlike the enforced paralysis on small business created by large banks reacting to their own bad bets in subprime real estate portfolios—which was to turn off the credit tap and, upon recovery, restrict it to those with the lowest perceived risk. It's cyclical, and despite the classic brokerage warning that historical results are no guarantee of future performance, follows a herd mentality to the current darlings of investment. Which leads us back to the story with which we opened this chapter, and an unfortunate truth: Whether Dr. Horn can ultimately realize the potential of IMT504 for influenza or diabetes may depend as much on cyclical, clinically agnostic investment trends as on whether it works in the clinic.

REFERENCES

[1] Dr. Horn D, Interview and personal communication with author SD, April 15, 2015.

[2] Chahin A, Opal SM, Zorzopulos J, Jobes DV, Migdady Y, Yamamoto M, et al. The novel immunotherapeutic oligodeoxynucleotide IMT504 protects neutropenic animals from fatal Pseudomonas aeruginosa bacteremia and sepsis. Antimicrob Agents Chemother 2015; 59(2):1225–9.

[3] US Centers for Disease Control. CDC presents updated estimates of Flu vaccine effectiveness for the 2014–2015 season. March 2, 2015. <www.cdc.gov/flu/news/updated-vaccine-effectiveness-2014-15.htm>; [accessed 16.04.15].

[4] Montaner AD, Denichilo A, Rodriguez JM, Flo J, Lopez RA, Pontoriero A, et al. Addition of the immunostimulatory oligonucleotide IMT504 to a seasonal flu vaccine increases hemagglutinin antibody titers in young adult and elder rats, and expands the anti-hemagglutinin antibody repertoire. Nucleic Acid Ther 2011;21(4):265–74.

[5] Bianchi MS, Hernando-Insua A, Chasseing NA, Rodriguez JM, Elias F, Lago N, et al. Oligodeoxynucleotide IMT504 induces a marked recovery in a streptozotocin-induced model of diabetes in rats: correlation with an early increase in the expression of nestin and neurogenin 3 progenitor cell markers. Diabetologia 2010;53(6):1184–9.

[6] Couzin-Frankel J. Breakthrough of the year 2013. Cancer immunotherapy. Science 2013; 342(6165):1432–3.

[7] Yahoo Finance. NASDAQ biotechnology index (^NBI). <http://finance.yahoo.com/q?s=%5ENBI>.

[8] Hron BM. Placebo or panacea: The FDA's rejection of ImClone's Erbitux licensing application. Harvard Law School, third year paper. 2003. http://dash.harvard.edu/handle/1/8889445>; [accessed 28.05.15].

[9] Altman RC. The great crash, 2008: a geopolitical setback for the west. Foreign Affairs, January/February, 2009.

[10] deCODE Genetics, Inc. FY2006 Form 10-K. Filed with U.S. Securities and Exchange Commission; 2006.

[11] Quandl. deCODE Genetics, Inc. (DCGN)—Market capitalization. <www.quandl.com/DMDRN/DCGN_MKT_CAP-deCODE-GENETICS-INC-DCGN-Market-capitalization>; 2008 [accessed 07.01.15].

[12] Vorhaus D. Meet the new deCODE, same as the old deCODE? Genomics Law Report 2010 January 25, 2010. www.genomicslawreport.com/index.php/2010/01/25/meet-the-new-decode-same-as-the-old-decode/.

[13] Baker M. Big biotech buys iconic genetics firm. Nature 2012;492(7429) 321–321.

[14] Weiss R. Death points to risks in research. *Washington Post* 2007 August 6, 2007. www.washingtonpost.com/wp-dyn/content/article/2007/08/05/AR2007080501636.html.

[15] Mease PJ, Hobbs K, Chalmers A, El-Gabalawy H, Bookman A, Keystone E, et al. Local delivery of a recombinant adeno associated vector containing a tumour necrosis factor alpha antagonist gene in inflammatory arthritis: a phase 1 dose-escalation safety and tolerability study. Ann Rheum Dis 2009;68(8):1247–54.

[16] González A. Targeted Genetics CEO resigns. *Seattle Times*. November 10, 2008. http://seattletimes.com/html/businesstechnology/2008374011_webtargeted10.html>; 2008 [accessed 28.05.15].

[17] MarketWire. Targeted Genetics corporation announces the sale of manufacturing assets to genzyme corporation. September 9, 2009. <www.ampliphibio.com/news/89-targeted-genetics-corporation-announces-the-sale-of-manufacturing-assets-to-genzyme-corporation.html>; 2009.

[18] Timmerman L. Targeted Genetics, re-invented as AmpliPhi, bets on anti-bacterials, moves HQ to London. Xconomy. March 9, 2011. www.xconomy.com/seattle/2011/03/09/targeted-genetics-re-invented-as-ampliphi-bets-on-anti-bacterials-moves-hq-to-london/>; 2011 [accessed 28.05.15].

[19] Huggett B, Hodgson J, Lahteenmaki R. Public biotech 2008—the numbers. Nat Biotechnol 2009;27(8):710–21.

[20] Booth BL. This time may be different. Nat Biotechnol 2016;34(1):25–30.

[21] Sohl J. The Angel investor market in 2008: a down year in investment dollars but not in deals. Center for Venture Research; 2009. March 26, 2009.

[22] Ernst & Young. The 2014 U.S. biotech IP market in 10 charts. <http://mcr.doingbusiness.ro/uploads/54b7839565ab7Blog%20infographic%202014%20IPOs.pdf>; 2015.

[23] Interview with author SD, February 4 2015.

[24] Greeley M. Head scratching data. <https://ontheflyingbridge.wordpress.com/2015/04/23/head-scratching-data/>; 2015.

Chapter 4

Velcade, a Biotech Success Story

It was after 10 p.m. when Ellen arrived in the emergency department of a Philadelphia hospital. She had just flown in from Israel and had gone straight from the airport to the hospital. She was accompanied by her husband, who had arrived with her, and her daughter, who lived nearby.

She was elderly and frail, clearly in pain, but handling it quietly in the way that people do who have already endured great suffering in their lives. Because of her pain, we were unable to move her from the wheelchair to the examination table.

Ellen had multiple myeloma, a cancer of the immune system, which had become resistant to all of the conventional chemotherapy drugs as well as to high-dose steroids. As a result, her disease had spread throughout her skeleton and was beginning to cause kidney failure. She was too sick for a bone marrow transplant, which would be the next logical step for a younger, stronger patient.

There was only one bed available in the hospital. We directly admitted her to that bed, bypassing the usual evaluation by the ER attending, to get her settled in as soon as possible. Once her pain was under control with morphine, we gave her bortezomib (Velcade), a drug that had just been approved by the US Food and Drug Administration for treatment of multiple myeloma and was safe for very sick patients because of its unusual mechanism of action.

If we reflect on how the Valley of Death (VoD) is *supposed* to function, Velcade may be the poster child for success. Alfred Goldberg, a Harvard University professor, was engaged in the type of basic research that is the bedrock of biotechnology … following a rabbit down a hole as he tried to answer a fundamental biological question. The question first occurred to him when he was a medical student: why do muscles atrophy when they are not stimulated by nerves? [1]. The simplest explanation would have been that muscle proteins were not made by the muscle cells, but this theory turned out to be wrong. Instead, Goldberg discovered that unstimulated nerve cells actually increased their rate of protein breakdown [2]. This occurred through increasing the activation of a large, intracellular structure that was responsible for protein degradation, which he dubbed the "proteasome." This work was so cutting-edge that

Preserving the Promise. DOI: http://dx.doi.org/10.1016/B978-0-12-809216-3.00004-X

follow-on studies of how cells select proteins for degradation by the protea-some (by linking them to a small polypeptide called ubiquitin) were awarded the Nobel Prize in Chemistry in 2004.

In 1993, the year after Human Genome Sciences (HGS) was founded, Goldberg started Myogenics, a company to synthesize proteasome inhibitors. His original plan was to make a proteasome inhibitor that could treat the muscle wasting that occurs in AIDS and cancer patients. At that time, nobody suspected proteasome activity was a target for treating cancer itself. From its beginning, Goldberg's company depended highly on close interactions with academic sci-entists, meeting monthly with Myogenics' scientific advisory board and estab-lishing research collaborations wherever possible.

A Myogenics team led by Julian Adams created a series of proteasome inhib-itors with increasing potency in vitro (in a controlled experimental environment rather than within a living organism). The company freely shared its proteasome inhibitors with academic laboratories, which led to two critical discoveries that guided the clinical development efforts. The first was when Kenneth Rock, then at the Dana-Farber Cancer Institute, discovered that proteasome inhibition did not immediately kill cells, as had been feared. The second was when Vito Palombella and Tom Maniatis at Harvard found that bortezomib inhibited the function of a key protein that drives the proliferation of immune cells, NF-κB, which is activated in rheumatoid arthritis and cancers of the immune system such as multiple myeloma [3].

Myogenics shifted gears, euphemistically known in the start-up world as "pivoting," to explore inflammatory disease and cancer, and changed the com-pany name to ProScript [4]. Their new CEO, Richard Bagley, sought deals with pharma companies while building new academic collaborations. He signed an agreement with Hoechst Marion Roussel (later Aventis), for up to $38 million plus royalties, to develop proteasome inhibitors for inflammatory arthritis and possibly cancer, as well as a smaller deal with Hoffmann-La Roche for cachexia (wasting syndrome).

On the academic side, Beverly Teicher at the Dana-Farber Cancer Institute discovered that bortezomib had activity in a mouse breast cancer model [5]. Teicher's strong preliminary data was bolstered by experiments led by the National Cancer Institute's Peter Elliott, who tested its panel of 60 human can-cer cell lines and observed antitumor efficacy in vitro and in a mouse model [6]. This was enough to encourage the NCI, CaP Cure, the Memorial Sloan Kettering Cancer Center and the University of North Carolina, to move bort-ezomib into Phase I clinical testing for cancer.

Despite rapid advances in collaboration-driven discovery, and a solid flow of initial capital that included venture capital (VC) investment and deals with two Big Pharma companies, ProScript's funding was almost completely gone by June 1999. This was in part because Hoechst decided to drop bortezomib. As Goldberg remembers, "Somehow they got to human trials but they decided to go ahead with their endogenous product. They didn't want two products for arthritis and they decided to get out of the cancer business. It was a crazy thing that some consultant told them" [7].

ProScript had also lost its main supporter when Wally Steinberg died of a heart attack at age 61. He had been the chairman of HealthCare Ventures, ProScript's lead investor, and was an industry leader and a key architect of the formation of HGS [8]. Remaining investors decided they would not continue to support the drug due to concern about its unexpected mechanism of action. "[Bortezomib] had already been stained so much. Every major company that was approached had never heard of the proteasome, so the VCs weren't going to put any further money in it. They decided to sell the company," Goldberg said. Eventually HealthCare Ventures sold Proscript to another of its companies, LeukoSite, for $2.7 million [4].

Less than a year later, LeukoSite was acquired by a larger company, Millennium, for $635 million [9]. This was primarily to obtain rights to the leukemia drug, alemtuzumab, then known by the trade name Campath. The Millennium announcement of the LeukoSite acquisition highlighted seven drugs that it would gain in the process, *but did not even mention bortezomib* [7]. According to Goldberg, "It was the failure of everything else from LeukoSite that gave bortezomib an opportunity. It was an agent that almost died on the shelf 3–4 times." Surprisingly positive Phase I results in multiple myeloma, along with championing by Julian Adams (by then working at Millennium), catapulted bortezomib to a top priority for the company.

Bortezomib proved highly effective in a Phase II trial of multiple myeloma patients who had failed previous therapies [10], and received approval of a fast-track IND for the (now-named) Velcade in May 2003. By 2013, global sales of the drug surpassed $2.6 billion [11], and Velcade remains one of safest and most effective drugs we have for treatment of multiple myeloma.

The story of Velcade's breakthrough success both validates and highlights fault lines in the medical research enterprise. Several features are instructive from the perspective of how new biotechnology can survive the VoD. When they first began, Goldberg and Adams had no idea they would be creating a drug for multiple myeloma. This is why we support basic research: we need to understand how things work before we can discover how they go wrong in disease, and we don't know everything that is wrong for every disease. Our multiple myeloma patient Ellen would not have been helped by a new drug that killed cancer cells in the traditional way, by damaging DNA. She was too debilitated by her disease. She needed something that could expose a vulnerability of her cancer cells, by gently modulating a cell process that would leave her normal cells essentially intact. Velcade could never have been imagined as a multiple myeloma therapy when Goldberg and Adams started, based on what was known about the disease at the time.

One of the problems Goldberg and Adams had was explaining the value of bortezomib to their investors. This communication challenge is intrinsic to innovation, which is fundamentally high risk because it builds on concepts that have never been executed before and can't be funded unless investors can be persuaded they'll achieve a return on invested capital. A drug that damaged DNA, while less differentiated from other cancer compounds, might well have found greater favor at the time from investors, simply because it worked by a familiar pathway, even if it worked less well.

Greater certainty in the short term gets conflated with reduced risk, when in fact there may be greater risk in an essentially "me-too" compound that is unable to establish a differentiated presence in the market. And in fact, there may indeed be less risk to investors in the short term from the similar drug than from the innovative one, because what investors are interested in is the probability of exit—which is to some extent driven by, but not necessarily a correlated of, the probability of major clinical impact [12]. Transformative innovation, the kind that ultimately commercialized Velcade, is just as likely to inhibit as to stimulate investment. This is because risk and expected time to exit are nominally, if not explicitly, calculated into the estimate of potential return on investment (ROI). The higher risk associated with greater innovation lowers the potential internal rate of return because of its impact on development timeline and probability of success. There's an intrinsic disconnect, driven by perspective—inventor versus investor versus clinician—between a discovery's value as an investment and its utility as a therapy.

The end of the Hoechst and Roche deals was the fatal blow for ProScript, as two of the main opportunities for VCs to obtain a return on sale of the company to Big Pharma were closed. But it's important to recognize that pharma has the same challenge as investors, in distinguishing potentially lucrative innovation from the noise of discovery research. Goldberg remembers a conversation with Frank L. Douglas, MD, PhD, who was Executive Vice President of Global Research and Chief Scientific Officer during Hoechst's restructuring as Aventis, and presided over the decision to drop Bortezomib. "[When he was] an emeritus professor at the MIT business school, he said to me, 'From your comments you seem to know a lot about proteasome inhibitors. We're thinking of buying a program from Millennium.'" Goldberg replied, "'Well, I think it is a good idea, but I should tell you, your company owned the program 10 years earlier.' He couldn't believe what I was talking about—but not only did they have it, it had never reached high up, he had no memory, no scientists still involved. They had made every possible error in predicting where the science would go" [7].

LeukoSite was acquired by Millennium primarily to obtain a leukemia drug, Campath (alemtuzumab). The purchase price of $635 million was an almost double premium over the share price at the time [13], so investors made a lot of money in the transaction … but what if they had realized the potential of this strange boron-containing drug with an unusual mechanism of action? LeukoSite may have sold for much more, as evidenced by Takeda's purchase of Millennium in 2008 for $8.8 billion in cash [14]. The same tensions are operative for early stage companies in the VoD, where too little innovation is seen as lacking competitive differentiation, and too much as undesirable risk that can send an investor elsewhere.

Velcade's success also demonstrates how critical it is that a new drug achieves scientific validation at it leaves the university. Academic collaborations were *required* to realize Velcade's potential, to discover its mechanism of action and antitumor effects. Today, many of these synergistic relationships are significantly delayed by legal process, shortsighted constraints on deals, or outright policy prohibitions. Conflict of interest policies divorce an inventor from his invention and the company that owns it, isolating a discovery from its most passionate advocate. Legal barriers to sharing materials and ideas before and after technology licensing slow scientific progress from weeks to months or longer. Inefficiencies and disincentives in the technology transfer process clash with the entrepreneurial process and kill innovations for the wrong reasons. The tensions between academia and industry are far worse today than they were in the era of Goldberg, Harvard, and Myogenics. In fact, this part of the Translation Gap, the process of transferring technologies from non-profit research institutions to the for-profit VoD, harbors some of the most powerful forces destroying technologies in the VoD.

REFERENCES

[1] Goldberg A. Bortezomib's scientific origins and its tortuous path to the clinic. In: Ghobrial IM, Richardson PG, Anderson KC, editors. Bortezomib in the treatment of multiple myeloma. Springer Basel; 2011. p. 1–27.

[2] Mitch WE, Goldberg AL. Mechanisms of muscle wasting. The role of the ubiquitin-proteasome pathway. N Engl J Med 1996;335(25):1897–905. http://dx.doi.org/10.1056/NEJM199612193352507.

[3] Palombella VJ, Rando OJ, Goldberg AL, Maniatis T. The ubiquitin-proteasome pathway is required for processing the NF-kappa B1 precursor protein and the activation of NF-kappa B. Cell 1994;78(5):773–85.

[4] Sanchez-Serrano I. Success in translational research: lessons from the development of bortezomib. Nat Rev Drug Discov 2006;5(2):107–14. http://dx.doi.org/10.1038/nrd1959.

[5] Teicher BA, Ara G, Herbst R, Palombella VJ, Adams J. The proteasome inhibitor PS-341 in cancer therapy. Clin Cancer Res 1999;5(9):2638–45.

[6] Adams J, Palombella VJ, Sausville EA, Johnson J, Destree A, Lazarus DD, et al. Proteasome inhibitors: a novel class of potent and effective antitumor agents. Cancer Res 1999;59(11):2615–22.

[7] Alfred Goldberg interview with author SD, August 26, 2014.

[8] Kolata G. Wallace Steinberg dies at 61; Backed Health Care Ventures. New York Times, July 29, 1995. <http://www.nytimes.com/1995/07/29/obituaries/wallace-steinberg-dies-at-61-backed-health-care-ventures.html>; 1995.

[9] The Pharma Letter. Millennium Pharmaceuticals set to buy LeukoSite for $ 635 million. <www.thepharmaletter.com/article/millennium-pharmaceuticals-set-to-buy-leukosite-for-635-million>; 1999 [accessed 29.12.14].

[10] Richardson PG, Barlogie B, Berenson J, Singhal S, Jagannath S, Irwin D, et al. A phase 2 study of bortezomib in relapsed, refractory myeloma. N Engl J Med 2003;348(26):2609–17. http://dx.doi.org/10.1056/NEJMoa030288.

[11] Live PM. Top 50 pharmaceutical products by global sales—2012 and 2013. <www.pmlive. com/top_pharma_list/Top_50_pharmaceutical_products_by_global_sales>; 2014. [accessed 29.12.14].

[12] Angell M. The truth about drug companies. The New York Review of *Books*. July 15, 2004. <www.nybooks.com/articles/archives/2004/jul/15/the-truth-about-the-drug-companies/>; [accessed 29.12.14].

[13] CBS.Marketwatch.com. Millennium to buy LeukoSite for $635 million. <http://www.market-watch.com/story/millennium-to-buy-leukosite-for-635-million>; 1999 [accessed 13.02.16].

[14] Feuerstein A. Japan's Takeda Will Pay $9B for Millennium. The Street, April 10, 2008. <www.thestreet.com/story/10411425/1/japans-takeda-will-pay-9b-for-millennium.html>; 2008 [accessed 29.12.14].

Chapter 5

Biotechnology and the Future of Pharma

Forty-one new compounds were approved by the US Food and Drug Administration (FDA) in 2014. Of these, almost 40% were specialty drugs targeting refractory diseases in small populations, and most of those were biotechnology products [1]. It is useful to pause in our discussion here, and take a close look at this subcategory that increasingly dominates the overall output of the pharmaceutical industry.

What is it? Biotechnology is broadly defined as the field of applied sciences intended to improve the quality of life by finding ways to manipulate and improve biological processes in living organisms. This includes manipulation of plant, animal, and human life forms and their molecules and processes in order to improve the diagnosis and treatment of disease. Biotechnology encompasses the field of Therapeutic Biological Products (Biologics), which are defined by the FDA as proteins derived from living material, e.g., monoclonal antibodies and growth regulatory molecules such as erythropoietin [2]. As biotechnology has continued to innovate, the definition has also expanded to include vaccines, gene therapies, single stranded RNA molecules, human tissues, and more.

Biologics are distinguished from so-called "small molecule drugs" such as atorvastatin (to manage cholesterol) or cyclophosphamide (an anticancer drug), which do not naturally occur in nature. Small molecules have historically been the province and bread and butter of the pharmaceutical industry. But the lines are becoming blurred, and it's clear that much of the action now—especially the action attracting investment dollars—is in biotechnology. Even in the small molecule realm, new drugs are being discovered directly or indirectly through biotechnology.

Revolutionary genetic studies of lung cancer, for example, found specific mutations that activate the epidermal growth factor receptor (EGF-R) in some tumors, resulting in uncontrolled cell proliferation [3]. Small molecules that reverse the effect of these mutant EGF-R proteins are extremely effective in reducing and stabilizing tumor size in these lung cancer patients. Much of the industry's small molecule discovery efforts now use such genetic analyses as a starting point for drug discovery. Insulin is clearly a biologic, even though it was discovered in

Preserving the Promise. DOI: http://dx.doi.org/10.1016/B978-0-12-809216-3.00005-1

33

1921 [4]. The distinction here is that modern insulin is produced in genetically engineered cells, whereas the original product was from cow pancreas.

There's another huge driving force behind biologics, with its origins in the enormous inroads generics make the moment a branded drug loses its patent. This "patent cliff" impacted many of the top-selling drugs in the industry over the past decade, and prompted a reexamination by industry of both how it undertakes "discovery" and which new drugs are worth pursuing. Faced with contraction of revenues on blockbuster brands, Big Pharma has reduced internal research and development spending to bolster returns in the short term, increasingly relied on acquiring technologies developed by smaller companies, and turned to biologics for additional protection from generics. Biologics are much more difficult to replicate, and the regulations on approval of so-called "biosimilars"—the conceptual equivalent to bioequivalent generics—are only beginning to resolve in Europe and still fairly muddy in the US. Biologics have the same patent life as any other pharmaceutical, but from a practical point of view there's a higher barrier to generic competition.

The efficacy of these compounds supports pricing for both early and mature biologics that is, in a word, breathtaking: $94,000 for 12 weeks' therapy with Harvoni, for example, for Hepatitis C. It's an attractive financial proposition, and that drives valuations for development-stage companies in the biologics space, which in turn encourages investors to open their wallets. With all of these factors at work, it is no exaggeration to suggest that biotechnology is at the core of modern drug discovery, and probably the future of the industry from both a financial and clinical perspective.

Biotechnology is seen by investors as a high risk but incredibly powerful investment opportunity. From 2013 to 2015, large institutional investors capitalized on a virtual flood of enormous, lucrative, and highly publicized exits, in the form of sales to Big Pharma or initial public offerings (IPOs). To capture and promote an early technology and bring it to the level required for such an exit can theoretically provide the 10-fold, 20-fold, or even greater return that is the de facto target for institutional investors. (The reason we say theoretically is that these returns need to be taken in context: the probability of success requires that the absolute figure realized on any winning investment needs to pay for a geometrically larger number of other investments that yield no return.)

Pharmaceutical and biotech companies are the ultimate beneficiaries of this process, in the form of sales revenue, and their calculation of return on investment (ROI) is the marginal cost of development against projected sales, which are greatest during the period of patent protection. This is a different calculation, and a different market from the one for early stage intellectual property. Most of the funding of early stage companies comes not from Big Pharma, but from investors, who expect to realize their return *before* the drug under development ever reaches the hand of a physician or patient.

To fully appreciate the biotechnology landscape it's necessary to understand the diversity of its constituents. At the ground level are scientists, who make the foundational discoveries. The US National Institutes of Health (NIH) funds discovery to the tune of tens of billions of dollars each year, most of it devoted to basic research. A US Federal law called the Bayh–Dole Act essentially deeds the rights to these inventions, the ability to license them to any other entity, and the proceeds deriving from those licenses to the originating university. Business service professionals package the technology and initiate the commercialization process. These include the patent attorneys who transform a concept into protected intellectual property and the advisors and managers who assemble and sell the business plan. This is all funded in the early stages by "friends and family," Angels, and other early stage investors.

Typically, the invention must navigate the Valley of Death (VoD) and progress to a later stage of development before it attracts the substantial funding required to get through clinical trials and final commercial development. The sources of that money include Venture Capitalists, big-company strategic partners, and public markets in the case of an IPO. It's not difficult to see that satisfying this range of stakeholders can be a comparable or even greater challenge than overcoming the technical barriers to development. And so, oddly enough, the constituents for whose ultimate benefit all of this development takes place, the patients, families, and caregivers, are almost always the ones furthest down the priority chain.

The authors of this book live and work in this domain because we believe that biotechnology is different from other areas of discovery or invention, and feel strongly that it deserves to be treated differently from other investment opportunities. As an investor, I may be able to make more money by investing in Apple. But if I or a loved one gets cancer or heart disease, do I really care about my Apple stock in the same way that I worry about what treatments will be available and how well they will work? Biotechnology matters, and it matters on dimensions that don't apply to other investments.

Beyond its intrinsic value for protecting our health, biotechnology is an economic engine of growth for the United States—in some regions, *the* economic growth engine. Jobs in the biotech industry are key to the overall US employment sector. There are more than 1300 firms in the US biotech industry, and in the first decade of this century the industry grew by 6.4% and added nearly 100,000 jobs—in a period when total employment for *all* US private-sector industries was falling by 2.9% and the economy suffered the loss of more than 3 million jobs [5]. Pharmaceutical Research and Manufacturers of America estimates 3.4 million US jobs are supported by the biotech industry [6]. Wages and benefits for the more than 800,000 individuals working directly in the industry averaged $110,490 per position, more than double the average private sector compensation in the United States. The Human Genome Project by itself converted a $14.5 billion investment over 1988 through 2012 into an estimated $965 billion in US economic impact, including more than 53,000 genomics-related jobs that paid $293 billion in personal income [7].

Appropriate to its mission and scope, the sector receives a massive amount of public and private investment. For instance, federal entities fund about 40%

of biomedical research. The NIH is the single largest funder of biomedical research in the world, with a budget exceeding $30 billion [8]. In 2014, US donations to health-related charities surpassed $28 billion [9]. Angel investors funneled almost $3.9 billion into the health-related sector [10]. In 2014, when estimated corporate R&D investment in the United States was $465 billion, about 20%, or $93 billion, supported life sciences, and 85% of that was specifically for biopharmaceuticals [11].

The pharmaceutical industry reaps a substantial return from this research investment, yet less and less of that income is being directed internally to new drug discovery. Big Pharma has increasingly outsourced discovery to pioneering companies in the VoD, not by contracting, but by limited partnering and acquisition of the output of those VoD companies' efforts late in development. At this juncture many of the risks of technological failure as internal overhead for the industry have been mitigated, and the risks of final development, manufacturing, and marketing are managed by the power of size and incumbency.

Biotech is clearly essential to the future of Big Pharma— a term which refers to the relative handful traditional companies that remain after consolidation of the chemistry-driven powerhouses that dominated drug development and sales in the last century. The complexity, cost and potential protection against generics are foils to the decline of profits as "blockbuster" drugs lose their patent protection. Sales of branded compounds can face a 90% drop almost immediately after patent expiration, as generic competitors enter the marketplace [12]. The industry is not particularly suffering financially, but it has been hurtling over a "patent cliff" which, by the end of 2015, devalued a stable of drugs worth $225 billion in annual sales [13]. Peak years of the patent cliff included 2012, with loss of patents on $54.7 billion in revenue, and 2015 at $47.5 billion. No industry prospers without a continuing flow of new or improved products, and dependence on patent protection makes this a particularly acute issue for Big Pharma.

The pipeline of new drugs is increasingly dependent upon biologics, for reasons of both uniqueness and high value pricing. In 2013, 907 biotech drugs were in clinical development [14]. For short-term financial reasons, the industry has divested itself of much of its internal discovery capability in favor of a licensing and acquisition model. This makes sense on paper, from the standpoint of reducing overhead and shifting the cost of discovery off the companies' balance sheets, but it only exacerbates the problem of funding for early stage discoveries. While innovation and creativity are more likely to flourish in smaller, more nimble companies than in very large organizations, the discovery effort doesn't survive without capital. And most of that capital is not available to a nascent biotech until it has somehow been able to get through the VoD to later stages of development.

As we've noted, compared with small molecules, biologics can be relatively resistant to the effects of patent expiration compared with traditional small molecule therapeutics. Biologics also benefit from a regulatory environment that fast-tracks specialty drugs for orphan diseases and other acute clinical needs. Orphan diseases are defined as those that affect less than 200,000 cases annually in the United States [15]. They receive special benefits from the FDA to encourage their development, including federal money for clinical trials, a tax credit on clinical testing costs and, most importantly, an exclusive right to sell the drug for 7 years following approval, even after patents have expired.

The idea behind this special treatment was to provide economic incentives to encourage development of medicines for critical but epidemiologically smaller populations. The reality is that the orphan market has become something of a revenue bonanza, companies achieving profitability far beyond traditional pharmacoeconomic models by taking advantage of a streamlined approval process and by pricing the new drugs at previously unheard-of levels. The poster child for this phenomenon is Soliris, a monoclonal antibody effective in the treatment of paroxysmal nocturnal hemoglobinuria (PNH) and atypical hemolytic-uremic syndrome (aHUS), both potentially fatal diseases. PNH can cause pain, fatigue, and devastating blood clots, and the only curative treatment is bone marrow transplantation, while aHUS can cause life-threatening hypertension and kidney failure requiring dialysis. Soliris has achieved blockbuster status, topping $2.5 billion in sales in 2015 to a population that numbers in the low thousands—that's thousands, not millions of patients [16]. While it is important to note that the company maintains a prominent compassionate use program for patients who cannot afford Soliris, it's equally of note that the drug sells in the United States for $669,000 per year [17].

The revenue potential means that orphan diseases, once bypassed as socially responsible but ancillary, have become a focus of development for the industry. The orphan drug market alone may reach $176 billion by 2020 [18]. Between October 2013 and June 2014, the FDA was reviewing an average of 40 orphan drug designation reviews a month. Twelve of the forty-one drugs approved by the FDA in 2014 were orphan drugs; five of these were biologics. The niche diseases that are often favored for a career in academic research have now been transformed from uninvestable "science experiments" (investors' pejorative for precommercial basic research) into high-potential opportunities. This is not because the industry has suddenly developed a greater predisposition to philanthropy, but because the business model for orphans has, at least for the present, become an irresistible one.

The biotechnologies traveling through, and occasionally emerging from, the VoD also have tremendous implications for personalized medicine. Personalized medicine refers to a treatment that is matched to a disease by a genetic or other biomarker test. The biomarker could evaluate almost any biological material or process, but most biomarkers test DNA, RNA, or protein. For instance, an RNA test of chronic myeloid leukemia cells is used to determine if the bcr/abl fusion gene is present; if so, the disease will probably respond to a drug such as imatinib.

Indeed, the fundamental driver of healthcare innovation in the VoD is often a novel understanding of how to treat a particular disease. If the discovery results in a biomarker that defines a rare subset of a common disease, you have essentially created an opportunity at the intersection of orphan disease, personalized medicine and biotechnology. For example, even though lung cancer is one of the most frequently diagnosed cancers, the specific type of non small cell lung cancer that harbors an EML4-ALK fusion gene comprises fewer than 5% of nonsmall cell lung cancers, likely less than 4000 cases per year in the United States [19]. On the surface, diagnosing a disease with an incidence of 4000 per year wouldn't seem to be much of a commercial opportunity. But the topline revenue potential of an orphan drug is amplified: first, by the orphan designation itself, which requires more targeted, and therefore smaller and less expensive, clinical trials; second, by the ability to obtain regulatory approval in less time; third, by the implications of that earlier approval for sales; and finally, by the nature of biotechnology which (at least for now) confers a longer effective patent-protected life in the marketplace.

So all appears to be on a solid path to success for Big Pharma: more effective medications based on biotechnology, more personalized medicine based on DNA sequencing, more financial return from orphan and other specialty drugs. Equipped with this roadmap, and addicted to cutting overhead through consolidation and outsourcing, the industry has been assiduously trimming the discovery portion R&D—closing facilities, providing some funds to early stage companies in the form of sponsored research agreements or modest upfront payments with milestones, and substituting targeted business development for internal discovery. Of the 41 approvals in 2014, 18 came from Big Pharma but only 6 of those originated within their own research divisions [1]. The rest were obtained by acquiring other companies or licensing their intellectual property.

The reduction in internal discovery initiatives is reflected in multiple basic science R&D facility closures by Merck, Pfizer, Roche, and others over the past several years, and in an acceleration of mergers and acquisitions activity. Inflation-adjusted R&D expenditures by the industry dropped by $12.9 billion between 2007 and 2012 [20]. The 2008 merger between Pfizer and Wyeth alone cut $5.5 billion in annual R&D spending by 2013 [21].

The thrust is that the pharma industry has increasingly shifted to "a buy, rather than build, model of discovery and development" [22]. In other words, start-up biotechnology, generally invented and progressed from preclinical through Phase I or Phase II clinical development *outside of Big Pharma's doors*, appears to be the future of clinical discovery—and the bet Big Pharma is making on its future. As Diego Miralles, head of Johnson & Johnson's California Innovation Center, put it, "At the end of the day, we are going to live or die by the success of the biotech start-ups" [23]. New drug initiatives surviving the VoD are, at once, more difficult and urgent than ever.

REFERENCES

[1] FDA. FDA approved drugs. <http://www.centerwatch.com/drug-information/fda-approved-drugs/year/>; 2014 [accessed 14.02.16].

[2] FDA. Drugs@FDA glossary of terms. <http://www.fda.gov/drugs/informationondrugs/ucm079436.htm>; 2014 [accessed 14.02.16].

[3] Gettinger S, Lynch T. A decade of advances in treatment for advanced non-small cell lung cancer. Clin Chest Med 2011;32(4):839–51. http://dx.doi.org/10.1016/j.ccm.2011.08.017.

[4] Rosenfeld L. Insulin: discovery and controversy. Clin Chem 2002;48(12):2270–88.

[5] Battelle/BIO State Bioscience Industry Development 2012. <https://www.bio.org/sites/default/files/v3battelle-bio_2012_industry_develop>.

[6] Pharmaceutical Research and Manufacturers of America. Profile: Biopharmaceutical Research Industry. Washington, DC. <http://www.phrma.org/sites/default/files/pdf/2015_phrma_profile.pdf>; 2015.

[7] Battelle Technology Partnership Practice for United for Medical Research (UMR). Economic impact of the human genome project. June 2013. <http://www.battelle.org/media/press-releases/updated-battelle-study-genetics-and-genomics-industry>; 2013 [accessed 14.02.16].

[8] Mervis J. Updated: budget agreement boosts U.S. science. Science. <http://www.sciencemag.org/news/2015/12/updated-budget-agreement-boosts-us-science/>; 2015 [accessed 14.02.16].

[9] Lilly Family School of Philanthropy. Giving USA 2015 report highlights. <http://givingusa.org/product/giving-usa-2015-report-highlights/>; 2015 [accessed 14.02.16].

[10] Sohl J. "The Angel investor market in 2014: A market correction in deal size." Center for Venture Research. <https://paulcollege.unh.edu/sites/paulcollege.unh.edu/files/webform/2014%20Analysis%20Report.pdf/>; 2015.

[11] Battelle. 2014 Global R&D funding forecast. <https://www.battelle.org/docs/tpp/2014_global_rd_funding_forecast.pdf>; 2013 [accessed 3.01.15].

[12] Bioassociate Consulting & Management Ltd. The significance and apparent repercussions of the 2009–2015 pharmaceutical patent cliff. Tel Aviv, Israel, 2012.

[13] Bailey J. Pharma patent cliff: why worst seems over. YCharts. <https://ycharts.com/analysis/story/pharma_patent_cliff_why_worst_seems_over#sthash.IFjAItUp.dpuf/>; 2014 [accessed 14.02.16].

[14] Pharmaceutical Research and Manufacturers of America. Medicines in development biologics 2013. <http://www.phrma.org/sites/default/files/pdf/biologics2013.pdf>; 2013 [accessed 14.02.16].

[15] Field MJ, Boat TF. Rare diseases and orphan products: accelerating research and development. Washington DC: Institute of Medicine, National Academies Press; 2010. <http://www.ncbi.nlm.nih.gov/books/NBK56189/pdf/TOC.pdf/>; 2010.

[16] Alexion. Alexion reports fourth quarter and full year 2015 results and provides financial guidance for 2016. <http://ir.alexionpharm.com/releasedetail.cfm?ReleaseID=953056>; 2016 [accessed 14.02.16].

[17] Palmer E. Alexion sues Canada over Soliris price cut attempt as drug cost debate explodes on center stage. FiercePharma 2015. <http://www.fiercepharma.com/story/alexion-sues-canada-over-soliris-price-cut-attempt-drug-cost-debate-explode/2015-09-25/> [accessed 14.02.16].

[18] EvaluatePharma. Orphan drug report 2014. <www.evaluategroup.com/orphandrug2014>; 2014 [accessed 14.02.16].

[19] Shaw AT, Yeap BY, Mino-Kenudson M, Digumarthy SR, Costa DB, Heist RS, et al. Clinical features and outcome of patients with non-small-cell lung cancer who harbor EML4-ALK. J Clin Oncol 2009;27(26):4247–53. http://dx.doi.org/10.1200/JCO.2009.22.6993.

[20] Chakma J, Sun GH, Steinberg JD, Sammut SM, Jagsi R. Asia's ascent—global trends in biomedical R&D expenditures. N Engl J Med 2014;370(1):3–6. http://dx.doi.org/10.1056/NEJMp1311068.

[21] LaMattina J. Biopharmaceutical industry consolidation diminishes future drug discovery. Forbes; 2014. <http://www.forbes.com/sites/johnlamattina/2014/06/10/biopharmaceutical-industry-consolidation-diminishes-future-drug-discovery/> [accessed 14.02.16].

[22] Burrill GS. Biotech 2014—Life sciences: transforming healthcare, Burrill's 28th annual report on the life sciences industry. San Francisco, CA: Burrill Media, LLC; 2014.56.

[23] Burrill GS. Biotech 2014—Life sciences: transforming healthcare, Burrill's 28th annual report on the life sciences industry. San Francisco, CA: Burrill Media, LLC; 2014.90.

Chapter 6

Why Pharma Should Care About the Valley of Death

The University City Science Center (UCSC) in Philadelphia is one of the oldest research parks in the United States. Founded in 1963 by a consortium of Philadelphia-area universities and nonprofit research institutions, including the University of Pennsylvania, Drexel University, and The Children's Hospital of Philadelphia, it is a high-profile spawning ground for new biotech companies in the mid-Atlantic region. The UCSC provides laboratory space, seed funding, mentoring and business guidance, and the immersion of a collaborative, entrepreneurial community. It is a natural landing spot for technologies that come out of these universities. In 2010, in the midst of the dark period that followed the burst of the 2008 biotech bubble, the authors were panel speakers at a UCSC-sponsored *Entrepreneur On-Ramp* colloquium. Many of those in the room were struggling to keep their start-up companies funded. The biotech initial public offering (IPO) window was closed, venture capitalists (VCs) had retrenched, and Angel investors were looking at diminished personal balance sheets and shifting their investments away from seed funding to follow-on rounds for companies in which they had previously invested [1]. Much of the discussion at the *On-Ramp* was about how to build a relationship with a Big Pharma company. To companies in the Valley of Death (VoD), the industry shift away from internal discovery efforts and burgeoning impact of patent expirations suggested opportunity.

Faced with an unprecedented patent cliff and declining productivity from internal research and development (R&D), Big Pharma had been failing to produce enough new drugs in the near term to offset displacement of blockbuster brands by generics. The industry was downsizing its internal research operations in favor of outsourcing, intensifying its focus on acquisition of technologies developed outside its own labs, and explicitly seeking the next big thing from biotech and other healthcare start-ups in the VoD. To those of us on the other end of the equation, it seemed almost self-evident that Big Pharma needed what we had and would be willing to pay for it. A deal with a strategic industry partner could go far beyond life support until the next funding round and give a technology a real opportunity to reach the clinic.

Preserving the Promise. DOI: http://dx.doi.org/10.1016/B978-0-12-809216-3.00006-3
41

This outsourced discovery model has intrinsic appeal from both sides. Research within Big Pharma has often been characterized, fairly or not, as intrinsically less innovative and creative than the research that occurs in a start-up environment. It's precisely the reason that spin-outs and acquisitions occur. A "buy technology" strategy allows pharmaceutical companies to focus their resources on acquiring (already) demonstrably groundbreaking technologies, or at least filling in the missing links to their own internal development. It also allows them to capitalize on the insight, motivation, and sheer force of will manifested by more nimble biotechnology start-ups. This strategy has yielded a fair number of high-profile deals for companies in later-stage development (as well as some in earlier stages), and an impressive stream of high returns to later-stage investors in biotechnology. Whether or not these marriages between start-up innovation and the commercialization power of Big Pharma ultimately generated big revenues, they clearly and repeatedly yielded some very large dowries.

Half of the motivation behind this shift is instinctively right: innovation does thrive in a more nimble, less bureaucratic environment [2]. But there's a catch, and it undermines the apparent efficiency of the argument. Aggregate overhead is increased geometrically through the inefficiency of independently running thousands of nascent ventures. In the VoD, every technology gets its own company, so the nonscientific expenses pile on: prosecution of IP, management (even if compensation is deferred), business development, lab and office space, contracts for materials and testing, assorted legal fees and so on. It is as though Pfizer decided to diffuse its R&D effort into 500 little companies, each with their own facility, management, lawyers, and scientists, completely siloed and buzzing away on their individual projects without regard to what anyone else was doing. It's not difficult for companies in the VoD to spend more money and energy on operations and fundraising than on research, extending the cost and duration of development.

Thus the rationale behind accelerators, incubators, and centers of innovation like the UCSC: to replicate the economies of scale for start-ups. Shared laboratory equipment and infrastructure, with common access to business, legal, and other advisors, provides support that would formerly have been part of internal R&D overhead for Big Pharma. The idea is to quickly assess, and determine whether to support or abandon new technologies while minimizing the cost at this very early stage. This reduces the financial demands of outsourcing innovation and it presumably increases aggregate harvest value at the back end. Almost one-third of US start-ups (all technologies) that raised a Series A in 2015 were graduates of accelerators, and this has been increasing every year for the last 8 years [3]. The UCSC alone claims to have produced ~150 stable companies that contribute almost $9 billion annually to the regional economy [4].

Our panel at the Entrepreneur On-Ramp considered the obstacles faced when seeking a deal with Pharma. The competition is great, as the number of VoD companies seeking these opportunities dwarfs the number of deals available. This may seem surprising, considering that in 2013 merger and acquisition (M&A) deals in the life sciences amounted to \$131.8 billion across 203 transactions [5]. However, upon closer inspection, most of this activity was directed at acquiring clinical stage or marketed products, rather than supporting early-stage biotech, which has very limited access to this level of activity until late in the game. In each of the years 2009–13, there were fewer than 10 M&A deals for preclinical programs [5].

Partnering activity, by contrast, in which Big Pharma provides limited funding for research collaborations but does not actually purchase an asset, is more accessible to VoD companies. This has been boosted in recent years by the high failure rate of mid- to late-stage internal programs, which has increased the interest of Pharma in new therapeutic targets, mechanisms, and technologies. One hundred thirty-three of these deals with values of \$20 million or more—the kind of deal that enhances exit potential for early-stage investors—occurred in 2013 [6]. Pharma partnering activity has migrated in some measure toward smaller deals, with many of these arrangements backloaded: they include a modest upfront payment with the option to license a technology, and include additional royalty payments as the technology achieves prespecified development milestones. But even these backloaded deals are difficult for VoD companies to achieve. They need to have a de-risked program that matches the needs of their potential Pharma partners. As a technology scout from a Big Pharma company related to us, "In the pharma world today, guys aren't looking for *stuff*—they're looking for very specific things. Perfect fits are really important."

The number of deals available is not tied to the number of VoD companies looking for them, and the probability of exit by acquisition has likely diminished due to industry consolidation. Over the past 30 years, more than 100 companies consolidated into fewer than 30 [7], and discussion of "Big Pharma" these days usually focuses on 6 or 7 monoliths. The results of these consolidations are clear. Any single company has less motivation than two separate companies to pursue parallel programs intended for the same indication, so following a merger programs targeting the same diseases are either blended or assimilated one into another, for the cost efficiencies that are the *sine qua non* of M&A. There are fewer buyers, with fewer development programs, with more targeted needs—while the number of start-ups looking to the same few pharma companies for an exit continues to increase. An early-stage company CEO summed it up this way: "There are thousands of companies in the US right now with a financing slide (in their pitch deck) that describes a sale to Big Pharma, but if you do the numbers, based on the actual number of deals, most of these companies will be left hanging."

It's not difficult to imagine a revolutionary approach to something refractory, like pancreatic cancer, going nowhere for reasons that have nothing to do with clinical medicine. Consolidation reduces the chances for any given discovery to enter the clinical development pipeline. This works against broader societal goals for clinical research, but it's also a devil's bargain that benefits late-stage investors at the expense of everyone else. As the top of the drug development pyramid continues to narrow, positive outcomes are fewer and further between for inventor/entrepreneurs, early-stage investors, clinicians, and patients. Even Big Pharma has effectively forced itself into a limited number of very large, very high-risk bets, as evidenced by a number of binary failures—dearly acquired technologies or companies that failed in Phase III.

Because of the enormous investment required to progress a drug through preclinical and clinical development, a deal or sale to Big Pharma remains the primary target for most start-ups in the VoD. As the financing available from all sources for progressing early-stage technology has become more difficult to access, the prime motive of any biotech venture is to accrue enough gravitas to attract a deal from Big Pharma that enables an exit for the investors. This is the subtext of every investor pitch. This is not to say that other types of deals, such as sponsored research agreements, grants, or other development support are no longer possible, and the 2013–15 reopening of the biotech IPO window may have changed the options temporarily, but the prime objective for entrepreneurs has definitively shifted from finding the next cure to finding the way to a Pharma deal.

In this role, Big Pharma has evolved from a unique, discovery-driven industry, to a small coterie of very large financial concerns trading on massive development heft. This is an industry that was founded and prospered on its distinction from every other commercial enterprise: the essential commitment to research in support of advancing human health. In a generation, it has, in a monumental push to maximize short-term shareholder "value" by reducing costs, consolidated into a few gigantic institutions whose real product—stock price and dividends—is undistinguished from other industries. If this seems extreme, consider the transformation during these authors' career lifetimes of Big Pharma: from one of the most esteemed industrial enterprises, to one of the most reviled.

What was part and parcel of the mission, and an integral part of the business model cost structure—spending considerably on basic research as well as development—has given way to a perpetual drive to shed overhead and offload risk. All of which leaves a horizontally diversified industry as simply the ultimate arbiter of the exit.

This isn't intended as an indictment of financial interests, which after all are the objective of most business pursuits. Nor do we mean to suggest that connecting the dots between university innovation and Pharma is as simple an equation as matching supply of technology to demand for deals. Our point, rather, is that much of the innovation coming out of university laboratories is simply not ready for a deal—yet. This is the first part of the Translation Gap: universities don't make what companies need.

Pharma doesn't want to pay for intellectual property in the early stages unless it provides a very specific missing link to an existing development program or otherwise supports a strategic push in a particular therapeutic area. The business development people responsible for acquiring IP, naturally enough, want a solid data package that proves the technology works in animal models of the disease and plots a realistic path to the clinic. This includes pharmacokinetic studies (how the body processes a drug), pharmacodynamic studies (what the drug does to the patient), and preliminary estimates of development and production costs versus revenue. These data are not the typical product of academic research and are also beyond the scope of what many new biotech start-ups in the VoD have so far achieved.

Pharma deserves credit for its continued efforts to partner with academic institutions to streamline the translation of academic discoveries into commercial development [8]. Nonetheless, with thousands of companies competing for a finite supply of Angel investor money, needing to survive ever-longer until VCs consider them a *safe enough* bet, most will stall or die before they can prove their technology is ready for acquisition by Big Pharma. After Big Pharma has cherry-picked the best early-stage opportunities for licensing and collaboration, and the most lucrative late-stage specialty drugs for acquisition, what will be left?

This is why the first component of the Translation Gap is so critical. When technologies leave academia and enter the VoD, they need to be far enough along for early consideration by a strategic partner—a slim prospect—or at least attractive enough that investors will provide support long enough to achieve a Pharma deal.

So why not just leave development to universities, and avoid the imperative for private funding entirely until the technology is ready for prime time? To begin with, the definition of success in an academic environment versus a commercial environment is different. On balance, academia rewards novelty over the mundane, but equally important process of drug development; it favors a paradigm shift in how we understand biology over an operational approach to solving the development puzzle. It's not that hard-and-fast, of course, and there are plenty of academic scientists working to merge academic innovation with drug discovery—a phenomenon most visible where universities and the start-up community are natural extensions of one another. Cambridge and Palo Alto come to mind, not coincidentally the homes of MIT and Stanford and the geographic launch pads for many high-profile biotechnology ventures.

The Center for the Science of Therapeutics at the Broad Institute in Cambridge, MA, for example, is a model of how to apply the creative power of academia to drug discovery [9]. A consortium comprising more than 1500 scientists in teams from Harvard University, Harvard Medical School-affiliated teaching hospitals, MIT, and the Broad Institute performs the full range of drug discovery activities, including genomics research, synthesis of novel chemical libraries, cell-based drug screening, and validation of novel disease targets. But in general, success in an academic environment is somewhat at arm's length from the commercial marketplace. The aspiration of the scientific researcher is to reveal something about nature that can lead to a new drug. The goal from a career and financial perspective is to establish a high enough profile and enough scientific progress for promotion, tenure and, of course, more grants—and certainly, if it comes, the opportunity to see the work commercialized.

The reward metrics in this environment also provide an incentive for extraordinary results that may not always be reproducible. Academia is a hypercompetitive system with limited opportunities for advancement [10]. Scientists need to support their salaries and research through grants, and successful research is required to receive grants. This "publish or perish" and "eat what you kill" mentality has seen enough high-profile missteps that regulations now exist to thwart even the possibility of conflict of interest, by rather bizarrely separating scientists from their inventions as they are being commercialized. We don't believe that publish or perish incentives necessarily undermine the objectivity of academic discovery, but they have created a hypercautious, defensive environment that can be counterproductive. Failure to reproduce a finding is part of research, and it's rarely because of intentional misdirection, but there is plenty of incentive for it and enough data for investors and Pharma to be cautious.

- Scientists at the biotechnology behemoth Amgen tried to replicate a selected series of key discoveries in academic cancer research, even working with the original researchers to ensure that they were adequately following the experimental protocols. As they described in the journal, *Nature*, only 6 of 53 could be replicated [11].
- A report from scientists involved in target validation at Bayer HealthCare described their efforts to confirm the results of academic research in the fields of oncology, women's health, and cardiovascular diseases. In the study of 67 projects over 4 years, they found that almost two-thirds of the projects had data inconsistencies that resulted in projects being significantly delayed or canceled [12].

In most cases, the operative variable is less likely to be fraud than misinterpretation, selective attention, or simple mistakes. If you accidentally get a result that proves your hypothesis, you might be less inclined to doubt it than you would a correct result that contradicts your expectations.

At the end of the day, and in most academic institutions, a different orientation to discovery, different aspirations, and different incentives demand that technologies be graduated from the university to begin their journey to the clinic in earnest. The necessity to do so highlights one part of the Translation Gap that we saw in the story of Velcade: academia produces a product that is generally not ready for commercialization. Goldberg needed to start a company to translate his mechanistic research of the proteasome into a drug candidate.

The VoD is the flawed but necessary commercial launch pad for almost everything leaving the university. This is where new technologies obtain funding and other support to confirm and extend academic results, and to create a data package that can appeal to later-stage investors and enable acquisition by Big Pharma. The same principles apply regardless of interim funding or eventual exit strategy: confirm, de-risk, extend, and create a vision of financial opportunity—which is in some ways coincident with, and in others distinct from, the pathway to the clinic itself.

If the VoD were functioning in the interests of all constituents, and in the historical model of the mission-based discovery engine that once described the pharmaceutical industry, it would identify the best technologies coming out of our universities and research institutes. It would select those most likely to have the greatest impact on health and society. It would sort out those that work from those that don't, or the ones that simply need more time. It might prefer drugs that can save lives rather than prolong them, or reverse chronic disabilities. It would favor innovation over incremental change, and it would intelligently match the limited funds available to support as many of these as possible. Gently guided by a free market competition for dollars, the best innovations would move forward steadily while those less compelling or unworkable fell to the sidelines.

But how can a process that destroys most of what comes into it, even some of the most revolutionary ideas from our most brilliant scientists, be considered to be working? The disconnect between what academia produces and what is needed to merit clinical development, combined with the limited availability of Pharma partnerships, and ultimately exits, challenges even the very best start-ups in the VoD.

REFERENCES

[1] Sohl J. The Angel investor market in 2010: a market on the rebound. Center for Venture Research; 2011. April 12, 2011.

[2] Scannell JW, Blanckley A, Boldon H, Warrington B. Diagnosing the decline in pharmaceutical R&D efficiency. Nat Rev Drug Discov 2012;11(3):191–200. http://dx.doi.org/10.1038/nrd3681.

[3] Tom M. One-third of US startups that raised a series A in 2015 went through an accelerator. <http://pitchbook.com/news/articles/one-third-of-us-startups-that-raised-a-series-a-in-2015-went-through-an-accelerator>; 2016 [accessed 16.02.16].

[4] UCSC. The University City Science Center: an engine of economic growth for greater Philadelphia. <http://issuu.com/sciencecenter/docs/full_report_-_science_center_is_a_regional_engine_?e=1878732/5347759>; 2014 [accessed 16.02.16].

[5] Burrill GS. Biotech 2014—life sciences: transforming healthcare, Burrill's 28th annual report on the life sciences industry. San Francisco, CA: Burrill Media, LLC; 2014.216.

[6] Burrill GS. Biotech 2014—life sciences: transforming healthcare, Burrill's 28th annual report on the life sciences industry. San Francisco, CA: Burrill Media, LLC; 2014.228.

[7] Davidovic D. The history of bio-pharma industry M&As, lessons learned and trends to watch. <http://www.pm360online.com/the-history-of-bio-pharma-industry-mas-lessons-learned-and-trends-to-watch>; 2014 [accessed 17.02.16].

[8] Huggett B. Academic partnerships 2014. Nat Biotechnol 2015;33(4):333. http://dx.doi.org/10.1038/nbt.3189.

[9] Center for the Science of Therapeutics. Home page. <http://www.broadinstitute.org/scientific-community/science/programs/csoft/center-science-therapeutics>.

[10] Alberts B, Kirschner MW, Tilghman S, Varmus H. Rescuing US biomedical research from its systemic flaws. Proc Natl Acad Sci USA 2014;111(16):5773–7. http://dx.doi.org/10.1073/pnas.1404402111.

[11] Begley CG, Ellis LM. Drug development: raise standards for preclinical cancer research. Nature 2012;483(7391):531–3. http://dx.doi.org/10.1038/483531a.

[12] Prinz F, Schlange T, Asadullah K. Believe it or not: how much can we rely on published data on potential drug targets? Nat Rev Drug Discov 2011;10(9):712. http://dx.doi.org/10.1038/nrd3439-c1.

Chapter 7

Porter's Five Forces and the Market for Angel Capital

We have already discussed how Big Pharma's internal investment in research and development (R&D) has declined, a migration from the more traditional gestation of new drugs within Pharma labs to outsourced discovery by smaller companies. Driven by the urgency of replenishing its development pipelines, a management predisposition to outsourcing, and the long development path for early stage technologies, Big Pharma has adopted an investment focus on later-stage properties with a nearer-term payoff. The industry now deploys substantial capital previously committed to internal R&D to buy late-stage, "derisked" ventures. While funds are still committed to sponsored research and codevelopment agreements with early stage biotech/healthcare companies, the amounts pale in comparison to acquisitions transacting at hundreds of millions of dollars each. The result of this emphasis is a less direct relationship between revenues from drug sales and the availability of funds to support innovation. The seed-stage activity in the Valley of Death (VoD) that Big Pharma does support has a nonlinear relationship with the financial success of the industry, and is more likely to respond to a vacuum in the pipeline than to reflect an historical percentage of sales.

An important consequence of these changes is that a substantial portion of drug discovery efforts, freed from the balance sheets of Big Pharma, are being financed with money "borrowed" from investors. This is a marked departure from historical practice whereby drug discovery was financed on an ongoing basis by revenue from drug sales, and the enormous R&D costs of each new drug that reaches the clinic were amortized across multiple development programs. Revenue from drug sales funded research, leading to additional revenue and more research, without the imperative of investors achieving short-term, high-multiple return on investments in start-up ventures. Of course there's a corollary expectation of return within the industry, driving extreme valuations on acquisitions, but the net effect is a shift *from internal business risk to external investor risk*. Much of the financial risk of R&D has been shifted to venture capitalists (VCs) and Angel investors, and across the board companies and investors are focused on achieving a shorter horizon to return.

Preserving the Promise. DOI: http://dx.doi.org/10.1016/B978-0-12-809216-3.00007-5

Apart from the impact on what gets funded, the fiscal inefficiency of this rush to outsourcing is obvious. It's not just that global discovery research has deconsolidated into thousands of start-ups, but also that each of them is gambling with someone else's money—money that is agnostic to clinical merit—in hopes of achieving a long-shot bonanza. Outsourcing has compounded the risk of scientific failure with the risk of financial failure for reasons unrelated to clinical merit. The ability to progress a research program depends entirely on the availability of investor dollars outside rather than inside the industry.

Fortunately for the biotech ecosystem, there's been a lot of money flowing through venture capital recently. The total biotech VC investment in 2015, according to the MoneyTree Report by PricewaterhouseCoopers LLP [1] was $7.4 billion, up from $6.3 billion in 2014. However, it's not being evenly distributed. Only 4% of the biotech companies funded by VCs in 2014 were seed-stage, which is consistent with historical trends [2] and therefore fails to compensate for the movement of discovery to research labs outside of Big Pharma. Seventy-nine percent of the biotech companies receiving VC investments were in product development: VCs, along with the pharma industry, increasingly prefer to leave the initial stages of biotech support, when drugs are still in the lab, to others.

We will no doubt be challenged on this point from investors pointing to their high-profile support of seed-stage companies, and it is true that there remains a small but active cohort of early stage VCs. Some are even creating and financing their own seed-stage companies, or creating portfolio funds that acquire collections of IP from universities. There's a degree of self-selection at work, of course, with a discernable focus on investments in "big name" scientists from major institutions and/or in entrepreneurs with a track record of successful efforts. Those with a less prominent profile will have a much more difficult time getting a high-level hearing. Whether that's a good thing in aggregate isn't clear. But at the end of the day, what is clear is that money is going in larger boluses to fewer companies, focused on more advanced, de-risked opportunities—and leaving the well somewhat dry for the large number of companies in earlier stages of their VoD journey.

There is also a heavy regional concentration, with the Boston/Cambridge and San Francisco Bay areas vying for leadership in the numbers of biotech deals and dollars invested [3]. Other prominent hubs include San Diego, Seattle, the Great Lakes Region, New York City, Washington DC, and Raleigh/Durham, but the ~$1 billion in biotech VC investments made in both San Francisco and Boston/Cambridge in 2013 dwarf the next on the list, San Diego, at $387 million. As you move farther from these hubs, the opportunities for VC investment in biotech drop precipitously. For example, Los Angeles and Chicago, the cities ranked 14th and 15th for biotech investment, respectively, pulled in only $46 million and $40 million. It should be no surprise that 6 of the 10 academic start-up companies receiving the largest Series A rounds in 2015 were located in Cambridge, MA, or the San Francisco Bay area [4].

Finally, as we noted earlier, the disposition of capital is both ephemeral and cyclical. The stock market in the first quarter of 2016 was more down than up, and for a while now institutional money has been getting redirected elsewhere, as biotech boom may be turning to biotech bust—again.

Most early stage companies are subject to this essential calculus of industry/ investor behavior, and that means most academic spinouts need to raise money from sources other than Big Pharma or VCs: government grants, other public funds, friends and family, and Angel investors. Because government and public funding sources are usually inadequate to fund a company through even the early commercialization phase, Angel investments are absolutely essential for virtually all early stage biotech ventures.

Companies in the VoD frequently raise early money in the form of convertible debt—money that is loaned with interest and will convert to equity when a share price is set in the future. Typically, convertible debt also includes the right to buy shares at a lower price, which may amount to a 20% or greater "discount." While other companies begin their journey with an equity investment— investors buy a percentage of the company based on current valuation—the funding dynamic is the same. Angels making an investment in your company want their money back, preferably at a very high multiple of what they put in, and most desirably within a limited time frame. Whether their investment is the debt incurred with a convertible note or equity represented by shares in the company is important for follow-on investment terms, but doesn't change the essential dynamic. In the final analysis, the start-up is taking on a financial obligation that needs to be paid back, plus interest, carrying charges and a substantial return on the Angels' investment.

The process of raising money from Angel investors typically goes like this: companies discuss the importance and scope of the unmet medical need and how their technology is a patent-protected, innovative solution to the problem that is better than everything else out there. One might expect this to be qualitatively different for companies developing advances in medicine, but it's not. In the competitive chase for funding, the truth is that a healthcare start-up is differentiated from other investment opportunities by the factors that determine every other transaction: money in, perceived risk, timing to execution, and absolute value of return.

For companies in the VoD, their apparent scientific, clinical, and technological diversity belies these fundamental common features:

- They are all very high-risk investments.
- They are all attempting to grow through the sale of financial obligations.
- They have a prolonged timeline to liquidity.
- The goal of obtaining an investment is to support efforts to obtain another investment.
- Success in achieving an exit depends on the company increasing its value with every round of fundraising.

At the end of the day, a novel, brilliant, and mankind-altering technology can only be advanced if it is effectively sold to investors, and they are not buyers of technology, but of equity and debt instruments. *The VoD is a market in which equity and debt are bought and sold.* Technology may be the point of entry, but the success of companies navigating the VoD depends entirely on their being able to maintain a continuing inflow of cash until they reach some kind of exit. Regardless of how technologies are differentiated by ingenuity, novelty, or clinical need, the essential factor for success in the VoD is whether they support an investment thesis that can maintain a continuous series of equity and/or debt transactions. For most of the companies in the VoD, the early customers in these transactions, the buyers, are Angel investors.

Angels are high net worth individuals who have achieved success, either as entrepreneurs or executives, and may or may not have deep expertise in the biomedical space. Some are in it for the "deal," others through attraction to a particular technology domain or an inspired scientific and management team. Some are motivated to solve a medical problem that has personally affected a family member or colleague. But there's a common denominator: the requirement that the technology be part of a cogent investment proposition. Anything else is either impulsive gambling or philanthropy.

Return on investment (ROI) may or may not be the primary driver of an investment, but the absence of perceived *probability* of ROI, as evidenced by a poorly conceived or unrealistic investment thesis, is fatal to an opportunity's prospects for investment. Investors need to hear an investment thesis that explains how and why they will achieve a return from this particular opportunity. Scientific founders of biotech and other healthcare start-ups, of course, want to talk about what they've discovered and how it works and what it may ultimately do for patients; but what they need to talk about is why their proposition is a better investment than the next guy's.

The challenge of converting a research project into an investment thesis is a considerable one, and it's poorly executed with frightening regularity by VoD start-ups. There's a lot of talk about the development challenges of translational medicine, but this is one of the earliest and most binary demands of the Translation Gap, the gatekeeping challenge that determines any chance of survival in the VoD. Innovation is not in and of itself an investment proposition, nor is greater innovation a positive predictor of investability or return.

When one considers the VoD as a marketplace in which investments are bought and sold, rather than as a commercial extension of academic research or a mechanism for creating new drugs, a number of curious dynamics become evident. For example, there is an absence of basic information that would normally inform an investment decision. If I invest in a mutual fund, I want to know the historical rate of return, the overhead and management fees, and as much detail as possible about the investment philosophy. The VoD is a marketplace with no reliable estimates of how many companies are selling investment opportunities, how much money they need to get to market, or what the returns on any given investment are expected to be. (Because of the high rate of failure on individual investments, investors are conditioned to think in terms of their aggregate return on a portfolio of investments.)

There's more information about the buyers, but it's not very granular with respect to the early stage money. There are certainly estimates of the number of Angels and what they spend in aggregate, as well as potentially reasonable ones about how much VC money is invested in healthcare, but for an individual company there's limited information about which Angels they should pitch, how to get to them, or how much money they should ask for.

The health of individual companies wouldn't matter so much in an ordinary consumer market like 3D printers, or a typical B2B market like enterprise software. The number of companies and their output would eventually equilibrate to match the number of printer variants and software solutions required to fulfill the need. But the VoD marketplace for medicine represents the fruits of university scientists' labors, the Mother's Day race money, the charitable donations, the government funding supported by taxpayers, and the hope for our children's future. Matching resources to value in the healthcare VoD is important in a way that matching demand to production of 3D printers is not. The downstream consequences of a healthcare technology being funded demand a close look at a system in which the money available to support companies in the VoD is not calibrated in any direct way to the number of companies seeking funding, and in which the societal value of those companies takes a backseat to investor return.

Most companies enter the VoD with a strong conviction that their proprietary technologies give them competitive advantage—which may well be true when we evaluate those technologies in the context of the market for therapeutics, diagnostics, or medical devices. The players on the VoD field, however, are not competing for the hearts and minds of clinicians, but rather for the wallets of investors. The difference between one VoD investment opportunity and another isn't a function of the specific technology or therapeutic target. In that sense, the one that matters most in the VoD, technologies are homogeneous except for the probability and size of return they can provide.

A PARADIGM FOR ANALYSIS

The number of companies and their aggregate funding needs are far greater than the resources available from early stage investors. Companies in the VoD are competing with each other to sell financial obligations, collateralized by their inventions, to investors. With this recalibrated perspective, where technology is essentially the collateral for a financial instrument, we can start to examine the dynamics of competitiveness in the VoD using business models that have been applied to other markets. We have found, for example, that Michael E. Porter's seminal "Five Competitive Forces That Shape Strategy" provides a useful starting point for understanding dysfunction in the VoD [5].

Porter's work describes the relationships between competitors within an industry and the groups that contribute to their success or failure. Key to his synthesis is that companies often define their competition too narrowly, considering only the product or service they provide and other companies that seek the same customers. A more comprehensive view of competitiveness, however, includes the pressures that determine whether a buyer will purchase a given means of satisfying a particular need rather than any other, a company's position relative to others providing the same solution, and the profitability of the entire industry in which it participates. The Five Forces provide a framework to identify competitive vulnerabilities that companies face, and to create better solutions.

In our application of Porter's model to the VoD, our goal is to improve the transition of technologies from the university to the clinic, and our unit of analysis is the start-up company (we address other stakeholders elsewhere). Once a decision has been made to build a company around a technology, then it is implicitly in everyone's interest for the company to survive, from the scientist who invented the technology, to the university that owns it, the entrepreneur who advocates for it, and the investor who pays for it. Failure of the company often leads to abandonment of the technology, the lost opportunity cost of time and money already committed, and of course the unrealized promise of a new treatment. Here, we focus on how to ensure the company's survival and progress through the VoD.

Our position is not that companies have some inherent right to success, with unfettered access to cash and astronomical returns on investment. Rather, we posit that companies exist within an imbalanced ecosystem, plagued by counterproductive practices that reduce the probability of success. The interests of companies need to be supported yet balanced by an environment that is optimized to reward forward movement and discourage the waste of time, effort, and money. This involves changes not only in their own practices but in the relationships that determine their success or failure. Porter coined the term "value chain" to describe how specific activities and relationships affect a company's competitive advantage: "The *value chain* has become shorthand for an activity-based view of competitive advantage; i.e., superior profitability can be traced to differences in activities that allow a company to lower costs or in its ability to charge higher prices" [6].

The activities of each of the constituents affecting the competitiveness of a company can be seen in terms of how they affect the value chain, by incurring expenses and affecting the rate of return on investment. Considering that the product being sold in the VoD is a collateralized financial obligation, the VoD value chain relates to how borrowed money is spent to advance the science toward the clinic and to support other activities that increase valuation. The objective at this stage is to support an increase in perceived valuation that exceeds the money already in, and thereby support both the eventuality and terms of the next financing transaction. The Five Forces that shape competition are a starting point to understand how key relationships and their activities contribute to the value chain of a company in the VoD [6]. They are:

1. Bargaining power of buyers
2. Rivalry among existing competitors
3. Bargaining power of suppliers
4. Threat of substitute products or services
5. Threat of new entrants

If we apply Porter's Five Forces to the purchase and sale of financial instruments in the VoD, the model translates into the following:

1. Bargaining power of buyers: leverage held by investors seeking to purchase equity in, or provide a loan to, a biotech company
2. Rivalry among existing competitors: competition among biotech companies vying for the same pool of investor money
3. Bargaining power of suppliers: leverage held by universities and other sources of biotechnology intellectual property, typically transferred in the form of a license to a patent or patent application, which the companies use to support their investment theses
4. Threat of substitute products: investment opportunities that are outside the VoD and siphon money away from biotechnology investments
5. Threat of new entrants: new companies in the VoD, which may disrupt the supply of money to the existing enterprises or provide a disruptive paradigm shift that changes funding patterns

The long-term health of companies in the VoD depends on assessing their competitive strengths and weakness in the *marketplace for financial support*. Our analysis of this marketplace in the context of the Five Forces suggests that the VoD can be functionally improved. Specific steps can be taken to mitigate self-destructive processes and to address structural imbalances in the VoD that make it difficult for early stage companies to thrive.

At this stage, it should be clear that the finite size of the funding pool imposes a unique structure and vulnerability to this transacting of technologies. For example, the mismatch between the number of companies and the number of early stage funding sources means that the Bargaining Power of Buyers (the ability of Angel investors to set the terms of an investment) and the Rivalry Among Existing Competitors (competition among biotech companies competing for the pool of investor money) are enormous. Furthermore, the fact that universities own the technologies that companies need to support their investment theses, that inventors are wedded to their inventions, and that the inventions are inimitable means that Supplier Power for a given invention is absolute. These three imbalances are at the heart of why the Translation Gap is insurmountable for many early stage companies. Assessing the dynamics that impede progression of technologies in the VoD starts with recognizing what the VoD really is,

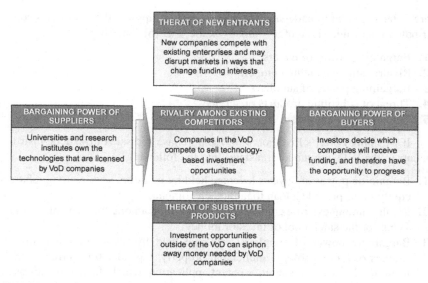

FIGURE 7.1 Porter's Five Forces. *Adapted to the VoD.*

why it functions the way it does, and how start-up companies can take advantage of these points of leverage (Fig. 7.1).

We'll first discuss Buyer power in the VoD, the leverage Angels hold when they consider whether or not to "buy" an investment in a start-up biotech company, and how excessive buyer power affects the progression of innovative technologies through the VoD. The factors that determine whether Angels invest in a company are key to understanding and overcoming the second component of the Translation Gap, that good innovation is not always a good investment.

All companies that carry technologies into the VoD need funding to survive, and, as we've noted, the primary source of early stage funding beyond grants, friends and family is Angel investors. The VoD is less a marketplace of technology seeking clinical or patient champions than a marketplace of investment vehicles vying for early stage money. Angels are the essential gatekeepers, in the sense that they (and a more limited cohort of early stage institutional investors) are the ones making a determination of the commercial value of a technology—years before there is any prospect of its being used in the clinic. Angel investment perspectives are idiosyncratic, and more likely to be motivated by the desire to achieve a meaningful return than to filter opportunities on the basis of whether they will transform medicine. We're not suggesting these are mutually exclusive, and prospective clinical impact is clearly one of the corollaries to commercial success. But it's not a necessary connection: questionable medicine can get funded because there's a opportunistic financial angle and important discoveries can languish or die because they are too risky or time-consuming to execute on.

Investors may decide to bet on a low-probability event based on the lure of a very high prospective rate of return, and/or for the same reasons scientific founders are in the game: passion for development, a personal connection to the therapeutic area, curiosity, energy, and desire to cause change. Investment motives are complex, and neither Angels nor scientists pursue their efforts for solely rational, or solely financial, or *solely any other* reasons—including the obvious one of which technologies are most likely to succeed or make the most money when they do reach the market. But the potential for important discoveries to go unrealized is not hypothetical. We have regularly seen shaky clinical propositions get funded and important clinical advances ignored. One example: a patch infused with "metal particles" intended to act like some kind of capacitor on the skin, the promise of pain relief backed by "black box" science and inventors who were possibly good marketers but questionable scientists, was funded because it's likely to make money on a late-night infomercial.

Each investor brings an individual perspective to evaluation of a company, so due diligence involves the questions that his or her experience has shown to be the most important in past business and entrepreneurial dealings. Due diligence is a somewhat formalized process (addressed in detail in chapter: Due Diligence and Angel Incentives) but the diversity of technologies and opportunities that need to be evaluated, and a compressed decision timeline can favor intuitive attraction over hard analytics, or lead to short cuts and inductive leaps in decision making [7].

Investors rely heavily, for example, upon the supposition that the past success of the management team is a key driver of success. This is not crazy: experienced people are more likely to be able to adapt to roadblocks; they know how to solve problems and those who have a network of connections in a particular domain are more likely to do well than those who don't. There's a self-fulfilling expectation that people who have achieved prior success carry with them the talent, temperament, luck, and network of associates to make it happen again. Plenty of literature from both academia and the commercial sphere promotes the common wisdom that you should "bet on the jockey" [8]. We agree that this is a hugely important component, and would never invest ourselves in a notably deficient management team unless it could be immediately supplemented or replaced. But we still want to know if the horse that the jockey's riding is a champion or lame.

This is not to say that Angel investing is a random or illogical process; only that it pretty consistently overweights variables other than the clinical implications of new healthcare technologies. "Innovation" and "value" from a human health perspective may be partially or wholly disconnected from the value of a technology as an investment proposition. To get funded, an inventor needs enough evidence to convince investors the idea will work (the so-called proof of concept), but also that the idea is supported by a critical mass of intellectual property, management—and other investors.

This means that early stage technologies offering important clinical promise but poor prospects for ROI may be unsupported, in favor of those offering incremental improvement. Consider the need for better treatments for Parkinson's Disease, which affects an estimated 7–10 million people worldwide [9]. One approach would be to reformulate carbidopa-levodopa, a drug already long on the market, but with an improvement in dosing, efficacy, and/ or side effects [10]. The other is a disease-modifying agent, a novel approach that promises better results, but has no track record with patients, limited data, and so a greater possibility of failure. Which one are investors likely to back? It's an open question, but implicitly the lower-risk proposition carries a shorter development timeline and a lower probability of failure due to safety or efficacy issues. For Parkinson's, this type of thinking resulted in the 2015 Food and Drug Administration approval of two new ways of administering carbidopa-levodopa, one by a long-acting capsule and one by a pump that delivers the drug to the small intestine [11].

THE PROSPECT OF TOTAL LOSS

Anyone brave enough to fund VoD companies is well aware that investing in a start-up may result in a total loss. To account for this, investors adopt a portfolio strategy for their high-risk investments, an adaptation of the diversified approach investors take to protect against downside in their equity and fixed income holdings. This "home run" strategy to high-risk investments invests on probability. A common rule of thumb is 10:1; the nine investments that fail entirely, or fail to return all of the capital invested, are covered by the one that hits it big.

William H. (Bill) Payne of Kauffman Venturing and Luis Villalobos of Tech Coast Angels analyzed a set of Angel portfolios that included 117 ventures. Almost 85% of the investment returns came from only 14% of the investments [12]. Most of the others broke even, lost money, or went out of business. This casino mindset may be attractive for a variety of reasons, but it doesn't feel like a very substantive foundation for selecting the most important inventions. To whatever extent investment is driven less by scientific or clinical merit than by "soft" influences such as intuition, peer influence (following co-investors), or prior success as a self-fulfilling predictor of the next win, we'd still rather hitch our ride on something other than probability metrics.

But here is where the wild card comes in. People making high-risk bets are driven by the emotional rush of investing and by the gratification of making something happen. Perhaps an Angel is looking for meaning and attachment, or to be inspired by supporting people doing something to change the lives of patients, or maybe the therapeutic target is something that has directly affected his or her own life. There's the intellectual gratification of the due diligence process, and the emotional and financial rush of making a good choice when an investment does pan out. There's engagement in the technology community, and exploring a new domain. (When one of us approached the other 7 years ago about an investment in his company, the approachee spent 2 weeks plowing through arcane immunology papers out of pure intellectual curiosity.) And of course, for those particularly oriented toward deal making, there's the intrinsic interest of negotiating the financial terms of the investment. As Jeffrey Sohl points out, "Angel investing is a full contact sport" [13].

So what does this have to do with the Translation Gap? Let's turn for a moment to the way projects are funded before they get into the private money arena. The National Institutes of Health (NIH) for example selects which projects to fund in academia. An NIH study section evaluates proposals on defined criteria: overall impact, significance, investigators, innovation, approach, and environment [14]. Overall impact and significance refer to the "likelihood for the project to exert a sustained, powerful influence on the research field(s) involved," and, whether the project "address[es] an important problem or a critical barrier to progress in the field?" Innovation and broad impact are a top priority: "Does the application challenge and seek to shift current research or clinical practice paradigms by utilizing novel theoretical concepts, approaches or methodologies, instrumentation, or interventions?," and are these paradigm shifts "novel to one field of research or novel in a broad sense?" These are scientifically cogent and appealing criteria, and they explicitly relate new technologies to their real-world impact. In other words, they are exactly what we societally want our academic investigators to achieve, yet not directly correlated with whether the research will produce a particular financial return in a given number of years.

This disconnect between what academia produces, and what investors and industry need, is a key contributor to the second part of the Translation Gap, that universities don't make what companies need. The scientific research that feeds the VoD is crafted to a standard different from the prime factor that determines whether a technology can progress toward commercialization, which is whether early stage investors find it attractive. The innovation that is an essential requirement for NIH funding may be exactly what makes an invention uninvestable in the VoD. And the factors that most determine an invention's success in raising money in the VoD are not the same as the criteria that determine its potential value to clinical medicine or society.

The potential for a big payoff notwithstanding, it's an open question just how viable Angel investing in early stage companies is, in aggregate. If the driver is return, and the returns are shallow, is it possible the entire pre-VC biotechnology commercialization process is built on sand?

Nobody is obligated to invest in the VoD. Funding for the VoD originates in the reserves of Angels and other early biotech investors, and the amount they have to invest depends on how flush they are with investable resources and their risk tolerance at any given time. There will always be reasons to put their money somewhere else, and there will always be opportunities for lower-risk investments. On any given day, an Angel investor may decide to keep his money in fixed income, or equities, or real estate, or a new social media company—instead of helping to fund a promising cure for Ellen's cancer (see chapter: Velcade, a Biotech Success Story). Angel participation in the VoD is entirely discretionary, not unlike the market for any indulgence, and we've heard more than one Angel refer to their group investment activity as very expensive book club. The ability of a company to survive in the VoD depends entirely on the motivation of Angels to buy a high-cost, high-profile investment that is more likely to depreciate than increase in value.

The financial realities are daunting. Any early stage biotech investment is so high risk that from a purely objective point of view it's almost farcical, like investing $100,000 on a space launch—a critical but small contribution to a company that will ultimately need tens or hundreds of millions to get to an exit, let alone to market. Multiple institutionally backed rounds of fundraising stand between an Angel investment and the clinic, during each of which the new investors, driven by their own financial imperatives, will dictate terms that dilute the holdings of previous investors. It's not unusual for Angels to participate in follow-on rounds or bridge financing, but when the numbers get exponentially larger in order to support clinical trials and later-stage development, it's no longer an Angel's game. The objective is to keep valuation ahead of the money already in, which works for early investors on the smaller share of a bigger pie principle, as long as valuation continues to increase. But if a follow-on round of investment takes too long and the company's cash reserves start to run out, new investors have the leverage to set terms for the next round and a financial interest in "cramming down" the percentage of the company held by prior investors. New money always trumps the old, and late investors take less risk for more return.

Anyone solely interested in exponentially increasing his or her money, or even in getting it back within a reasonable period of time, should probably not be investing in biotech. A colleague who has been in the life sciences for a long time told us a story about a company he ran in the early 2000s, at which time the firm was almost 10 years old. When the company finally achieved an exit in 2014, the original investors had been in for up to 18 years, and realized a net return on capital of 1.2 ×—i.e., they held equity in the company for the better part of two decades and realized a 20% return, or just over 1% per year (before adjustment for lost interest and inflation).

Angels and Angel groups are understandably private about their disposition of assets. Aggregated data on success rates is difficult to come by, so it's hard to know how many Angel investors in biotech are growing their capital and how much they're earning over time. But with long dry spells between exits, and a probability model that expects *no* return of principal from 90% of investments, one might ask how long it takes for a bruised and bloodied Angel to realize he might want to do something else with his money.

In the future of healthcare, Angels serve a higher function than simply providing capital. The decisions they make delineate the pipeline of innovation coming out of universities and the start-ups that universities spawn. Does it make sense that the efforts of our best scientific minds should be parsed for commercialization by individuals who may or may not be expert in a particular therapeutic domain and whose interests are guided as much by investment return as by our collective healthcare needs?

Regardless of whether this is what we would choose, it is what we have now. It is therefore absolutely critical to protect and encourage the interests of these key gatekeepers. Because if the dynamics of the market for investment opportunities in the VoD continue to undermine incentives for early stage investment, reduce the prospects of return on capital, and emphasize the high-roller component of the equation over informed investment in innovation, we may all find ourselves one day battling our own drug-resistant infection, our own degenerative neuropathy, our own heart disease, cancer or whatever—and wondering why $30 billion a year in NIH funding so rarely turns into a cure.

Finding better ways to bridge the translation gap, to best match the needs of medicine and society with investors' financial prerogatives, is essential to preserve the benefits of our healthcare research enterprise. After all, Angels have complete buyer power: if they want to, they can just walk away. It is foolish to suggest that they will ignore return; they are, after all, *investors*. But in facing the Translation Gap, there is room for an explicit shift in incentives, working within the context of buyer power to de-risk investments while moving in personally and societally valuable directions, and creating agents of change that extend beyond the financial value of a portfolio.

REFERENCES

[1] PricewaterhouseCoopers. National venture capital association. MoneyTree™ report Q4 2015/full year 2015 summary. <http://www.pwc.com/us/en/technology/assets/pwc-money-tree-q4-2015-summary-fullyear.pdf>; 2016.

[2] Huggett B. Biotech's wellspring—a survey of the health of the private sector in 2014. Nat Biotechnol 2015;33(5):470–7. http://dx.doi.org/10.1038/nbt.3218.

[3] The top 15 cities for biotech funding. *FierceBiotech*, March 6, 2015, <http://www.fierce-biotech.com/story/top-15-cities-biotech-venture-funding/2014-03-06>; 2015 [accessed 18.02.16].

[4] Huggett B. Innovative academic start-ups 2015. Nat Biotechnol 2016;34(1):19. http://dx.doi.org/10.1038/nbt.3447.

[5] Porter ME. The five competitive forces that shape strategy. Harvard Bus Rev 2008;86(1):25–40.

[6] Porter ME. On competition: updated and expanded edition. Boston, MA: Harvard Business School Publishing; 2008.

[7] Maxwell AL, Jeffrey SA, Lévesque M. Business angel early stage decision making. J Bus Venturing 2011;26:212–25.

[8] Shipley T, Kos J. Betting on the right jockey—the number one indicator of investment success. Angel Capital Association Webinar 2014 January 28, 2015. <http://www.angelcapital-association.org/webinars/>.

[9] Parkinson's Disease Foundation. Statistics on Parkinson's. <http://www.pdf.org/en/parkinson_statistics >; 2016.

[10] Arnst C. Start-ups progress with novel drugs for Parkinson's disease. Xconomy. <http://par-kinsonsaction.org/fda-approves-two-parkinsons-drugs/>; 2012 [accessed 20.02.16].

[11] Act4PD. FDA approves two Parkinson's drugs. <http://parkinsonsaction.org/fda-approves-two-parkinsons-drugs/>; 2015 [accessed 20.02.16].

[12] Payne WH, Villalobos L. Start-up pre-money valuation: the keystone to return on investment. Kauffman Foundation. <http://entrepreneurship.org/resource-center/start-up-premoney-valuation--the-keystone-to-return-on-investment.aspx>; 2016 [accessed 20.02.16].

[13] Interview with the authors, February 26, 2015.

[14] National Institutes of Health. Grants and funding: peer review process. <http://grants.nih.gov/grants/peer_review_process.htm#Criteria>; 2016 [accessed 20.02.16].

Chapter 8

Out of the Frying Pan: The Fire's Not So Great Either

Thus far, we have focused on what happens to a technology once it arrives *in the Valley of Death (VoD)*. We now turn our attention to *how it gets there*, which in itself can be a tortuous journey. It often takes an extraordinary effort to get a technology out of a university and on the path to commercialization. Once again, there's the potential for significant misalignment of objectives, in this case between the charter of technology transfer offices (TTOs) and the goals of founders, investors, and the marketplace. This is because universities are focused on a mission and metrics that have a tenuous connection to the clinical value of any given technology.

The execution of a deal enables "launch" of a technology out of the lab and into the VoD. Perhaps surprisingly, it's not only money that differentiates technologies successfully launched out of the university from those that aren't—rather, it is a function of multiple factors: a particular university's role in the regional start-up ecosystem, the visibility of the founding scientist, institutional reputation, priority assigned to nurturing faculty relationships, and proactive or defensive risk tolerance. What constitutes a good technology licensing deal has as much to do with the metrics by which a given TTO is evaluated as with the ultimate prospects for a particular technology, and it's not difficult to find organizations that seem to be more focused on avoiding "bad" deals than on championing or executing good ones.

The VoD as we know it was born in 1980, when Congress passed the Bayh–Dole Act [1]. Of course, the Act's goal was not to create a VoD; rather, it was intended to stimulate the commercialization of technologies invented in US universities. Bayh–Dole enables organizations that receive federal funding for research to retain the title to innovations developed with that support. Because university scientists are required to assign their invention rights to their employers, the net result of Bayh–Dole is that US universities own the majority of publicly funded research. This rule also applies de facto to research supported by charitable contributions funneled through educational institutions, for two reasons: Universities will not accept charitable funding that doesn't grant them

Preserving the Promise. DOI: http://dx.doi.org/10.1016/B978-0-12-809216-3.00008-7

ownership of invention rights, and most charitable giving in this context supports work that has some component of federal funding.

By defining ownership, Bayh–Dole provides incentives for inventions to be patented and exclusively licensed. This has been the linchpin of the biotechnology revolution in the United States, because it established the university's prerogative and motivation with respect to science emerging from its labs. An invention needs to be owned, as well as defined, in order to support an investment thesis. For technologies outside of the healthcare arena, e.g., a software application or consumer electronics, the bar to commercialization may be lower—not because companies aren't interested in patenting their inventions (one has only to look at the patent portfolio of an Apple or Samsung), but because of a much shorter development timeline and the first-to-market imperative for rapidly evolving technology. In biotechnology, where the gestation period for getting a technology to the market may be 7–10 years or more, intellectual property (IP) is paramount because the ability to generate continuing investment interest demands assurance that no one will be able to replicate the technology. By patenting and licensing biotechnology inventions, universities create investment opportunities—the chips that companies and their investors will bet on.

Prior to Bayh–Dole, the government retained commercial rights for inventions created with its funding. It would only grant nonexclusive licenses to its inventions, based on the belief that discoveries were a public resource that would do the most good if they were available for everyone to use. This practice actually had the opposite effect; virtually nothing that originated in a publicly funded setting was licensed. As Joseph Allen, a former staffer of Senator Burch Bayh and one of the Act's most fervent advocates said, "Before Bayh–Dole, there were 26,000 inventions sitting on the shelf." And the truth is that Bayh–Dole has worked very well, in spite of its many unintended consequences. A BIO-sponsored study published in 2015 estimated that the Bayh–Dole Act has boosted gross industry output by almost $1.2 trillion and supported as many as 3,824,000 US jobs [2]. Bayh–Dole has performed an enabling role with respect to development of new drugs, and has no doubt been instrumental in making the United States the undisputed global leader in biotechnology development.

So where is the problem, and why are we talking about this? As originally envisioned, ownership by the universities that received the funding and conducted the research was a logical starting point. As nonprofit organizations functioning in the public interest and dedicated to discovery, it would be natural to think that institutions of higher learning could achieve the right balance, selecting the best technologies to support and fairly nurturing their passage into the VoD. After all, universities are primary sponsors of innovation and discovery, as well as champions of the efforts and reputations of their faculty. As gatekeepers for which technologies advance, universities would logically be expected to act in the best interests of their faculty inventors *and* society.

But the Bayh–Dole Act did not come with a playbook, so universities have had to devise their technology transfer practices from scratch. Most of those generating even a modest volume of inventions started TTOs to facilitate the emergence of their science into the commercial realm. The results have been quite variable. In places like Cambridge or Palo Alto, there's a baked-in disposition that facilitates organic flow of ideas and technology, both into and outside of university labs. Elsewhere, process-oriented culture and risk aversion tend to inhibit translation of inventions into medicine. But the culture in universities, business programs to train budding entrepreneurs notwithstanding, is typically less than entrepreneurial. It is, in our experience, more likely to be risk-averse than risk-taking, and no less prone to legal and administrative obstructionism than is any other bureaucracy.

Seeking to balance the demands of entrepreneurial activity with the historical nonprofit orientation that money is granted or donated rather than earned, TTOs labor in an environment of variably defined research and business objectives. As agents of universities they are also expected to perform under the yoke of inconsistently defined ethical, financial, and legal priorities. This has led to a patchwork of tech transfer policies and practices throughout the country.

There has probably never been a more challenging time to be running a TTO. Many universities and research institutes are in crisis mode, primarily due to cuts in federal funding of research initiatives. Recent pronouncements from Washington notwithstanding, funds from the National Institutes of Health (NIH) have for years failed to keep pace with even modest inflation, and the purchasing power of those dollars is down by 25% over the past 10 years. Sally Rockey, NIH Deputy Director for Extramural Research and Francis Collins, MD, PhD, NIH Director and genomics pioneer, wrote, the "NIH's ability to support vital research at more than 2500 universities and organizations across the nation is reeling from a decline in funding that threatens our health, our economy, and our standing as the world leader in biomedical innovation" [3].

The dampening effect on research institutions has been far worse than even a 25% drop might suggest, because of the way the NIH funds research. This was first explicated by MIT professor Richard Larson and his colleagues [4]. Most NIH grants provide support for 4 years, so a proportion of each year's spending is dictated by grants approved in prior years. The remaining funds go to new grants. When there is an increase in funding, a higher number of new grants will be approved. But if in the following year the funding goes down, the obligations of the prior years must be met first, leaving less money to support new grants.

The roots of the present crisis can be traced to the years 1998–2003, a period during which NIH funding doubled. Universities expanded their commitments to research, hired new investigators, and started building new research space. The plan was to stuff the new space with scientists who would bring in more NIH grants, each of which comes with an "indirect cost" component, up to 70% in some cases, which goes directly to the university [5]. This overhead allocation is a necessity for universities, to provide research infrastructure and balance their budgets.

Then, in 2004, NIH budgets stopped growing—and therefore began dropping in terms of inflation-adjusted dollars every year. The effect of this steady decrease in funding has been to markedly reduce basic research. The impact was massive in the year following the sequester of 2013, resulting in 650 fewer new grant applications funded compared to the year before [4]. From 2000 to 2013, the NIH grant success rate dropped from about 35% to less than half that, or approximately 17%. This has decimated research divisions and converted many scientists into desperate grant-writing machines.

We mentioned renewed noise about research funding from the federal government, the most recent example being a billion dollar cancer "moonshot," which calls for a $195 million increase in NIH cancer funding in 2016 and an additional $755 million in 2017. It's worth putting this in perspective, even apart from the uncertainty of the initiative from a political standpoint [6]. "The good news is that the budget is no longer being cut," said Dr. Peter Adamson, the chairman of the Children's Oncology Group, which conducts national clinical trials. "But we're not going to the moon on $1 billion. The administration's $1 billion commitment is not enough to fund even half of the cost of a [single] new cancer medicine" [6].

So prospective new funding notwithstanding, the long-accumulating deficit in funding isn't likely to resolve any time soon. As a result, the revenue potential of the IP, funneled through TTOs, is increasingly seen as a potential money-maker for cash-strapped institutions. How much to fund a TTO can be a tough decision for a university—we've seen data suggesting it amounts to an average 0.6% of the entire university operating budget—so TTOs are simultaneously under pressure to be frugal *and* to bring in the next big licensing deal that will net millions [7]. Walter D. Valdivia of the Center for Technology Innovation at the Brookings Institution estimated that in 2012, 84% of TTOs were operating in the red [8]. The funnel of inventions is always exponentially larger, and therefore requires more attention than the resources available to advance them toward commercialization. At major universities, the number of invention disclosures submitted is in the hundreds every year. Vetting them all, while keeping faculty happy, and achieving the metrics that justify their existence to a university impatient for deals, is a Sisyphean task.

JUGGLING INTEREST, SUPPORT, COMMITMENT, AND IP

The large number of invention disclosures means that TTOs need to make tough decisions about which of their discoveries are worth the time and money of a patent filing—generally $5,000–$10,000 just for the initial, provisional application. But it is also about the very difficult job of predicting the future importance of a discovery, something that may be without precedent and the effects of which could transform practice. Would even futurists have been able to anticipate the impact of the smartphone on politics, social interaction, and consumption of media? It's a tall order, made more difficult by operational constraints. Paradigm shifts need champions, and by definition TTOs have to serve a lot of constituencies. It's perhaps too much to ask for long-term vision and passion, when the context is short-term budget justification and juggling multiple masters.

We alluded to the same phenomenon when we talked about investors trying to understand how Velcade as an innovation matched up with its potential as an investment. There's no crystal ball to be had, and TTOs cannot possibly be staffed with an endless range of expertise to accommodate all of the faculty technologies they review. It may be possible to sort the wheat from the chaff, but how does one objectively select the best commercial prospects from among the mix? As James Elmer, Director of the TTO at St. Jude Children's Research Hospital, said, "It's frustrating, but look at the reality—we patent 10 things and if two of them actually are successful we're doing a decent job, financially successful. So we're not that good. We're given an impossible task of trying to assess embryonic inventions" [9].

So, while Bayh–Dole offers an opportunity for tremendous financial gain, it is basically an unfunded government mandate imposed on institutions that receive federal research support. *It demands that cash-challenged, nonprofit organizations engage in high-risk, entrepreneurial activities that are more likely than not to lose money.*

As difficult as this mandate is on its face, the task is complicated further by the role that TTOs are supposed to play as advocates for faculty discoveries. The politics of scientific reputation and policies that minimize inventors' financial share of their discoveries virtually assure that TTOs will be in conflict with their faculty, the same scientific founders with whom the TTOs must ultimately negotiate licenses. It is not hard to find an academic scientist who will enthusiastically excoriate the TTO staff for failing to appreciate what he has done or for mismanaging his IP. For their part, TTOs are understandably frustrated by scientists who don't understand why their inventions cannot be commercialized, or who do not cooperate in the licensing process, and have a limited appreciation of how monumentally complicated technology transfer has become.

We're actually pretty empathetic. TTOs struggle with internal incentives that prioritize deal volume yet chase high-visibility "wins," and with administrations that pay lip service to, but won't modify policies that impede deal quality and fail to adequately support commercial innovation. They're subject to internal political pressures from the faculty and administration, needing to balance their budgets through licensing and administrative fees while assembling a credible IP portfolio, while constrained by metrics that have less to do with getting drugs to market than with rationalizing a balky process. They need to somehow find business advisor/entrepreneurs for the new companies who will accept deferred compensation, because they work with budgets and deal structures that won't compensate top talent. And like every deal-making organization, they can sometimes get stuck. It's no secret that technologies have died trying to avoid a "bad" deal—which might variously be one that doesn't retain enough equity, is attached to some unacceptably high legal or public relations risk, or simply costs too much time and money to move forward.

From the perspective of Porter's Five Forces, the Bayh–Dole Act has given universities absolute supplier power over the fruits of their research enterprise. Whereas prior to Bayh–Dole, nonexclusivity and government bureaucracy were the barriers to commercialization, the Act has made TTOs the sole arbiters of whether a university technology can be transported into the VoD and how much it will cost to do so. If a university doesn't want to license or otherwise release the technology to a third party to develop, for whatever reason, they don't have to—even if the technology could lead to a badly needed cure, and even if there is no other viable route to development. Clinical need is a secondary consideration, because the suppliers are too often underfunded organizations operating in a risk-averse environment and trying to accommodate irresolvable demands of their many constituencies.

This means that some important and innovative technologies will never have a chance for commercialization. It also means that those that do enter the VoD carry a monkey on their backs, fees imposed by TTO deal terms long before inventions have created any clinical value, in order to cover overhead and patent expenses. Someone needs to bear these transfer costs, and that's typically the early stage investors who are already assuming enormous risk. Any extra fees increase the size of the debt incurred or the amount of equity that needs to be sold by a start-up company, reduce the amount available for actual development, or both. As Dale Pfost, General Partner of Advent Ventures observed, "It falls under the umbrella of appreciating how hard it is to raise money ... any baggage that you attach to the licenses that make it a challenge for the company to go off and raise a Series B or a C or do a public offering ... [just] don't. It's just impossible to raise money, so anything you do that will be a burden on the company is not good" [10].

A FULCRUM OF TENSION

TTOs sit at the intersection between universities' historical mission of scholarly activity and society's need for technology that will improve our lives. It's not an easy place to be, nor is it an abstract issue in the current economic environment: witness the most recent state administration in Wisconsin under Governor Scott Walker explicitly changing the espoused mission of the University of Wisconsin from a "search for truth" to "meeting the state's workforce needs" ... and cutting $250 million from the budget in the process [11].

Nobody wants to lock up academia in silos of pure intellectual inquiry, but universities are beneficiaries of public money and ought to be good caretakers of the research enterprise, responsive to the needs of society. But from the perspective of Five Forces, it is hard to imagine how companies in the VoD can be expected to do well when the suppliers of their technology, TTOs, are almost all losing money in the process. This creates a vicious cycle, inflating the costs of licensing without elevating the quantity or quality of the technologies transferred.

For TTOs, this is an especially big deal because of the second part of the Translation Gap we defined earlier: that universities don't make what companies need. TTOs somehow need to bridge the gap between what they have to offer, i.e., early, untested technologies, and what Big Pharma and healthcare investors need: mature entities with a clear path to the clinic. They also need to find ways to bring industry funding into their institutions without compromising their academic value system, balancing problems of disclosure, collaboration, IP ownership, and conflicts of interest. This will require cultural changes in licensing practice, perhaps via reaffirmation of the values of open-ended inquiry that have defined great institutions of learning throughout history.

THE SPECIAL CASE OF CONFLICT OF INTEREST

One of the greatest challenges associated with the shift from invention for its own sake, to discovery with commercial ambitions, relates to conflict of interest (COI) policies within tech transfer. The Department of Health and Human Services defines COI as a situation "when two or more contradictory interests relate to an activity by an individual or an institution" [12]. The National Academy of Sciences describes this more specifically in the context of scientific research: "A conflict of interest in research exists when the individual has interests in the outcome of the research that may lead to a personal advantage and that might therefore, in actuality or appearance compromise the integrity of the research" [13]. This is still rather vague, and certainly open to interpretation, but one example would be a researcher who may be inclined to falsify data if it would enable his company to make a deal with Big Pharma or a Venture Capital firm.

COI policies attempt to avoid impropriety by defining acceptable behaviors and proactively preventing activities from which a conflict *could* arise. Most institutions have a COI committee that "manages" conflicts of interest: asking, for example, whether they should only sanction activities that are "beyond reproach" or also those that are "reasonable policy."

The intent is sound, and good fodder for debate, but the consequence of COI practices is often to place a wall between the inventor of the licensed technology and the company that has licensed it. Recall that Alfred Goldberg was not allowed to work in his Harvard laboratory with Velcade, the drug his company invented, so he had to study a related molecule instead. In most cases, the inventor of the technology is also not allowed to hold a significant ownership stake in a company, or even to accept sponsored research funding from the company to work on the technology in his own laboratory. This again is variable by institution, but too often imposes a nanny-like structure where the ability to conduct collaborative research is proscriptively constrained.

We asked Dora Mitchell, Director of the UPstart commercialization program at the University of Pennsylvania, about this. Her thoughts were that "any institution getting government funding must comply with a variety of legislation—that obligates them to have systems and procedures for disclosure, avoidance of misconduct [and so forth]. So, there are certain things that all of them will do—like disclosures and transparency, certain types of reporting. From then on, it varies tremendously. Every university makes up its own policies, and US academic institutions vary immensely." The University of Pennsylvania "allows licensees to put dollars back into the lab of the founder but the relationship has to be disclosed and subjected to review by a conflict of interest committee. Princeton does not allow companies to put money back into the founder's lab, with the exception of Phase I SBIRs. MIT does not allow faculty to own equity in companies, thus avoiding conflict when company money flows into the lab in the form of sponsored research" [14]. In all of these instances, COI policies introduce barriers that separate a technology not only from the university, but also from its most fervent and qualified advocate, the inventor who created it.

Confusion over COI policies, the tendency of some scientists (and the rest of the human race) to focus on their own self-interest, and the reactionary stance of most university legal departments wastes clinical and financial opportunity. It encourages institutional paralysis and restricts reasonable university/industry synergies that could save time and money. Many TTOs are innovating new structures for industry/academic partnerships, as we'll discuss in a subsequent chapter. The proliferation of new models, especially around finding better ways to collaborate with companies that have licensed academic technologies, both reveals the fault lines and demonstrates the value of increasing efficiency in the third part of the Translation Gap: technology transfer wastes money and innovation.

REFERENCES

[1] 37 Code of Federal Regulations 401. Chapter 18—patent rights in inventions made with federal assistance. <https://www.gpo.gov/fdsys/pkg/USCODE-2011-title35/pdf/USCODE-2011-title35-partII-chap18.pdf>.

[2] Pressman L, Roessner D, Bond J, Okubo S, Planting M. The economic contribution of university/nonprofit inventions in the United States: 1996–2013. <https://www.bio.org/sites/default/files/BIO_2015_Update_of_I-O_Eco_Imp.pdf>; 2015.

[3] Rockey S, Collins F. Sally Rockey and Francis Collins: one nation in support of biomedical research? <http://nexus.od.nih.gov/all/2013/09/24/one-nation-in-support-of-biomedical-research/#comment-3940>; 2013 [accessed 24.02.16].

[4] Larson RC, Ghaffarzadegan N, Diaz MG. Magnified effects of changes in NIH research funding levels. Serv Sci 2012;4(4):382–95. http://dx.doi.org/10.1287/serv.1120.0030.

[5] Ledford H. Indirect costs: keeping the lights on. Nature 2014;515(7527):326–9. http://dx.doi.org/10.1038/515326a.

[6] Harris G. $1 Billion planned for cancer 'Moonshot'. New York Times, February 1, 2016, <http://www.nytimes.com/2016/02/02/us/politics/dollar1-billion-planned-for-cancer-moonshot.html>; 2016 [accessed 22.02.16].

[7]   Abrams I, Leung G, Stevens AJ. How are U.S. technology transfer offices tasked and moti-
      vated—is it all about the money? Res Manag Rev 2009;17(1):1–34.

[8]   Valdivia WD. Center for technology innovation at brookings. <http://www.brookings.edu/
      research/papers/2013/11/university-start-ups-technology-transfer-valdivia>; 2013 [accessed
      24.02.16].

[9]   Elmer J. AUTM 2015 annual meeting. Releasing IP rights to inventors: alternatives and expe-
      riences. <http://www.softconference.com/AUTM/sessionDetail.asp?SID=371140>; 2015.

[10] Pfost D. AUTM 2015 annual meeting *Venture Forum*. <http://www.softconference.com/
      AUTM/sessionDetail.asp?SID=371165>; 2015.

[11] Strauss V. Gov. Scott Walker savages Wisconsin public education in new budget. Washington
      Post. <https://www.washingtonpost.com/news/answer-sheet/wp/2015/07/13/gov-scott-walker-
      savages-wisconsin-public-education-in-new-budget/>; 2015 [accessed 24.02.16].

[12] Korenman SG. Teaching the responsible conduct of research in humans (RCRH). <http://ori.
      hhs.gov/education/products/ucla/chapter4/default.htm>; 2006 [accessed 24.02.16].

[13] Committee on Assessing Integrity in Research Environments, National Research Council,
      Institute of Medicine. Integrity in scientific research: creating an environment that promotes
      responsible conduct. Washington, DC: National Academy of Sciences Press; 2002. <http://
      www.ncbi.nlm.nih.gov/books/NBK208712/pdf/TOC.pdf>.

[14] Interview with author SF, January 29, 2016.

Chapter 9

Getting to Australia

Lisa's mother knew something was wrong shortly after Lisa was born. The baby cried continuously, as though from chronic colic. "There was obviously something wrong with me. I would stop feeding for about 5 days and get into all sorts of contortions, which was obviously, in hindsight, to alleviate stomach pain. I think at the age of 2 my Mum gave me loads of chocolate buttons to stop my 'incessant crying'. And that made me come out in the yellow fat spots, as I knew them" [1].

Her mother took Lisa to the Great Ormond Street Hospital in London, United Kingdom. Three months in the hospital resulted in a surprising diagnosis: lipoprotein lipase deficiency (LPLD), a lack of the enzyme that breaks down dietary fat so it can be removed from the bloodstream and metabolized by the liver. The yellow spots were "xanthomas," collections of undigested fats beneath the skin, and the pain wracking Lisa's body was pancreatitis, inflammation of her pancreas caused by the high levels of circulating fat.

Recurrent, severe pancreatitis is one of the most devastating consequences of LPLD. In addition to the painful attacks, which often require hospitalization, recurrent pancreatic inflammation can lead to diabetes and increase the lifetime risk of pancreatic cancer [2]. Managing the symptoms of the disease requires strict adherence to an extremely low fat diet (between 5 and 20 grams per day, less fat than in a single hamburger).

Lisa recalled, "I seemed to be very prone to severe stomach pains. Back in the 1970s you had to order skimmed milk from the milkman because it wasn't widely available. I was constantly ill, especially through my teenage years and my early twenties. I've never been diagnosed with pancreatitis, but when I used to get stomachaches I would kind of go into a room for 5 days and take solpadeine, which is a kind of paracetamol, codeine, and caffeine, and not eat or drink for 5 days. But now I have diabetes, so I would imagine that I must have had pancreatitis, and my pancreas must have been damaged through these attacks."

In her mid twenties, Lisa resolved to accept the restrictions of her illness and control her symptoms as best as she could through her diet. She married a man who is a good cook, and while limited in what she can eat, she attempts through

Preserving the Promise. DOI: http://dx.doi.org/10.1016/B978-0-12-809216-3.00009-9

diet and yoga to maintain a steady baseline. She had three children, despite the gestational diabetes and worsening pain caused by her pregnancies. "I was under a lot of pressure to not have a baby because it was very risky. Having children is really difficult with this condition because your baseline triglycerides go up … that becomes risky because triglycerides over 20 leave you open to pancreatitis, and if you get pancreatitis as a pregnant woman there is a risk for both yourself and your baby."

Today, much of Lisa's daily life revolves around managing her diet, and social situations involving food are problematic. "It is always an effort to ensure that I will be able to eat what is provided for me, and I often either take my own food or make sure I have eaten before I go out … [this] can be extremely stressful" [3].

Reaching out to others, Lisa established an online community for patients with LPLD and other rare diseases. Looking forward at age 50, she wonders what the disease has in store for her. "Not much is known about how aging affects LPLD, and I live in fear of losing my mental faculties and not being able to explain what I need to be fed to keep healthy."

A deficiency like Lisa's is the classic target for gene replacement therapy. LPLD patients have gene mutations that cause little or no LPL to be produced, so a cure should theoretically be possible by providing a normal copy of the gene. Glybera (alipogene tiparvovec) is a genetically engineered adeno-associated virus (AAV) that introduces a functional copy of the LPL gene into patients' muscle cells [2]. It is given as a one-time series of approximately 20 intramuscular injections.

Glybera cuts in half the clinical symptoms of pancreatitis, has only minimal side effects, and has shown benefits that can extend at least 6 years [2]. A drug like Glybera can reduce the overall cost of a patient to the health system and increase that patient's ability to be productive. This is the kind of advance that is likely to be embraced by clinicians, investors, insurers, industry—and of course patients. As Lisa says, "My God, do I want it! Because living with LPLD is an absolute pain in the ass. It invades every single aspect of my life. If you gave me something that cures me and I never had pancreatitis again and I could work fully and I would be able to achieve my full potential because I could work solidly, then maybe what I put into the economy—taking away all of the hospital costs—is actually worth it, on balance" [1]. (Ironically, she is not eligible to receive Glybera, because she has been able to achieve and maintain a disciplined lifestyle.)

Glybera would appear to be a role model for academic and industry collaboration resulting in a success for patients. The therapy has its roots in academia, with the original gene replacement studies in animals performed by the geneticist Dr. Michael R. Hayden, University of British Columbia, Vancouver, BC, and his colleagues [4]. The second-generation AAV vector used to make Glybera originated in Dr. James M. Wilson's laboratory at the University of

Pennsylvania [5]. Most of the development work was performed by the Dutch gene therapy company, Amsterdam Molecular Therapeutics (AMT).

Like most triumphs in biotechnology, the story of Glybera followed anything but a straight line of success from its academic origins. The IP for the AAV vector was licensed from Targeted Genetics, the company that went out of business after a young mother died during its clinical trial of an AAV drug (see chapter: Clinical Promise ≠ Investment Practice). AMT itself collapsed when it failed to meet its primary clinical endpoint of reducing blood lipid levels in its patients. AMT was liquidated and the Glybera program was acquired by Amsterdam-based uniQure. Continued follow-up of treated patients showed a promising reduction of rates of pancreatitis. uniQure performed a third clinical trial, which demonstrated the safety and efficacy of Glybera and led to its approval in Europe.

A great technology originates in the university lab, follows a typically circuitous path that's part rigorous development and part serendipity, almost fails for want of sustained funding, but ultimately realizes a potent clinical outcome. So what's the issue? Well, in addition to its status as the first approved gene replacement therapy, Glybera has the distinction of being the most expensive drug ever made. Its list price is over $1 million [6]. Gene therapies are expensive to develop, and they reach the clinic with value-based pricing strategies. The calculus underlying such pricing is this: a drug useful for a small group of patients is no less costly to develop than one for a larger cohort, these patients have limited or no alternatives, and taking care of them with existing options is inadequate and exorbitantly expensive. Furthermore, a gene therapy like Glybera may achieve prolonged effects from a single course of treatment, meaning it fails the traditional development target of an ongoing income stream from chronic treatment (in contrast to enzyme replacement therapies or anti inflammatory drugs, which need to be taken for a lifetime).

Of course there's a powerful humanitarian argument that supports paying for Glybera for patients like Lisa. But, with prescription drug spending in the US at $374 billion annually [7], there's a lot of pressure being exerted from multiple directions: formulary restrictions from insurers, galloping copays, media coverage of patients cutting pills in half to make their prescriptions last longer, highly publicized congressional hearings on "predatory" pricing. "Access really is a problem for a lot of patients in relation to these very costly medicines," notes Jerry Avorn, a professor at Harvard Medical School and chief of the Division of Pharmacoepidemiology and Pharmacoeconomics at Brigham and Women's Hospital. "We sometimes think, 'Well, people have insurance, and under Obamacare there's a lot more coverage,' but what that doesn't take into account is that there is a very big copayment that the patient has to come up with that is often many, many hundreds or thousands of dollars" [8]. For many patients, and even for drugs with less stratospheric pricing, this means they simply cannot access the treatments needed to prolong their lives.

This hasn't been without pushback, some of which is coming directly from clinicians. A team of oncologists at Memorial Sloan Kettering, Peter B. Bach, Leonard B. Saltz, and Robert E. Wittes, rebelled against the price of Zaltrap (ziv-aflibercept, Sanofi) a colorectal cancer drug, which was twice as high as a similar drug, Avastin (bevacizumab, Genentech), even though it was not demonstrably better. They published an editorial in the Op-Ed pages of the *New York Times*, in which they explained that they would not prescribe Zaltrap because of the financial burden it placed on patients, which may require over $2,200 per month in copayments [9]. Sanofi has since retreated on the pricing of the drug in a move that earned Zaltrap a spot on Fierce Biotech's list of the 10 Top Biotech Drug Launch Disasters [10].

An international group of over 100 chronic myeloid leukemia (CML) specialists questioned whether the high prices of the tyrosine kinase inhibitors (TKIs) available for CML treatment prevent patients from getting the medicine. They noted that CML patients in the United States had lower survival rates than in Sweden [11], suggesting that high TKI prices may be standing in the way of fully treating the CML patient population. Globally, 70–75% of CML patients are not receiving TKIs for their disease in spite of drug access support programs maintained by the manufacturers.

Another pricing protest was lodged by David M. Orenstein, Director of the Antonio J. and Janet Palumbo Cystic Fibrosis Center and the Chair of the Ethics Committee at the Children's Hospital of Pittsburgh, and four of his pediatric specialist colleagues. In an open letter to Vertex Pharmaceutical's CEO, Jeff Leiden, they complained about the decision to charge $294,000 annually for the cystic fibrosis drug, Kalydeco (Ivacaftor). He writes, "This action could appear to be leveraging pain and suffering into huge financial gain" [12].

And finally, Glybera has failed to achieve any commercial traction and continues to lose money for uniQure, which has turned EU sales over to an Italian drug maker and reportedly dropped plans for US approval [13].

Drug companies are under fire to explain why their prices are so high. US Senators Grassley and Wyden initiated an 18-month investigation that challenged Gilead's pricing as Medicare spending on Sovaldi and Harvoni topped $8.2 billion [14]. Their report concluded that the price was set solely to maximize profits, without consideration of patient need and access, and asserted that, " Gilead knew these prices would put treatment out of the reach of millions and cause extraordinary problems for Medicare and Medicaid, but still the company went ahead." The result? Only 2.4% of Hepatitis C patients were treated in 2014. Senator Wyden further said, "If Gilead's approach to pricing is the future of how blockbuster drugs are launched, it will cost billions and billions of dollars to treat just a fraction of patients. America needs cures for cancer, Alzheimer's, diabetes and HIV. [What] if those cures are unaffordable and out of reach to millions who need them?"

Express Scripts, a pharmacy benefits manager, has also pushed back on the high price of Hepatitis C drugs. Upon approval of Abbvie's lower cost treatment for Hepatitis C, Viekira Pak, they excluded three more expensive drugs, Sovaldi, Harvoni, and Olysio (simeprevir, Janssen) from their formulary [15].

The industry's defense cites a combination of the high cost of development, currently estimated at $2.6 billion per drug [16], short payback due to patent expiration, the need to funnel profits back into R&D, and the value-based calculation we described earlier. While drugs like Glybera, Kalydeco, and Harvoni would not exist without the critical basic studies performed in publicly funded academic laboratories, it's also true that they would not exist without the industry assuming the much greater financial risk of development. Despite all the media attention, drug pricing is not a simple problem attributable to a rapacious villain. It is, rather, a multifaceted and multiconstituent problem, driven by financial incentives that can be traced, at least in part, from university ownership of academic research through Bayh–Dole.

More than 900 biotech drugs are in clinical trials worldwide, and at least one estimate suggests that as many as 100 of these could gain market approval in the next 5–10 years [17]. Biologics are a prospective victim of their own success. EvaluatePharma, a market intelligence company, focused on the life sciences, reports the number of US orphan drug designations increased by 12% to 291 in 2014 and rose an incredible 62% to 201 in Europe. By 2020, orphan drug sales alone are projected to reach $178 billion, representing almost one-fifth of global drug sales excluding generics [18]. Express Scripts calculates that the newer biotech drugs account for 32% of drug spending, even though they are only 1% of prescriptions written [19].

It doesn't follow that we can or should, as a society, be without these new biotechnologies from Valley of Death (VoD) start-ups. But it's not hard to imagine drugs in the current pharma pipeline exceeding the healthcare system's ability to pay for them.

The momentum for exerting controls over US drug pricing may spur change. Free market effects will present opportunities for less expensive alternatives, there will be regulatory pressure to modify the period of exclusivity for biologics, and there is already activity around new legislation to enable approval of biosimilars [20]. Rationalization of drug pricing would seem reasonable to enable the greatest number of biotechnology innovations to reach the greatest number of patients. Allowing Medicare Part D to negotiate drug prices, a measure proposed by the Obama administration, has even been supported across the political aisle [21]. All in all, the forces at work here are considerable, and despite industry lobbying, a negotiated or mandated reduction in pharma prices is probably inevitable.

Changing the pharma reimbursement paradigm, however, could have a devastating effect upstream on the biotech VoD. Remember that the VoD is fundamentally a market in which investments are bought and sold. Pricing strategies for biologics are stunning, but the math behind them drives a value chain that supports the early-stage development ecosystem. The Angel money that enables translation from the university to commercial development is part and parcel of how we get to a cure for Hepatitis C. Investors, including those coming in at an early stage, are attracted to the lucrative development pathway that produces drugs that: (1) have no therapeutic alternative; (2) can be brought more quickly to market; and (3) capitalize on orphan and breakthrough drug designations to achieve stratospheric pricing. This mindset drives investment at every stage of technology development. If the pricing paradigm shifts and no exits can be achieved at enormous multiples because there's not enough money in the system to pay for breakthrough drugs, then early-stage investors will have much less incentive to participate in these very high risk bets.

REACHING THE LIMITS

Investing in a biotech start-up is inarguably a high-risk activity, and the first money in is only the first table stake in a process that will ultimately demand an enormous kitty. If this sounds a lot like gambling, it is. Angels have limited tolerance for the long play, and follow a conventional wisdom investment strategy that's based on probabilities: achieve one win so big that it generates a handsome return and pays for the other nine losses. It's like the high roller room in Las Vegas, except that the stakes are medicine's future.

That some healthcare investments continue to get funded, and a few yield enormous investor returns, doesn't mean we should continue business as usual. Healthcare costs are a political hot potato because they're straining the economy. We can barely afford all of the drugs we have now, we can't afford all of the drugs that are in the pipeline, and we couldn't afford all of the drugs that would be available if we weren't killing most of them in the VoD. So we'd better look at making the formula work better, and that starts with eliminating some of the costly friction in the system. The moving parts, as always, are time and money.

Improving the efficiency and output of the VoD means reducing the dysfunction underlying the three Translation Gaps. More specifically, it means:

- Overcoming the disconnect between a technology's innovation and investment potential.
- Enhancing the relative attractiveness of biotechnology as an early-stage investment. High risk of failure demands a very high prospective return to offset the risks of capital and time needed to progress the technology.
- Reducing unnecessary impediments to the progression of medical discoveries from universities to the clinic. The inconsistency of technology transfer practices increases the time and money needed for technologies to attain the standard of validation required by investors and strategic partners.

Effective allocation of capital should nurture, not destroy, potential new therapies. A rationalization of the flow of money within the VoD would reduce the risk for later-stage investors, while preserving the value and the motivation of those coming in early. It would also, ultimately, improve the return to the public on our massive investment in biomedical research, financially and from the standpoint of human health.

It is, of course, impossible to impose some external standard of rational behavior on the VoD. We do not claim that solutions to the problems of the VoD can be easily implemented. The VoD has developed as a free market for investment theses supported by biotechnology, in which each of the actors attempts to maximize his own success in terms of his perceived incentives. Subsequent chapters will present specific prescriptions for modifying the structure of incentives and encouraging better alignment. We'll begin here with an instructive story about incentives. Alex Tabarrok, a Professor of Economics at George Mason University, featured *Planet Money* guest and TED talk speaker, and founder of the economics blog Marginal Revolution, uses the story of Britain's colonization of Australia to illustrate how essential incentives are to outcomes [22,23]. We've paraphrased it below.

In 1787, Great Britain began sending prisoners to Australian penal colonies. The Government of Britain paid sea captains to transport the prisoners, but the outcomes were atrocious, with many of the prisoners dying en route due to privation and abuse. This caused a scandal in England; newspapers protested, and one could argue that the British Government was certainly not getting its money's worth. Obvious changes were tried. New laws were passed to require better conditions for prisoners, medical care was improved, and the clergy tried to appeal to the ship captains' higher nature. But these measures did not work: on one of the trips, one-third of the prisoners died.

An economist was consulted, who suggested that the government should not pay for sending prisoners to Australia. *Rather, the government should pay for getting them to Australia.* When the new system was instituted in 1793, the prisoner survival rate immediately rose to 99%.

This story is a useful analogy for the problem of crossing the VoD with a new technology. The main problem with the Australian transport was that people could earn money from the system before a "product" was finished and delivered—the product being successful arrival of a prisoner in Australia. The ability of the sea captain to make money by a variety of means that did not contribute to live prisoners actually arriving in Australia—for instance, saving money by not carrying enough rations, for example, while nevertheless being paid for making the voyage—led to the diversion of resources from the government's objective. Prisoners died, but from the perspective of the sea captains, who increased their personal wealth, the process was entirely successful.

In our adaptation of this story, the technologies are the prisoners, the VoD is the ocean, Australia is the clinic where patients receive treatment, and the boat captains are those of us charged with getting the technologies to the clinic safely. Many of those technology "prisoners" are dying, despite our best intentions.

Throughout the VoD, smart people, acting in their own apparent self-interests, actually harm the prospects of the technologies they are supposed to support. Commonly accepted practices in the VoD focus on short-term gains rather than long-term clinical impact. It's possible for investors to make a great deal of money without anything ever getting to the clinic; and it's becoming routine for pharma/biotech companies to generate enormous sales revenues by focusing development on very small groups of patients instead of solving bigger epidemiological problems.

Incentives can be adjusted to align self-interest with social interest. Modifying incentives within the VoD to bring them in line with broader societal objectives is the ethos of this book: to support our economy and research institutions, to enhance financial returns for investors and the pharma industry, and to improve the health of mankind. In short, we fully subscribe to the notion of doing well by doing good.

If the VoD continues to operate the way it has, we will continue to pay sea captains to transport prisoners, alive or dead, to Australia. The cost of our inefficiency is hard to quantify, but the implications are easy to understand. Every technology that cannot make it to the clinic is a wasted opportunity to change someone's life, and we will never know what *could* have been done. As Bob Wills once sang, "dreams don't make noise when they die" [24].

REFERENCES

[1] Lisa is a pseudonym. Interview with author SD, June 1, 2015.

[2] Scott LJ. Alipogene tiparvovec: a review of its use in adults with familial lipoprotein lipase deficiency. Drugs 2015;75(2):175–82. http://dx.doi.org/10.1007/s40265-014-0339-9.

[3] Email to author SD, April 21, 2015.

[4] Excoffon KJ, Liu G, Miao L, Wilson JE, McManus BM, Semenkovich CF, et al. Correction of hypertriglyceridemia and impaired fat tolerance in lipoprotein lipase-deficient mice by adenovirus-mediated expression of human lipoprotein lipase. Arterioscler Thromb Vasc Biol 1997;17(11):2532–9.

[5] Bryant LM, Christopher DM, Giles AR, Hinderer C, Rodriguez JL, Smith JB, et al. Lessons learned from the clinical development and market authorization of Glybera. Hum Gene Ther Clin Dev 2013;24(2):55–64. http://dx.doi.org/10.1089/humc.2013.087.

[6] Morrison C. 1-million price tag set for Glybera gene therapy. Bioentrepreneur Trade Secrets 2015 March 3, 2015. <http://blogs.nature.com/tradesecrets/2015/03/03/1-million-price-tag-set-for-glybera-gene-therapy/>; [accessed 24.02.16].

[7] Silverman E. Why did prescription drug spending hit $374B in the US last year? Wall Street J 2015 April 14, 2015. <http://blogs.wsj.com/pharmalot/2015/04/14/why-did-prescription-drug-spending-hit-374b-in-the-us-last-year-read-this/>; [accessed 24.02.16].

[8] Tirrell, Meg. The $84,000 question: Will focusing on drug prices rein in costs? CNBC, May 22, 2014. <www.cnbc.com/id/101694293>; 2014 [accessed 27.05.15].

[9] Bach PB, Saltz LB, Wittes RE. In cancer care, cost matters. New York Times, October 14, 2012.

[10] Carroll J, Staton T. 10 top drug launch disasters. Fierce Pharma; 2012. November 27, 2012. <www.fiercepharma.com/special-reports/top-10-drug-launch-disasters>; [accessed 27.05.15].

[11] Experts in Chronic Myeloid Leukemia. The price of drugs for chronic myeloid leukemia (CML) is a reflection of the unsustainable prices of cancer drugs: from the perspective of a large group of CML experts. Blood 2013;121(22):4439–42.

[12] Orenstein DM, Quinton PM, O'Sullivan BP, Milla CE, Pian M. Open letter to Jeff Leiden. July 19, 2012. <http://www.medpagetoday.com/upload/2013/5/17/CFletter.pdf>; 2012.

[13] https://www.technologyreview.com/s/601165/the-worlds-most-expensive-medicine-is-a-bust/.

[14] United States Senate Committee on Finance. Wyden-Grassley Sovaldi investigation finds revenue-driven pricing strategy behind $84,000 Hepatitis drug. <http://www.finance.senate.gov/ranking-members-news/wyden-grassley-sovaldi-investigation-finds-revenue-driven-pricing-strategy-behind-84-000-hepatitis-drug>; 2015 [accessed 25.02.16].

[15] James D. Express Scripts to Cover Viekira Pak, Exclude Sovaldi. December 23, 2014. <http://www.specialtypharmacytimes.com/news/express-scripts-to-cover-viekira-pak-exclude-sovaldi>; 2014 [accessed 25.02.16].

[16] Tufts Center for the Study of Drug Development. Cost to develop and win marketing approval for a new drug is $2.6 billion. November 18, 2014. http://csdd.tufts.edu/news/complete_story/pr_tufts_csdd_2014_cost_study; 2014 [accessed 25.02.16].

[17] Evens R, Kaitin K. The evolution of biotechnology and its impact on health care. Health Aff (Millwood) 2015;34(2):210–19. http://dx.doi.org/10.1377/hlthaff.2014.1023.

[18] EvaluatePharma. Orphan drug report, 2015. <http://info.evaluategroup.com/rs/607-YGS-364/images/EPOD15.pdf>; 2015.

[19] America's Health Insurance Plans. Specialty drugs: issues and challenges. July 8, 2015. <http://www.ahip.org/Issues/Specialty-Drugs/>; 2015 [accessed 25.02.16].

[20] Monroe-Yavneh N, Royzman I. Twelve years, or fewer? two current debates on the exclusivity period for biologics. Biologics Blog. February 24, 2015. <www.biologicsblog.com/blog/twelve-years-fewer-two-current-debates-exclusivity-period-biologics/>.

[21] Shih C, Schwartz J, Coukell A. How would government negotiation of Medicare Part D drug prices work? Health Affairs Blog 2016. <http://healthaffairs.org/blog/2016/02/01/how-would-government-negotiation-of-medicare-part-d-drug-prices-work/>; [accessed 25.02.16].

[22] Cowen T, Tabarrok A. Modern principles: macroeconomics, 3rd ed. New York, NY: Worth Publishers; 2015.

[23] Interview with the authors, August 14, 2014.

[24] Walker C. Going Away Party. Recorded by Bob Wills on *For the Last Time*. United Artists; 1974.

Translation Gap 1

Universities Don't Make
What Companies Need

Chapter 10

When Is an Experiment Ready for the Valley of Death?

One of the conversations that started this book was about "Eureka" moments. Clearly, they're qualitatively different for scientists than for investors, and it's hard to weigh the gratification of discovering a novel means of antibody engineering compared with making a lot of money on an investment. But we'll start this chapter with the scientist. His or her impetus for entering the Valley of Death (VoD) is the desire to realize the potential of a novel platform or drug that can ultimately make a difference—clinically, societally, and not incidentally, financially.

Even to lay observers, it's clear that what's intended by all those walkathons, ice bucket challenges, and lemonade stands is support for scientific research in search of a cure. But scientific exploration is a nonlinear walk; it's inspired by curiosity and sustained by doggedness, the result of which, if successful, is discovery of something not previously understood or conceived. In the world of healthcare, this is a potential therapy, brought to life through the agency of people whose careers are focused on changing what we know about biology and how that can lead to better lives. Investors aren't always generous in their perceptions of scientists, because they are seen to lack business acumen (a sweeping but common generalization), but no one denies the enthusiasm with which they advocate for their inventions. They have been dedicated to advancing their fields for years or decades. They have a profound understanding of the "big questions" and what needs to be done to solve apparently intractable problems.

And so the scientific process of discovery often reaches a point where it feels a real commercial pull. An experimental system, built in a laboratory to model a disease, answers a question that is initially agnostic to the demands of, or odds of survival in, the VoD. It is, rather, focused on mission: we have a brand new way of solving a problem that re-sets the clinical paradigm, something that works differently than what has been tried before. Physicians don't necessarily need to know the details of how, commonly referred to as mechanism of action, to help their patients. Investors probably don't care that much either, except to the extent that uniqueness renders the invention commercially viable and reduces the uncertainty of market competition. This moment of transition

Preserving the Promise. DOI: http://dx.doi.org/10.1016/B978-0-12-809216-3.00010-5

is accompanied by a sense of urgency to get started right away, transferring the discovery into commercial development before someone else figures it out or creates an alternative, and the commercial opportunity goes away. This isn't strictly a commercial or a scientific urge but a human one.

People have a variety of good reasons for doing what they do, and they're neither wholly scientific nor wholly commercial. One of the authors watched a well-known academician and management consultant advise 100 first-year MBAs at a prestigious business school that the only criterion for deciding whether to start a small business was to compare the expected return on investment (ROI) to the founders' current income. This seemed breathtakingly deaf to the higher-order aspirations that define us. There are great reasons to start a company that have little to do with financial return. New technologies are intrinsically exciting, and entrepreneurs and the Angels who finance them can easily become devoted to the promise of something that may effect change for patients.

It's also incorrect to ascribe a life of scientific inquiry to pure curiosity or altruism. From inside as well as outside, a life in academia can feel isolated from the "real world"; and indeed it is possible to be in medical science for a lifetime without actually impacting human health. So it is natural to pursue another avenue of self-fulfillment, by commercializing one's discoveries in the laboratory. The other author of this book was in the audience at the American Society of Hematology Conference at which Brian Druker first presented his clinical experience with imatinib. This was the first-in-class drug that inhibits tyrosine kinases in cancer cells and the first oral therapy for Chronic Myelogenous Leukemia. A disease formerly treated with a bone marrow transplant would now be treated with a once-a-day pill! The look on Druker's face as he walked up the aisle to give his talk said it all; he knew the data he was about to present would change medicine forever.

Science is also personal. Doug Melton, scientific founder of Semma Therapeutics, pivoted his research program from embryonic development in the African clawed frog, *Xenopus laevis*, toward the creation of pancreatic islet cells from human pluripotent stem cells when both of his children developed Type I diabetes [1,2].

In other words it's not, as that business professor pointed out with such assurance, the pursuit of ROI that drives healthcare invention. Passion for discovery and its implications is the elixir that fuels excitement in the VoD. It's embodied in the classic American success story, a good idea translated to something great through courage and elbow grease. Before we get carried away with Norman Rockwell optimism, however, it is worth pausing to note that the pace of commercial development of a discovery, especially within a university setting, ranges from measured to impossibly slow.

The experiments and resources required to validate may be outside the scope of the original discovery program. Making a prototype drug suitable for testing in animals and humans, performing pharmacokinetics, replicating and extending the original result with new material—it's goal-oriented work, prone to technical glitches and requiring experience and intuition. Such development needs money of course, beyond what can be accomplished with grants, and that means commercial funding. The hard reality is that whatever aspirations initially drove them, worthwhile inventions need to get out of the university environment that nurtured them.

While this can be an uncomfortable transition for scientist inventors, moving a discovery to the commercial realm is also an antidote for increasing distress in the world of academic research. Continued shrinkage of public funding affects everyone working in biomedical science. The strains on principal investigators, charged with defining the research program and writing grants, have never been greater. They are assigned lab space, teaching and/or administrative obligations—and saddled with the requirement to find grants that will pay for their salary, staff, research expenses, and overhead costs such as space, infrastructure, and administrative support. If you're far enough along and/or sufficiently prominent, it is not a huge problem to support your research from grants. But the reality of decreasing National Institutes of Health (NIH) grant resources in real dollars, and a declining ability of younger or less prominent investigators to receive the critical R01 investigator-initiated grants, have cut deeply into the ethos of academia and created a pressure-cooker environment where scientists continually write grant proposals to keep their research funded.

The old adage "publish or perish" has given way to "fund yourself or be marginalized." A tenured colleague at a major academic medical center recently lost his NIH funding despite having a productive research program in red blood cell disorders, thalassemia and sickle-cell anemia [3]. His division Chairman channeled him a $100K bridge loan, but when that money ran out and his grant proposals continued to return disastrous reviews, his lab was shut down. His equipment and supplies were arrayed on the benches in his laboratory and his colleagues were encouraged to drop by to see if there was anything they would like to scavenge for their own labs.

Because he was a tenured physician, he couldn't be fired outright, but this traditional academic perk doesn't mean much if you're a researcher without a laboratory in which to do research. Without sufficient grant funding, work is deferred and momentum lost. The university may neither have wished to, nor been able to, discharge him, but of course loaded him up with additional administrative, teaching, and clinical duties.

This physician is now working to improve protocols for care of sickle cell disease patients, certainly a worthy aim but not the same as basic research into the disease itself. "This is not where I thought I would spend the last 2 or 5 or 10 years of my career." After almost three decades of study, grant writing, and teaching, he laments "I'm sick and tired of academia. I can't do it any more. Even when you are doing well, you're still fighting the whole time."

The prospect of commercialization and clinical implementation of an invention is an attractive goal that can sustain researchers through long periods of delayed gratification, technical complications, and unpredictable grant reviews. It carries the possibility of being responsible for a cure, of scientific or clinical fame, and not incidentally of equity and royalties that overshadow typical academic financial rewards. In fact, for the newest generation of scientists entering academia, starting a company is pretty much part of the plan.

Scientists are optimistic people who believe they can usually find a way to make things work, so the odds of a biotech start-up failing in the VoD may not feel that daunting, even if they have a concrete idea of just how long those odds are. There's a deep-seated sense that important ideas will intrinsically have the power to succeed. And the VoD presents an opportunity to make that happen; for all its tribulations, how much more difficult could it be than trying to keep the lab funded by grants and supplication to department chairmen? Isn't seeking private sector funding essentially the same process as seeking grant funding? And isn't starting a company just another type of experiment?

The financial risk proposition also has less immediacy for scientific founders that it might for hired CEOs, who join a start-up for deferred compensation, or for investors interested in keeping the company going just until they get a return. Most founders won't give up academic jobs, reasonably stable employment with benefits, to devote themselves full time to starting a company. This is a commitment problem that makes investors wary, since they want 110% from founders. But that in no way diminishes how much this matters to founders, or the fact that, among all of the people involved in an early-stage company, they need to be accounted for as the technology champions.

While investors have many technologies from which to choose, scientific founders are naturally wedded to their own creations. Serial entrepreneurs notwithstanding, most scientists will only move a small number of inventions toward the clinic over their careers. This is a simple function of time, energy, and research focus. The decision to exert the time and effort to commercialize a particular technology is thus one of the most important decisions an academic scientist will ever make.

WHY NOT SIMPLY LICENSE THE TECHNOLOGY TO A BIG HEALTHCARE COMPANY?

An alternative to creating a start-up around a technology, acquiring funding and working toward an exit, may be to license it to an existing company that has the staff and resources to support clinical development. The fundamental problem, of course, is that the imputed value of the technology will be much lower at such an early stage. There are other barriers: a high ratio of available technologies to potential licensors, the problem of obtaining visibility, and the absence of commercial proof of concept. And as we have discussed, most of what comes out of university laboratories is not ready for pharma. At the Bio-Europe conference in 2013 in Vienna, Austria, author Dessain participated in a panel discussion entitled "Building the drug pipeline of tomorrow: Capturing the potential of the academic research enterprise." The discussion topic was how to encourage academic/industrial collaborations. Considering the gulf between what academia makes and what her company, Merck, needs, panelist Suzanne Mandala commented, "Academics start with the mouse knockout, and then they have the best idea for the future, and we in drug development see the long, hard road ahead where brilliant ideas [fail] ... Very few of them actually pan out" [4].

As a potential strategic partner, any pharma company understandably would prefer to see a substantial data package. They want a drug to be thoroughly characterized, with an explicated mechanism of action, pharmacokinetic profile, therapeutic activity in at least one animal model, and a clear rationale for effectiveness in humans. Furthermore, the drug candidate must fit into an existing development program, a broad strategy targeting a therapeutic domain, or a defensive market strategy where acquiring control over the new invention will protect an existing franchise. Lastly, pharma needs to be convinced that the data set is fundamentally valid and can be replicated—and this is the case even if the research has been published in a reputable journal [5].

Like all industries, Big Pharma does pass through phases, including periods of excitement about new platform technologies, which provide an impetus for early-stage deals. With the ascendancy of cancer immunotherapy, messenger RNA therapeutics, and gene editing with CRISPR-Cas9 [6–8] platforms were temporarily back in vogue. Propelled by these discoveries, biotech in general experienced a period of early- (as well as late-) stage investments at dizzying valuations. But that boom just as quickly settled into quiescence, and lately it's out of fashion to invest in anything that doesn't have a clearly established therapeutic target. As FierceBiotech's Damian Garde reported from the 2016 J.P. Morgan Health Care Conference in San Francisco, CA, "Many emerging biotechs, only a year or so removed from going public, seemed to abandon talk of 'platforms,' of 'product engines' and of R&D 'operating systems,' instead harping on comparatively unsexy things like 'execution,' 'validated endpoints' and 'FDA meeting minutes'" [9]. Scientific fads notwithstanding, pharma will always gravitate toward what it does best, creating value by getting products approved, and that means acquiring validated therapeutic candidates.

This is the core of the first translation gap, that universities don't make what companies need. The science may be either too early or a bad fit, or maybe not yet credible, despite its apparent innovation, prospective importance, or highly credentialed scientist/inventor. There is an active industry initiative to move beyond these traditional barriers, reaching further into the academic research enterprise to accelerate early discoveries. For example, Gilead and Yale have a multiyear, multimillion dollar collaborative effort in cancer genomics and drug discovery [10]. As important as they are, however, these relationships are too few to dramatically change the commercialization prospects for most new technologies.

Some may flip the equation in our first translation gap, and argue that of course companies need what universities make, just not all of it. That's true, and not the crux of our argument. The issues are that universities make an enormous amount of things that companies don't need, or at least don't want, or that aren't nearly ready for commercial development. This means that to overcome the first Translation Gap we also need to think about the relationship between academia and what start-up biotechnology companies in the VoD need. The question is not just whether something is scientifically sound, but whether it is ready to support the investment thesis of a company in the VoD?

The barriers to entry (as opposed to success) into the VoD are low, and the number of companies already there is high. From a Five Forces perspective, the threat of new entrants and rivalry among existing competitors are high and probably not modifiable. Further, nobody is going to be served by arbitrarily reducing the number of companies that go into the VoD seeking funding or by prematurely culling the companies that are already there. The VoD is a market for investments and sorting things out is what markets are supposed to do. Our goal is to help healthcare companies better survive the challenges of the VoD, to give the best ones a fair chance of surviving, and to lower the logistical barriers that harm important technologies.

What universities make is intellectual property, in the form of a scientific discovery supported by a patent application. Of course, they also provide education and student services, but in the realm of commercialization, intellectual property (IP) is their product, and the product needs to match the needs of their customers—licensors of their technology. Absent a match, healthcare IP never has an opportunity to reach the clinic. To understand how we may be able to address the first Translation Gap, let's begin by analyzing the process whereby an invention becomes property.

COLLABORATION AND CONFLICT

Once a scientist decides to bring an invention into the VoD, the next steps are constrained by law and policy. Employment contracts at academic institutions are based on work for hire laws and assign all employees' rights to any inventions to their university employers. Bayh–Dole goes further, granting the academic institution exclusive ownership of inventions produced with Federal support. Some technology transfer offices (TTOs) have policies enabling inventors to reclaim rights to their inventions under certain circumstances, if the university has no intention of submitting a patent application to support the invention. In practice, the process is complicated and very rarely done, and reinforces risk-averse behavior that, instead of facilitating commercialization, may put the inventor and technology at even greater disadvantage. From a practical perspective, if a TTO will not support the technology, its prospects for commercialization will be severely compromised if not eliminated entirely.

So, barring a reputation that attracts private investors or companies to the party even before the university issues an invitation, the first step for a scientist working at an academic institution is to ask the TTO what, if anything, the university will do with his/her creation. This is the beginning of what's often a major culture clash, the schism that underlies the first part of the Translation Gap. And though TTOs play a role in this, it is only one of several missed opportunities for alignment, on all sides. This first Translation Gap, universities don't make what companies need, reflects a *collaborative dysfunction* between inventor, TTO, university administration, and the functions and needs of the pharma and investment communities.

Most prominent academic institutions doing healthcare research have established "translational therapeutics" initiatives because, in healthcare research, the putative objective for all parties is translation: changing some unlocked secret of nature or technology that has the potential to improve human health into a worthwhile clinical tool. To get there, the invention must become IP that can be owned and sold. There are lots of definitions around IP, but it is pretty well described by the words themselves: the product of someone's thinking, the rights to which are owned and protected. That typically means the protection/ validation of a patent application. If a patent application is written support for the strength and potential of the idea, the issued patent is something of a merit badge that transforms a budding idea into an investable one.

Solid IP, especially in biotechnology, is tangible evidence that the technology is novel, nonobvious, and potentially useful. None of these is a guarantee of anything, but they are usually prerequisites for investment. Investors put their money behind differentiated technologies, innovative companies with practical solutions, and people who can make things happen. In this context, IP is essentially the collateral for the investment, and its absence is a significant barrier to obtaining capital.

From the perspective of the inventor, their invention should be submitted as a patent application at the earliest possible date. Like parents trying to make an objective assessment of their own children's potential, however, scientists may overestimate the commercial value of their discoveries, assume a small market opportunity is sufficient, conflate innovation with commercial potential, and/ or underestimate the risk of failure. They also feel pressure to submit patent applications quickly because it is entirely possible that someone else may have made either the same discovery or one that accomplishes the same purpose, and will blunt the opportunity. At the same time, patent laws mean they are unable to discuss details of the invention publicly or publish results connected to the patent. This carries over to grant proposals, which are nominally confidential disclosures but will be reviewed by other experts competing in the same field. This transitional period is something of a limbo in which a basic feature of the academic work—communication of research findings to others—is suspended. So the patent filing acquires some urgency.

TTOs are the screening authorities for what gets filed, and often disagree with the inventor's opinion. In 2014, 24,117 invention disclosures were filed with TTOs at the 161 academic institutions that contributed to the AUTM licensing survey, but only 13,907 patent applications were filed [11]. If scientists are subject to magical thinking about the compelling value of their inventions, that's intrinsic to the creative process of discovery. TTOs generally have their feet planted more firmly on commercial ground. Most profess that their primary goal is to translate research results and serve the interests of the faculty, but they are not granted unlimited funds or staff by their administrations and they need to judiciously allocate their time and resources [12].

First, they need to satisfy themselves that there is a need for the invention and the presence of potential development partners or acquirers. This isn't a casual analysis, and it's generally more realistic than an inventor's sense of "if I build it they will come," but it is too often conducted at a 10,000-foot level. Some places are better at it than others. For example, Stanford's bar for submitting a provisional patent application is a potential lifetime ROI of at least $100,000 [13]. Factors at work in this assessment include the tech transfer officer's experience, expressions of interest from companies or industry experts, and the track record of the inventor.

TTOs and inventors operate within a paradox, tasked with patenting noncommercial academic research for commercial development. Academic patenting occurs at a point that is usually quite distant from a package that can allow acquisition by Big Pharma, support from deep-pocketed institutional investors, or an exit from the VoD [14]. The cardinal feature of patentability is that it is "not obvious to one skilled in the art," so in biotech a novel means of manipulating a biological system is the kernel of the decision whether to file a patent application. But at this juncture, there is a broad chasm between innovation for its own sake and something that is able to support an investment thesis or be taken up by a strategic partner.

Research programs that seem far from any medical relevance have yielded paradigm shifts that impacted medicine in unanticipated ways. Studies of gene regulation in the nematode, *Caenorhabditis elegans*, gave rise to the understanding of microRNAs and a drug to treat familial amyloid cardiomyopathy, a fatal disease that results from abnormal protein deposition in the heart [15]. Studies of the HIV genome in the mid-1990s yielded a means of genetically manipulating T cells, which recently enabled chimeric antigen receptor-modified T cells to cure acute lymphoblastic leukemia [16,17]. One of the first clinical applications of CRISPR-Cas9 gene editing, which was discovered through the study of the bacterial immune system, may be for the debilitating bleeding disorder, hemophilia [18].

The technology transfer process is more than just the conversion of novelty into property; it is the narrowing of the infinite possibility of scientific exploration into a discrete number of what investors call "shots on goal." When scientists take the long view and operate in faith that the unexpected is a wild card for innovation, they are in conflict with TTOs, university administrations, entrepreneurs, and investors, who all want greater specificity and immediacy. The products of this tension, each a decision of whether to patent a new discovery or not, are the seeds of success or failure in the VoD—the preservation or loss of a promise for cure.

The first Translation Gap, *universities don't make what companies need,* recognizes that we, the community that creates and commercializes biotechnology, are not as good as we think we are at converting innovation in its raw state into IP that has a clear, investable path to the clinic. When the number of patents dwarfs the number of approved drugs by a factor of thousands, and most of the companies in the VoD fail, we should ask what we are really getting for our efforts—and whether we can do better.

REFERENCES

[1] Pagliuca FW, Millman JR, Gurtler M, Segel M, Van Dervort A, Ryu JH, et al. Generation of functional human pancreatic beta cells in vitro. Cell 2014;159(2):428–39. http://dx.doi.org/10.1016/j.cell.2014.09.040.

[2] Cook G. Son's disease propels a stem cell pioneer. The Boston Globe, March 20, 2005, <http://www.boston.com/yourlife/health/diseases/articles/2005/03/20/sons_disease_propels_a_stem_cell_pioneer/?page=full>; 2005.

[3] Interview with author SD, December 23, 2015.

[4] E.B.D. Group. Building the drug pipeline of tomorrow: Capturing the potential of the academic research enterprise. Bio Europe conference, November 4, 2013, Vienna, Austria, <http://www.partnering360.com/insight/showroom/id/424>; 2013 [accessed 15.03.16].

[5] Ioannidis JP. Why most published research findings are false. PLoS Med 2005;2(8):e124. http://dx.doi.org/10.1371/journal.pmed.0020124.

[6] Hoos A. Development of immuno-oncology drugs-from CTLA4 to PD1 to the next generations. Nat Rev Drug Discov 2016;15(4):235–47. http://dx.doi.org/10.1038/nrd.2015.35.

[7] Sahin U, Kariko K, Tureci O. mRNA-based therapeutics—developing a new class of drugs. Nat Rev Drug Discov 2014;13(10):759–80. http://dx.doi.org/10.1038/nrd4278.

[8] Doudna JA, Charpentier E. Genome editing. The new frontier of genome engineering with CRISPR-Cas9. Science 2014;346(6213):1258096. http://dx.doi.org/10.1126/science.1258096.

[9] Garde D. Biotech rehearses its 'difficult' second album at #JPM16. Published January 15, 2016. <http://www.fiercebiotech.com/story/biotech-rehearses-its-difficult-second-album-jpm16/2016-01-15?utm_medium=nl&utm_source=internal>; 2016 [accessed 10.03.16].

[10] Hathaway B. Yale and Gilead Sciences extend cancer research collaboration. Published October 23, 2014. <http://news.yale.edu/2014/10/23/yale-and-gilead-sciences-extend-cancer-research-collaboration>; 2014 [accessed 17.03.16].

[11] Hippenmeyer P, Hawkins S, Mroz MA, Robertson R, Ruey N, Stevens AJ, editors. AUTM U.S. Licensing Activity survey: FY2014. <http://www.autm.net/resources-surveys/research-reports-databases/licensing-surveys/fy-2014-licensing-survey/>; 2015.

[12] Abrams I, Leung G, Stevens AJ. How are U.S. technology transfer offices tasked and motivated—is it all about the money? Res Manag Rev 2009;17(1):1–34. <http://www.bu.edu/otd/files/2011/02/How-are-US-Tech.-Transfer-Offices-Tasked-and-Motivated.pdf/>.

[13] The patent approach of stanford's OTL: If no licensee is reimbursing patent costs. <http://otl.stanford.edu/inventors/resources/inventors_patapp.html>; 2016 [accessed 19.03.16].

[14] Silva R, Allen DN, Traystman RJ. Maturing early-stage biomedical research; proof of concept program objectives, decision making and preliminary performance at the University of Colorado. Med Innov Bus 2009;1(1):52–66. http://dx.doi.org/10.1097/01.MNB.0000357626.97020.e5.

[15] Suhr OB, Coelho T, Buades J, Pouget J, Conceicao I, Berk J, et al. Efficacy and safety of patisiran for familial amyloidotic polyneuropathy: a phase II multi-dose study. Orphanet J Rare Dis 2015;10:109. http://dx.doi.org/10.1186/s13023-015-0326-6.

[16] Naldini L, Blomer U, Gallay P, Ory D, Mulligan R, Gage FH, et al. In vivo gene delivery and stable transduction of nondividing cells by a lentiviral vector. Science 1996;272(5259):263–7.

[17] Maude SL, Frey N, Shaw PA, Aplenc R, Barrett DM, Bunin NJ, et al. Chimeric antigen receptor T cells for sustained remissions in leukemia. N Engl J Med 2014;371(16):1507–17. http://dx.doi.org/10.1056/NEJMoa1407222.

[18] Park CY, Kim DH, Son JS, Sung JJ, Lee J, Bae S, et al. Functional correction of large factor VIII gene chromosomal inversions in hemophilia A patient-derived iPSCs using CRISPR-Cas9. Cell Stem Cell 2015;17(2):213–20. http://dx.doi.org/10.1016/j.stem.2015.07.001.

Chapter 11

Unintended Consequences of Applying for a Patent

From an economic perspective, there is never an easy time to start a biotechnology company, just difficult times and more difficult times. Companies begin when innovation and a commercial opportunity appear to converge, but this is a bit of a mirage early on, resting more on the excitement of new possibilities than the actualization of a drug and a matched clinical pathway. People start companies when they have a good idea that seems to make sense and they can convince other people to go along for the ride. All of this begins with submitting an invention disclosure form to the technology transfer office (TTO), which also begins the inventor's long slide from autonomy. This is the first step in a process that ultimately ratifies the IP as a patent and enables entry to the Valley of Death (VoD), and it comes with a natural tendency to inflate expectations—and a variety of unintended consequences.

The first filing is a provisional application. The Patent Office simply records the receipt of the document, giving the inventor a priority date, but it does not evaluate the contents of the application. Patent prosecution does not begin until the provisional application is converted into a utility application 1 year later.

Any patent filing rests in part on a search for prior art: a survey of existing patents, patent applications, and the scientific literature, to assess whether there are previous inventions that may render the new discovery unpatentable (if it is not sufficiently differentiated or makes claims already held). A favorable patent search supports the novelty of the scientific discovery and suggests a measure of exclusivity that will provide protection from competitors trying to copy the invention.

But patentability and exclusivity do not automatically mean that an invention has practical utility or can be practiced without infringing on anyone else's IP. Beyond novelty, the security of a patent depends upon its scope of coverage, promise of utility, and ability to withstand competitive onslaught—including, if necessary, the ability to prosecute infringing technologies. Yet in an academic setting, and in many start-up companies, a comprehensive legal opinion on whether an invention has "freedom of operation" may not be obtained due to its high cost. Furthermore, uncertainties around performance, application and

Preserving the Promise. DOI: http://dx.doi.org/10.1016/B978-0-12-809216-3.00011-7

95

competitive response cannot be fully anticipated at the provisional application stage. The question of whether any patent application will ultimately demonstrate enduring commercial value is thus a difficult one.

Nevertheless, the provisional and subsequent full patent filing is the *sine qua non* of a technology worthy of investment. Intellectual property is foundational to qualifying biotech and other healthcare ventures as investable [1]. The premise is that, in absence of an officially protected technology, an investment in the long-term prospects that characterize most healthcare opportunities would be too great a risk. In other words, the value proposition needs to include not just a great technology and management team, but a US Patent Office "warranty" of unique differentiation and merchantability. Being worthy of advancement is a broader issue, but secondary to the prerequisite of *fundability*. Without the unique pathway implied by a patent or the ability to obtain one, an invention will be unable to generate investment and the trip across the VoD will end before it has even started.

Investing in IP that is in the process of being evaluated by the patent office may provide comfort, but at the end of the day, even if an inventor is awarded a claim that protects against someone else creating the same thing, or using the same method, he cannot protect himself from someone *solving the same problem in a different way*. This is especially salient in the context of a multiyear development program for a device, or the even longer development path for a therapeutic. A patent gives a head start, but earning a competitive advantage in the VoD demands expert execution of the scientific plan as much as ownership of an exclusive concept.

Even a well-executed and bulletproof patent doesn't mean that the prospective competition is going to sit back and let a new technology siphon off their market share. One of us saw a pitch recently for a nicely researched, designed, and executed prototype of a home diagnostic tool that will compete in a market currently dominated by a few major players and worth hundreds of millions of dollars. The founder was smart, passionate, driven—and firmly convinced that her positioning and IP would provide a reasonable path to market. She was right on the first count but dead wrong on the second. It's virtually certain that if she doesn't make a distribution deal or get acquired by one of these major players before launch, immediately upon any meaningful capture of market share she will get completely buried by blunt force marketing and legal challenges to her IP. This isn't speculation; incumbents have hard-won franchises to protect, and protect them they will.

Hence, the first flaw in relying on IP to reduce investment risk: IP is more a toehold than a resting place. The second flaw is that the science underlying a particular patent may not be fully vetted prior to submission of the patent application, especially if it passes the litmus test of generating potential interest from a commercial partner.

Many universities have a patent committee to evaluate the invention disclosures and decide what merits patenting. Academic convention can mean that the decision to submit a patent application is filtered through multiple departments and, institutions being what they are, it's not unusual to find a political undercurrent reflecting broader university objectives. For example, we know of a prominent US research university with a 17-member IP committee that includes three administrators, a librarian, a French horn player, a professor of theology, representatives from management, education, social work, the law school, and the honors college (a professor of Renaissance rhetoric)—and only five members from the entirety of the sciences.

This may make historic sense within the context of academia, as a community of scholars with complementary and equally important perspectives, but it's not quite the same thing as assembling a cross-functional team for commercial ideation. The diversity of such a committee is without doubt of value, but may underestimate the technical and legal complexity of biotechnology patenting and the associated challenges of commercialization.

Where formal TTOs exist, the decision reflects a more commercial culture and the decision about what to patent is largely the province of the TTO. These offices are more connected to their regional entrepreneurial and investment communities, priorities and interests, and of course understand the patenting process, although the level of activity varies as a function of funding and institutional priority. Most TTOs spend more money than they take in from licensing and royalties, and are more focused on the science and patentability than on market opportunity factors. Yet it's the latter that will ultimately determine fundraising success and commercial viability.

It may not always be possible to do more, but it is a problem down the line when resource constraints force TTOs to take scientists' interpretations of their data at face value. There's a body of published evidence, and it's common knowledge among academics and industry, that a substantial portion of published scientific experiments cannot be replicated (see chapter: Why Pharma Should Care About the Valley of Death). But for short-term financial reasons there's not a lot of demand from TTOs for replicating discoveries prior to licensing, even though this might enhance confidence and perceived value among investors and strategic partners.

University TTOs apportion investment in a given technology as a function of personnel and financial resources. Provisional applications are relatively simple exercises, basic data sets with some interim claims, or maybe a draft of the scientific paper that will be submitted to a journal. Legal expenses are minimal (normally under $10,000) and most of these are reimbursed when the application is licensed to a company. Prosecution of a full utility patent is another matter entirely.

Patenting decisions do not happen in isolation, so it's worth having a look at how much a patent actually costs, not just in legal and filing expenses, but in terms of the entire VoD ecosystem. Filing a provisional application sets into motion a chain of activity that accumulates costs for the new venture. Ultimately, those costs need to be paid out of the money raised to support the company. So it's important to examine both the technology and the quality of its patent application. The first question, of course, is does it work and can it support an investment thesis in the VoD? If some aspect of the invention is not well considered or supported experimentally, if the idea has no clear path to the clinic, or if the business model has not been evaluated in terms of whether it can generate sustained interest from investors and partners, it is a money sink waiting to happen.

It is also worth noting that the strength of any IP depends on the foresight, expertise, and billable hours with which it has been prosecuted. Start-ups want to create a supposedly airtight envelope of invincibility around their inventions. But they usually don't have much money in the early stages, and the quality of their legal representation depends upon a host of factors including their network, access to a top firm, access to specific expertise within that firm (i.e., understanding of the technical intricacies, competitive landscape, and clinical implications of the technology), time pressure (often a function of fundraising imperatives) and, of course, the peccadillos of a particular patent reviewer.

THE DOLLARS BEGIN TO FLOW

Generally speaking, there is no "intermediate state" in which a nonprovisional patent application is submitted without a license or licensing prospect. In other words, no one is likely to front the money unless there's someone in line to pay for it. TTOs simply don't have the budget to file for all of the inventions that come through their doors, let alone prosecute a large portfolio of unlicensed patents. Most of the submitted patents we described in Chapter 10, When Is an Experiment Ready for the Valley of Death?, for example, had a company willing to license them.

TTOs are naturally reluctant to do deals with parties with limited intention or capability to commerciale the patents, or to have their IP end up in the hands of so-called "patent trolls" who accumulate patent rights for financial leverage against future companies. For inventors and universities, it's important that the patent process be rational, fair, and financially sound, given limited TTO resources and the high ratio of invention disclosures to potential partnerships.

Patenting has two key deadlines. The first is at 12 months, when the provisional patent must be converted to a utility application for prosecution in the United States, and a Patent Cooperation Treaty application for those seeking foreign rights. The next is 18 months later, when an application is designated for entry into the national phase, where individual countries are identified and costs pile up quickly. Prosecution of the national phase applications can reach $100,000 or more.

Submitting a patent application therefore opens a transient window of opportunity: the IP has to be funded by a partner or the TTO will be hard-pressed to continue to support the filing, especially once the patent office responds to the application (often with an initial rejection) and the process of back-and-forth negotiation with the patent office ensues. If a patent application is abandoned, the opportunity for commercialization supported by a foundation of IP is gone. So if they're going to file, it becomes time-sensitive for the TTO and scientist to find an investor or partner. Conversations with Angels, economic development organizations, accelerators and incubators, venture capitalists, and potential industry partners pressure test the scientific discovery. The story needs to be saleable, a deal needs to be closed, and this needs to occur sooner rather than later.

Upfront licensing and acquisition deals with pharma (as distinct from sponsored research agreements) are rare, and new companies are typically formed to progress the invention, acquiring rights to the patent application in the form of an option or license agreement. These agreements almost uniformly demand that patent costs be paid by the licensee, so the new company now needs to raise money for legal costs as well as development and proof of concept. TTOs facilitate the recruitment of financial and business advisors committed to the founders and their technology, who see its commercial potential and are willing and able to sign on—typically on a deferred compensation basis—for the fundraising roadshow. The first and primary advocate at this early stage is the scientist/inventor, and the usual pattern is to reach out to friends, family, business associates and Angel networks for financing, attend educational seminars, access whatever free advice is available, and if possible engage a business advisor or CEO. Solid institutional affiliations and a research track record are important but insufficient. Prior successful venture experience is a huge plus, because the story needs to be told and told well. In fact, the most innovative science raises the bar higher than for other investment theses from the standpoint of communication, credibility and achieving buy-in.

There's plenty of research on the character, temperament, and performance of effective CEO/entrepreneurs, and we won't review those data here, except to make the point that a great CEO is an absolute requirement for survival in the VoD. We've both observed pitches with essentially identical foundations and content, delivered by two different people—in some instances for the same company but a year or two apart—with dramatically different results in terms of generating investor buy-in. Even, perhaps especially, if the founder/scientist is no longer at the podium, the passion behind and fervent belief in the technology need to be evident. Sellers of investment theses, those pitching new companies to investors and potential strategic partners, have power in the VoD based on: (1) their own credibility; (2) the extent that the invention reflects a unique, approvable and therefore lucrative solution to an important clinical problem; and (3) the potential for the whole package to achieve an early exit. (Note that the initiative doesn't need to achieve the clinical solution, only substantiate that it offers one long enough to achieve an exit!) CEOs are the catalyst that converts a scientific concept into a data package suitable for investment by a fund or strategic partner.

The point of hiring a CEO for a start-up is objectivity as well as fundraising experience. It's too easy for the scientist/inventor to be seduced into thinking the technology is so special that it does not need to support a hard-nosed investment analysis. Those guiding an early stage company need to execute an unflinching

SWOT (Strengths, Weaknesses, Opportunities and Threats), guide the company through investor due diligence, and develop a business plan that won't be side-tracked by opportunistic money. The healthcare entrepreneur needs to be cre-dentialed and experienced in his or her scientific/clinical sphere, credible as a business leader, effective at building investor networks, and a profoundly effec-tive marketer. He or she needs a track record running companies and raising money, that helps investors feel comfortable.

Great CEOs are rare and expensive. They have the option of earning money in real time, from established companies, rather than deferred income from a start-up (albeit at a higher, but speculative, return). Investors expect founders to be free or a nominal early expense, since everything they do is tied to an eventual payoff, both psychically and financially. Start-up CEOs can be brought in at relatively modest cost; there are a lot of "business advisors" available who don't seem to have that much else to do, and reduced or deferred immediate compensation is offset by equity participation in the company. But a bad one is probably worse than sticking with the scientific founder, and ultimately costs a lot more than a great one, especially if their efforts inhibit progress or lead to the demise of the company altogether.

Lots of scientific founders choose to be their own CEOs, at least for a while. This saves cash outflow in the short term, but much of the time it's not a great fit with commercial culture, and there's also the matter of executive inexperience. The genius of innovation is mysterious and often cloaked within a behavioral profile that can be wildly successful, incredibly destructive, or both: obsessive, narcissistic, neurotic, self-absorbed, inflexible, unwisely transparent, too cer-tain, overprotective, unremittingly driven … these are traits that drive people to invent things that other people find hard to understand. Anyone who has attended technology-oriented business pitches has likely heard all of these strains com-ing through: the scientist who can never make a declarative statement about his work without dissembling on the details of what uncertainty remains, the visionary inventor who doesn't need to do market research because "there is nothing else like this out there," the researcher who can't tell you exactly what he is doing because you might steal it from him, and the budding scientist/entre-preneur oozing desperation because he doesn't understand how anyone could pass on investing in his amazing idea.

Some scientific founders assume and carry the CEO mantle with ease; there are those who stumble somewhat but grow into it, and there are those who really, for everyone's benefit, need to stay out of the boardroom. Part of this has to do with the difference between a research and a business temperament. Everyone chooses a career path based on "fit" of the academic versus business mantle, but that's bit facile; the "personality disorder" of innovation is pretty easy to find among CEOs as well as scientists. There's a more immediate and practical issue: investors demand full-time attention to the new venture from whomever is running things, and people with secure academic appointments rarely want to leave their day jobs. At the end of the day, for whatever reasons, many scientific founders have a hard time fulfilling all of the roles of a CEO, especially the one that involves marketing the venture to funding sources.

At the same time, there's too often a reflexive tendency to discount scientists' ability to engage in the commercialization effort, and an associated expectation that they'll step aside (or be pushed out) when the "business guys" take the reins. There's some justification to this, but it's hardly a one-size-fits-all proposition. The key here is self-awareness on the part of founders. If they're not comfortable with presenting, or good at fundraising, or tolerant of changes in direction necessary to satisfy critical constituents, then it's probably a good idea to move laterally into the role of Chief Scientific Officer or head of the Scientific Advisory Board.

Being a scientist-founder-CEO is difficult, especially in dealing with the concerns of the board, directional changes in the business or scientific plan, and—as the person who birthed the invention—the very real possibility of commercial failure. Most company founders realize sooner or later that running the whole show is not something they can "wing." As expressed by Didier Jean-Francois, a Canadian executive with extensive experience in biotechnology deal making, "There are a lot of companies where you go to the one-on-one meeting [and] you are facing the primary inventor who is a CEO and who is negotiating with you. Obviously I appreciate their genius, but now would be a good time to hire someone who actually knows what they should be doing at this meeting" [2].

THE REAL COSTS OF A PATENT APPLICATION

A patent application needs to be licensed, which requires a company, which in turn requires someone to run the show, a founding or hired CEO who can raise money to pay for the license, the costs of filing, and his own upkeep. Lab space must be rented and equipped, scientists hired, regulatory oversight addressed for safety, animal, and human experimentation. Administrative overhead needs to be covered, including insurance, accounting services, and legal representation. And as we have already noted, the process of raising money in the VoD is itself a drain on time and capital, with ongoing costs for travel, networking, and legal support. Bringing a technology out of a university is like adopting a baby from an orphanage. Everybody can agree it's a good idea, but the baby will require a lot of effort and money before it will become a fully realized and financially productive member of society.

All of which has to be paid for by bartering equity in the company or taking on debt, most often from Angel investors. Within the context of our first Translation Gap—*universities don't make what companies need*—it is evident that sending discoveries into the VoD immediately upon filing saddles companies with financial liabilities that are out of proportion to their *real* value at that time, especially when one considers the limited scope of assessment likely to have been performed on the application and invention prior to licensing. Essential but still preliminary work, such as replicating the original research findings and establishing initial proof-of-concept for a therapeutic, is paid for by early investors, who are meanwhile supporting company infrastructure, management expenses, business development, legal, and other costs. This is on top of paying for the license for the patent application and all of the patent prosecution costs.

Every financial obligation incurred along the way, whether debt or equity, imposes the burden of repaying creditors, who naturally want to get their money back along with an attractive return. Debt financing needs to be repaid, with interest and within a specified time frame. Equity participation may not be repaid in cash until a liquidity event occurs, but terms such as warrants that give a discount upon conversion into equity also reflect an obligation to pay. The structure of the deal depends upon where the company is in its fundraising journey, what milestones have been achieved, what valuation can be mutually negotiated, and the prospective impact of deal terms on future fundraising rounds. Needless to say, all of these have a lot more to do with positioning the company to current and future investors than with technology or clinical endpoints, and they amplify the cost of the money the start-up company needs to raise.

Thus, the simple and relatively inexpensive act of submitting a patent application sets into motion a cascade of spending and activity that needs to be absorbed by the VoD ecosystem and paid for, primarily, by Angel investors. A VoD start-up requires a substantial appropriation of resources by other activities, that might otherwise be dedicated to research and development. Since most or all of the money being spent is acquired as equity or debt, even the dollars actually spent on research come with an expectation of a high-multiple return. This is an abrupt turnabout for a technology that had been previously nurtured within an academic setting, by money with no commercial expectations attached.

The enlightened intent of Bayh–Dole clashes with the long timeline between innovation and actualization, while patent considerations, academic culture, and increasingly cash-strapped university balance sheets force innovations into the commercial realm before they are ready to support a company. The VoD burdens each technology in a vicious cycle of chasing milestones and funding, where survival means the ability to continually raise money, and that depends on keeping imputed valuation ahead of investment. It demands changes of direction that aren't necessarily warranted by the science, or even by market needs, but are instead driven by the relentless pursuit of the most lucrative exit.

Whatever humanistic or clinical motivations underlay the original intent, ultimately the interests of the scientists, entrepreneurs, and early supporters are subsumed into an opportunistic financial power play. This couldn't be further from the thrill of discovery that the scientist first carried from his laboratory to the TTO.

We're not expecting commerce to be driven by selfless motives. But if noble aims have little sway in this environment, then perhaps the practical imperatives of improving probability of success, increasing yield from a given number of investments, and maximizing financial return may have greater influence. It only makes sense that finite resources be directed to the most likely and profitable outcomes, and that the patent applications which feed new ventures are ready to survive the challenges of the VoD.

In the translation of IP from the university to the VoD, we believe that an emphasis on quality over quantity, readiness over urgency, and transparent explication of interests can be leveraged to increase efficiency. One of the reasons that discoveries die in the VoD is that they are not ready to be there. Embryonic and incompletely validated, burdened by galloping debt and the *a priori* high likelihood of failure, they fail to attract the sustained investor interest required to advance beyond speculative science projects. They never become drug candidates that can successfully navigate the development pathway. We need to give them a softer landing, let them gestate a bit longer, before we place on them the burden of supporting a company and providing an investor with an expectation of a 10× or 20× return.

REFERENCES

[1] Gogoris AC, Clarke PJ. Patent due diligence in biotechnology transactions. Bioentrepreneur. <http://www.nature.com/bioent/2003/030101/full/nbt0201_175.html/>; 2016.
[2] Interview with author SD, July 22, 2015.

Chapter 12

What if It Doesn't Actually Work?

Venture capitalists and pharma business developers say "no" to most of the opportunities that present themselves, and those of course include university technology transfer property. These investors have specific objectives based on therapeutic domain and investment return, among other factors: they decide what they are looking for, the terms, and if they don't see what they're interested in from a deal, they don't pursue it. The parameters may be less rigidly circumscribed for Angels and other early-stage investors who inhabit the Valley of Death (VoD), and, while they often walk away, they are also more likely to engage with early-stage technologies coming out of the universities. Those technology properties at this juncture are innovation converted into intellectual property (IP)—patents and patent applications, packaged in the form of licenses.

A fairly pervasive view of university-originated investment opportunities is that they are speculative science projects, with potential for an outstanding upside, along with a very high expected failure rate. In our experience, apparent differentiation on the basis of scientific novelty and the potential for serving an unmet medical need often muddle up the process of consideration by high-net-worth investors who have variable knowledge of a particular domain. Biotech, small molecules, devices, and diagnostics may find appetite or resistance based on very broad "category" definitions: a lack of interest in a vascular device, for example, among a group of investors who had been burned by a large investment in a diagnostic (actual event). Opportunities to license healthcare technologies are fraught with tension between high hopes and low expectations, risk aversion due to very long timelines, and ambiguity associated with the earliest of early-stage investments.

It is not surprising, then, that IP assumes such a prominent role as a de facto risk-reducer. IP is the collateral for the financial instruments bought and sold in the VoD. IP that is poorly conceived or cannot be replicated renders success in the VoD improbable, diverting time and money that could be better dedicated to other opportunities, including IP that is intrinsically more worthy

Preserving the Promise. DOI: http://dx.doi.org/10.1016/B978-0-12-809216-3.00012-9

105

of commercialization, has a reasonable chance of supporting a development program, and can therefore attract a continuing stream of investment. From this perspective, it is clear that the nature of the collateral deserves scrutiny, because the perceived quality of the IP is the independent variable underlying the prospects of any technology launched into the VoD. In a broader sense, IP is a primary driver of success or failure in the healthcare VoD ecosystem, which determines which academic discoveries will be able to help patients. It needs to be both experimentally valid and capable of supporting an investment thesis that will sustain investor interest.

Universities transact their IP in the form of a license, with full awareness that the IP will be used to attract investor dollars. It follows that universities have—or should have—a fiduciary responsibility to entrepreneurs and investors supporting commercial development of their IP, whose decision to invest rests on the perceived strength and scientific validation of the IP. For entrepreneurs, this is a decision about investing their time, and depends on the resources and quality of financial and strategic partners. For investors, this is a go/no-go decision based on the implicit warranty of academic integrity supporting the IP.

Except that there is no warranty. Technologies are valued based on what entrepreneurs and investors are willing to pay for them, not some intrinsic quality scale for IP. Even if the value of a license is pegged to prior deals in a given category, it is clear that any investor in university IP has a right to ask for basic validation of the collateral. Likewise, entrepreneurs should ask whether the IP they are using to start a company or extend a development portfolio is sound— at least before they quit their day jobs and hit the road trying to raise money.

In a later chapter, we discuss the difficulty of scientific and IP due diligence, with a focus on how Angel investors can best balance risk between scientific uncertainty and the likelihood of return on investment. But here we are still focused on the first Translation Gap, that universities don't make what companies need, because the linchpin of success or failure in the VoD is the existence of solid IP as collateral for raising money and prospective commercial value. Biases in the decision processes about what to patent and when, and not infrequent problems reproducing academic research findings, seriously challenge the *prima facie* acceptance of academic IP as valid.

As we have seen, the origin of a patent application is in the laboratory, often without a definition of the final product, and the decision to file an application may be only loosely informed by any market-driven evaluation process. Yet it is precisely these elements—characterization of unmet market need and product definition—that provide rationale for a patent and render an idea able to support an investment thesis in the VoD [1]. While the decision to patent and license IP is subject to the same temporal and political forces that inform commercial due diligence, universities take no responsibility, legal or financial, for whether their patent applications describe replicable experiments or are suitable for supporting a VoD investment.

Here is actual language taken from a license executed between a major US university and a start-up biotechnology company:

> *Except as otherwise expressly set forth in this agreement [the licensors] make no representations or warranties of any kind concerning the patent rights and the tangible property, and hereby disclaim all representations and warranties, express or implied, including without limitation warranties of merchantability, fitness for a particular purpose, noninfringement of intellectual property rights of [the licensors] or third properties, validity, enforceability, and scope of patent rights, whether issued or pending, and the absence of latent or other defects, whether or not discoverable.*

It's hard to decide which of these phrases is most incredible. "Including without limitation warranties of merchantability, fitness for a particular purpose" means that the licensor will not guess whether there is a market for the technology or that the technology will be suitable for that market. "Noninfringement of IP rights of [the licensors] or third properties" means that they won't even assert that the licensed technology doesn't infringe on one of their own patents, let alone any other existing IP. But the most stunning one has to be "the absence of latent or other defects, whether or not discoverable," which means that they won't guarantee that the technology works, and that if it doesn't, it's not their problem, whether or not you ever figure it out by yourself.

Apart from the obvious defensive legal calculation, the problem is that technology transfer offices (TTOs) engage in process, with success metrics that depend on the number of patents filed and licenses issued, rather than the long-term impact of that effort. TTOs are confronted with a constant influx of new disclosures, constrained budgets, irritable faculty, aspirational demands from university administration, and mixed messages about their mission that echo the identity confusion faced by everyone in academia: the conflicting values of commitment to public service and the need for economic viability [2,3]. Whatever their commitment to service and preserving the value of their faculty's discovery efforts, no TTO can assemble and support a large pool of unfunded patent applications.

As we explored common practices in patenting and licensing, a pattern became clear. Like mortgage originators incentivized to provide loans to high risk borrowers and repackage them for investors into mortgage-backed securities, TTOs are incentivized to originate licenses. The goal is to execute as many deals as possible that immediately generate cash (in the form of an upfront payment), with as little investment of time and money as possible, and virtually no exposure to losses if the transacted IP fails. We're not trying to suggest that TTOs are the same as unscrupulous mortgage originators, only to note that the incentive calculation is similar. Profits were generated by mortgage originators from the process, which was only tangentially associated with creating value, and the result wasn't so great for homeowners. Likewise, TTOs file patent applications, license these to companies for a fee (upfront and in downstream royalties), and then require that the companies pay all of the prior and ongoing patent costs. The net effect is that they can achieve their metrics—reputational, relational, and financial—from transaction and downstream fees, without assuming any risk or responsibility if there is a failure of their licensed IP.

Some might argue that it is not the role of the university to validate what it sells, that fair licensing is sufficient, and investors and entrepreneurs should be sophisticated enough to understand the risks and make their own informed choices. Furthermore, it is not the culture of a university to conform its activities to what is best for business. There's already plenty of concern that the accommodations that academia has made with industry are a threat to its core values and credibility. Yet putting constraints around university licensing activity to deflect such criticism doesn't really answer the question: Is the claim that the university is not suited to perform replicative experiments, or commercial due diligence, sufficient justification for *caveat emptor*—the right to sell something that may or may not work?

Again, we don't mean to trivialize the work of TTOs, who in our experience are among the most intelligent and motivated practitioners of this essential first stage of technology commercialization. We simply observe that common metrics for evaluating the success of a TTO do not assess the quality of the products sold or (with the exception of high-profile, high-return-via-royalty deals) their success or failure in the VoD, and that this is an institutional, rather than an individual issue. The simple execution of a license is not evidence that the technology is ready for commercialization and is not, in itself, a measure of the success of the commercialization process.

Porter's Five Forces, described earlier, provide a useful framework for analyzing why the situation exists as it does. The Bayh–Dole Act confers upon universities absolute supplier power over the inventions created by their faculty. This means that they determine exactly what portion of their research portfolio will be patented and when, and under what conditions it will be licensed. Patent applications are made with the intention of generating revenue in the short term through licensing, which helps support TTO operational costs, and in the long term through either retained equity in the company or a royalty arrangement that pays downstream revenues. The near-term endpoint is the execution of a license; the more speculative long-term one is revenue from financial, not developmental, participation in the creation of sustainable value.

Because of this, with annual targets that have more to do with short-term revenue and deeply ingrained policies of not participating directly in development, universities have limited motivation to spend money to validate what they are selling. TTOs thus have few if any mechanisms for obtaining definitive proof-of-concept (POC). They are further constrained by the patent clock, which starts ticking upon demonstration of scientific innovation rather than commercial viability and demands that they identify a suitable licensee and license the IP as soon as possible. Short-term financial incentives, rather than the prospects for long-term success, dominate IP production.

Fueled by a desire to satisfy important faculty and by the advocacy of the scientists who created the IP, even flawed patent applications can approach the VoD with an apparently credible endorsement and garner a license agreement. The large number of licenses executed annually testifies to the success of a business model dedicated to creating saleable IP as much as it may be interested in creating long-term value. Of course, entrepreneurs and investors are free to "take it or leave it," but the impetus to take it is strong, because they are the essential connectors between the *possibility* generated by the university and the *reality* of clinical medicine. It's incumbent upon those in the early-stage ecosystem to support not only a more efficient process, but a more productive outcome.

A focus on process in the short term does not make long-term fiscal sense for the university. Academic scientists with patent applications pending are already predisposed to overestimate the commercial potential of their discoveries, and an application is an imprimatur of commercial validity and merchantability in the VoD. Thus encouraged, they start a venture, which demands considerable time and energy for engaging investors, satisfying due diligence, attracting business advisors or executive management, developing partnerships—all in addition to continuing to apply for grants and championing the science within the company. This can diminish their availability for primary academic duties (e.g., writing papers and raising grants that supplement university resources), raise questions about their motivation, and affect their relationships with their colleagues and trainees—to say nothing of the discouragement if a venture fails and the attendant sense that there is little connection between their scientific efforts and the possibility of success in the VoD.

The effect on resources available within the VoD ecosystem can be equally profound. A poor patent application can doom a company, but *failure still takes time and money.* The patent application alone is insufficient to guarantee success, and it doesn't even have to be lacking in technical or legal merit to fail, because a thousand other factors can doom a nascent company. Legal process, infrastructure, management, investments, and/or grant support all need to be in place before the first POC experiments can be done. Then, the POC experiments have to be conducted simultaneously with an aggressive fundraising effort, so that the company can stay in business while it learns more and refines what it has. It may require months or years, and millions or tens of millions of dollars, before a definitive experiment clarifies that it is simply time to walk away, that the technology will never be able to support the entire journey through to an exit.

Licenses to IP supporting questionable concepts squander time and effort that could be allocated to better ideas. Investors often participate in follow-on rounds, loathe to give up on ideas to which they have previously committed, until substantial sums have been spent chasing ideas that simply won't work.

People with lots of resources may be able to absorb a lousy ROI, but the cumulative effect is diminished confidence in early-stage biotechnology investment as a whole. Too many companies in a particular domain (healthcare), achieving too few successes, can overwhelm the capacity of a regional Angel investing community to support new and existing ventures, and will encourage investors to put their money elsewhere (Porter's threat of substitutes).

In this way, every failure in the VoD has the potential to harm the system as a whole, weakening the availability of capital for the best companies while it supports the marginal ones. Failing to connect the licensing potential of an innovation with its therapeutic potential, especially as the result of filtering to the wrong metrics, nullifies what the university wanted to achieve when it built its laboratories, supported its scientists, and started its TTO. There's obviously no way to ensure success, but it is important to recognize the extreme consequences of failure, not just for a particular technology or company but for the start-up ecosystem as a whole. The decision by an academic institution to produce and license a patent application is one of the most critical decisions made in the entire process of biotechnology commercialization.

We advocate a rigorous and tempered evaluation of the process that determines which patents are applied for, and thereby nominated for potential commercialization. In a competition-free development environment, technologies would be afforded the time they need to prove their mettle before filing a patent application. In the real world of the VoD, they need to be protected as soon as possible, both to maintain a lead on competition and to become an attractive investment proposition. This needs to be facilitated by a focused and nonadversarial ecosystem in which they can quickly and efficiently establish their worth, without needing to prematurely become the basis of an entire commercial enterprise. Clinical value may be the ultimate measuring stick, but the data are too limited and gradations of apparent merit not fine enough, in these early stages, to identify the best candidates for commercialization. It will always be difficult to distinguish those discoveries with the greatest long-term potential, but that is not an argument for conceding scientific merit to faculty prominence, or clinical importance to the shortest ROI timeline. Healthcare discovery carries with it an intrinsic moral responsibility and the need to select and prepare the best discoveries for their next steps toward the clinic.

This could happen within academia or without, but it needs to occur if Angels are to continue shouldering the financing burdens and extraordinary risk of supporting unrealized discoveries. Appropriately nurturing these technologies—as contrasted with the "fast kill" model being popularly practiced by technology accelerators—should be about building a bridge between academic innovation and the commercial sector. It needs a greater focus from university TTOs on market need, commensurate with how the Angel community decides where to spend its investment dollars. This involves better IP due diligence, market research, and replication of the key experimental findings. It is the opening salvo to the detailed due diligence process that is essential to effective Angel investing.

If we delay the race to a provisional patent application, despite the risk, and expand our ability to nurture inventions prior to throwing them into the VoD, one of the consequences may be that fewer patents are submitted. Another is that those that are filed will be stronger—possibly more innovative, certainly better validated, better able to support an investment thesis, and with a higher probability of success. We're not oblivious to the competitive threat of a delay, and our recommendation may be construed as heresy, but a headlong rush into provisional applications is like taking bread out of the oven while it's still gummy just to make sure guests don't fill up on something else.

A process that involves greater nurturing of early technologies, before they are thrust into the VoD, demands a more entrepreneurial technology transfer approach: selecting what to advocate based on a more intensive review of market opportunity, assuming mutual risk by coinvesting in the cost of patent prosecution rather than insisting that all risk be assumed by licensees, lobbying for university funding built on specific prospective opportunity rather than last year's budget, and emphasizing outcomes over process.

This of course means applying different metrics. The value of patents and licenses, for example, could be evaluated by long-term metrics, such as the number of licensees who achieve Series B funding and federal grants, who have research efforts ongoing 3–5 years after licensing, who have a deal with a pharma company, or other outcomes that suggest the patent and company were reasonably conceived. Metrics for determining long-term value, such as the Innovation Scorecard developed at PricewaterhouseCoopers, may be useful but themselves need to be validated [4]. A lack of concrete outcomes data can easily stifle innovation by obscuring the effects of improvements and allowing inefficient practices to become ossified as habits.

A more rigorous and multifaceted process that reduces the number of patent filings, while devoting more resources to those that go forward, will demand that TTOs make even more difficult choices than they do already. But innovation in the laboratory is the consequence of choices, what experiments to do and what experiments not to do. Scientists live or die on the basis of their decisions. As any investor knows, participating in the upside reward of innovation is not a zero-sum game and requires something other than a business-as-usual approach to risk. A willingness by universities to embrace and share risk will foster collaboration rather than conflict. It honors the intellectual contribution of scientists, ratifies the academic mission, and fulfills a societal obligation to see that important advances are ultimately available to patients.

We recognize that there are many within universities who seek to increase, rather than further restrict, the numbers of patents submitted: faculty who want to see their innovations protected and will chafe at policy changes that reduce the number of patent applications supported and TTOs that are interested in expanding their influence. We also take an open-minded view that much of what comes from a university, more than is being realized now, has potential to be transformative—if it can be validated and find its place in the commercial landscape. This is justified *a priori* because scientists live at the boundaries of our knowledge; they have the most future-oriented appreciation of what is new and what needs to be known. How can we manage these competing interests, to be more selective yet more inclusive? The solution to this problem is to provide motivated scientists with a parallel path to commercialization, one that doesn't automatically require universities to front the costs of patent filing.

If universities are to accept the opportunity provided by the Bayh–Dole Act, the opportunity to reap financial returns from selling their IP, they cannot be excused from taking reasonable steps to promote commercialization internally simply because they are resource constrained, it is not their habit, or it is not consistent with their academic mission. Bayh–Dole charges universities with an obligation to effectively translate the innovation we support into something that is commercially viable, for the benefit of their licensees and society, as well as their own balance sheet. The uncomplicated ideal of an academic community engaged in the pursuit of pure knowledge for its own sake was lost the minute universities went into the business of selling their technologies, a fact that is obvious to anyone who has ever negotiated a license with a TTO.

The moral obligation is theoretical, and could reasonably be rejected by cash-strapped not-for-profit institutions, but it actually makes financial sense for everyone in the system. The first Translation Gap, that universities don't make what companies need, is a model case for how incentives that promote short-term interests can subvert the long-term survival of a technology as well as the mission of the entire drug development ecosystem.

REFERENCES

[1] Silva R, Allen DN, Traystman RJ. Maturing early-stage biomedical research; proof of concept program objectives, decision making and preliminary performance at the University of Colorado. Med Innov Bus 2009;1(1):52–66. http://dx.doi.org/10.1097/01.MNB.0000357626.97020.e5.

[2] Abrams I, Leung G, Stevens AJ. How are U.S. technology transfer offices tasked and motivated— is it all about the money? Res Manag Rev 2009;17(1):1–34. <http://www.bu.edu/otd/files/2011/02/How-are-US-Tech.-Transfer-Offices-Tasked-and-Motivated.pdf/>.

[3] Valdivia WD. Center for technology innovation at brookings. <http://www.brookings.edu/research/papers/2013/11/university-start-ups-technology-transfer-valdivia>; 2013 [accessed 24.02.16].

[4] Levy D, Wasden C, Reich A. If innovation isn't measured, how can it be managed? PricewaterhouseCoopers; 2011. <http://www.pwc.com/us/en/health-industries/publications/if-innovation-isnt-measured.html/>.

Chapter 13

Building a Better Mousetrap

Adaptation of patenting and pre-licensing practices can better prepare university scientific innovation for the investment marketplace. Optimizing the quality of licensing output is an important way to minimize the risk of failure in the Valley of Death (VoD) and improve the long-term success of the drug research and development (R&D) process. Ideally, the numbers of new companies formed and products developed would be appropriate to the capacity of the VoD marketplace, not only to support an initial investment but to carry through to institutional financing. The number of companies that fail to sustain funding in the VoD suggests that participants in the VoD ecosystem continue to make questionable selections and chronically exceed available capital. However, it is possible that the capacity to support exceptional companies could be increased over time if Angel investors could achieve a better aggregate return on investment (ROI). The starting point in both cases is better validation of technology, before Angel investments are raised to support a company and its intellectual property (IP).

It will no doubt be argued that this would incur an unacceptable delay in a competitive environment and slow innovation. We think the opposite is true. An analysis of technology transfer data in the University of California system showed that successful licenses require an average of 9 years to achieve their first $1 million in income and that revenue generation follows an invention disclosure by an average of 10 years [1]. There's variability by domain and institution, but the extended time to revenue argues even more strongly for thorough vetting at the earliest stage. Collecting long-term outcomes data would be ideal but impractical, so we need surrogate endpoints that can be used to gauge the quality of the patents produced. The objective is to move the VoD ecosystem forward from its historical reliance on probability investing, by aligning selection of which technologies to patent with better predictors of success. As it stands, succeeding one out of 10 times is considered an acceptable ratio by investors. But is it really necessary to settle for 9 abject failures?

Shifting incentives to a greater focus on long-term outcomes will require changes in institutional thinking about tech transfer budgets and expectations. On a philosophical level, such changes may be welcome. Incentivizing TTO professionals on the basis of process and short-term deal flow, rather than

Preserving the Promise. DOI: http://dx.doi.org/10.1016/B978-0-12-809216-3.00013-0

long-term success, doesn't exactly leverage the unique expertise that these professionals bring to their jobs.

According to David Allen, Vice President of Tech Launch Arizona (TLA), the TTO at the University of Arizona, a decision to patent an invention should be a collaborative process that evaluates the substance of the patent itself, the commercial potential of the invention, and whether there is a good fit between the invention and the entrepreneurial ecosystem within which it will exist [2]. In developing the TLA business model, he has built a continuous, well-integrated evaluation process that is "done by lots of eyes." Oddly enough, TLA's detailed investigation of market opportunity and commercialization prospects as leading indicators seems to be a relative rarity in the TTO world.

When a scientist submits an invention disclosure at TLA, it is assigned to a Licensing Manager who works closely with the submitting scientist to perform the initial patentability and market assessment. This process incorporates the efforts of student fellows and the assistance of a Business Intelligence Unit (BIU), which is a novel collaboration between the TLA and the University of Arizona Libraries. According to Cindy Elliott, a member of the Research Services Team at University Libraries, she and other librarians "find, analyze and synthesize available industry and market data in those areas where our BIU colleagues have identified demand for their technology may lie. This relationship allows the BIU to have unprecedented access to pinpoint in-depth, actionable information pooled from every accessible University library, database, catalog, publication and article" [3].

If the initial assessment is encouraging, then the findings are shared with so-called Commercialization Partners, who have personal experience in one or more aspects of technology commercialization and serve as Entrepreneurs-in-Residence, Executives-in-Residence, or Investors-in-Residence [4]. Many are later-career executives with a personal connection to the University of Arizona and/or the local business community. Allen describes them as tech-savvy individuals who are seeking an opportunity to "be part of something big" [2]. Only *after* positive engagement of these Commercialization Partners is a patent application filed.

If an invention is deemed not ready for a journey into the VoD, or could realize improved chances of commercial uptake with additional effort, TLA has funds available to perform extended market research, proof-of-concept (POC) experiments, or prototype development. Over $1.5 million in such funding has been provided to UA scientists since 2012. "We put greater resources into crafting better, stronger applications than in years prior to TLA," said Allen.

The process remains difficult, and including many different inputs doesn't necessarily temper the challenges of dealing with, and potentially saying "no" to, disgruntled faculty. Allen offered: "You have to be empathetic, listen hard, and take a lot of sh#t and turn the cheek. But, if they feel like you're not working for them, they won't trust you." Nonetheless, the response overall has been positive, and the relationships the TLA is building through their process are just one aspect of a broad effort to engage regional inventors, entrepreneurs, investors, and established businesses in strengthening their entrepreneurial ecosystem.

The North Carolina Biotechnology Center (NCBiotech) also recognizes the value of extending support for new inventions at the pre-licensing stage. Kenneth Tindall, PhD, Senior VP at NCBiotech, described one aspect of their commercialization program: "We take an invention at the [time of] disclosure—pre-company, pre-IP, still in the university researcher's laboratory—to help assess whether the university should move forward. The key here is that we're trying to connect the professor with a business professional, entrepreneur, tech development specialist" [5]. Together, they set business and technical milestones that can help move the discovery along the commercialization pathway, which might include better defining the IP or identifying a key POC experiment. Scientists in academic research laboratories in North Carolina can apply for a Biotechnology Innovation Grant (BIG), which provides up to $100,000 to support studies that evaluate *whether a patent application is warranted*. "Typically, funding will support studies that yield a 'go/no-go decision' regarding the pursuit of intellectual property protection and/or commercialization of the invention" [6].

Once filing of a provisional patent application has been initiated, but before a license or option has been executed, the TTOs themselves are able to apply for a technology enhancement grant (TEG) [7]. The TEG specifically supports the efforts of TTOs to conduct research, such as market or IP due diligence, that will contribute to the ability of the university to execute a license. Together the BIG and TEG grants help to establish and strengthen the confidence that new IP is workable, and suitable to support an investment thesis in the VoD, before it forms the basis for a start-up company. It is helpful that the NCBiotech is independent, funded by the state, as a 501(c)(3) nonprofit corporation. "We can work easily with all departments, with everyone, we're not a part of UNC or Duke—we have a neutral status," notes Tindall. This standing insulates them from academic politics and helps them adhere to their mission of promoting biotechnology innovation in North Carolina.

Such POC programs have objectives that extend, by intention, beyond academic research. Their small grants embrace high-risk, high-reward concepts, precisely targeted to meet "smart money" investment milestones identified through interaction with business advisors. These may be basic science or replication of prior results, and there's no *a priori* expectation that favors innovation per se or publishable data—it's all directed toward prospects for commercialization. The objective is to help build a data package around a patent application, a concrete market-based validation of investability. These are de-risking activities designed to encourage (or deny) investment in technologies based on the likelihood they can succeed in the VoD, proceed to institutional funding, and be realized in the clinical marketplace that follows.

This approach conceptually overlaps other Entrepreneur-in-Residence or Executive-in-Residence (XIR) programs. Columbia University in New York City started an XIR program to help its TTO accommodate an onslaught of increasingly diverse and cross-disciplinary inventions and a rapidly evolving regulatory and reimbursement landscape [8]. Columbia brings in 4–6 XIRs each year, for a period of 3–9 months each. They are selected for significant entrepreneurial or executive experience, a substantial technical background, and willingness to commit up to 20 hours per month for nominal compensation (~$1000/month). Business advisors are commonly asked to sign standard confidentiality and limited IP assignment agreements.

Author Fishman has provided similar executive-led guidance for evaluating technologies at the pre-license stage as Program Executive of the Wharton Commercialization Acceleration Program (CAP) at the University of Pennsylvania (UPENN) [9]. CAP is a consultancy staffed by Healthcare MBAs and undergraduates from the Roy and Diana Vagelos Life Sciences Management Program. The organization has worked with over 85 start-up ventures originating in UPENN and affiliated laboratories, providing market and technology assessment services and support for business strategy. CAP has contributed to successful fundraising efforts in the millions of dollars, as well as acquisition of multiple start-up initiatives in the region. Fundamental to these efforts is explication of the market opportunity surrounding each company's IP.

The Massachusetts Institute of Technology has a prominent POC initiative in the Deshpande Center for Technological Innovation [10]. Founded in 2002 with a donation from Gururaj "Desh" Deshpande and his wife, Jaishree, the Center has funded over $11 million in grants for early-stage technologies. Each award pairs the scientist with a catalyst/mentor: a seasoned executive who helps coordinate the scientific progress with an analysis of market needs and opportunities, business planning, and networking with investors and entrepreneurs. According to MIT associate provost Karen Gleason, "The Deshpande Center continues to help MIT researchers defy the 'Valley of Death' faced by so many inventions. The Center supports innovators as they grow and shape nascent ideas into viable and scalable technologies" [11]. In 2015, the Center awarded $1.2 million to 15 MIT faculty initiatives, including 8 projects in biotech or health-related fields. Leon Sandler, the Executive Director of the Center, has seen the idea of supporting innovators spread: "At a high level the Deshpande Center model is generalizable, in fact there are many institutions that have programs that were inspired by the Deshpande Center. However each one has adapted their program to their own unique environment and circumstances" [12].

There's a solid rationale, but relatively limited funding, for public initiatives such as National Institutes of Health (NIH) Small Business Innovation Research (SBIR) and Small Business Technology Transfer Research (STTR) grants [13]. The two programs differ in that the SBIR is intended for small businesses themselves, whereas the STTR grants support academic research in collaboration with a small business. The latter are probably most adaptable to help overcome the first Translation Gap. The STTR regulations currently stipulate that at least 40% of the research work needs to be performed by the small business and that a minimum of 30% of the work needs to be performed by the partnering research institution [14]. The downside of this workload split is that it demands the small business establish a research infrastructure and hire research staff, which precludes a virtual model for a start-up. It's possible that funds might be more efficiently utilized in developing POC, if the work could be wholly subcontracted to the academic institution.

STTRs could also go one step further and emulate the NCBiotech program. What if academic institutions could apply for STTR funding directly, to fund explicitly commercial POC experiments? This would be consistent with the goals of the program, "to stimulate a partnership of ideas and technologies between innovative small business concerns and Research Institutions through Federally-funded research or research and development (R/R&D)" and "to assist the small business and research communities by commercializing innovative technologies" [14]. Expanding the scope of STTR funding would ideally be accompanied by an increase in the size of the program.

An expansion of POC grants, STTR grants, and other sources of funding provided for validating the commercial potential of academic IP would add a level of quality filtering for patenting university technologies. Scientists and TTOs could use the support to build a commercial data package, perform market research, and network with the entrepreneurial community to assess the barriers and opportunities a technology may face, when and if it becomes the basis for a company.

To this end, it's not a bad idea for universities to create investment funds to support early-stage commercialization efforts, covering patent costs, POC experiments, market research, and business development. The University of Oxford, e.g., has implemented a number of ways to fuel commercialization of its early-stage technologies. These are all overseen by Oxford University Innovation [15], a wholly owned, for-profit subsidiary of the University, which manages all of its technology transfer activities. Oxford University Innovation provides a broad suite of services, including:

- Staffing so-called "hot desks," weekly meeting points located within departments that provide informal opportunities for university researchers to interact with TTO professionals [16].
- Running the University Challenge Seed Fund (UCSF), an evergreen fund established with a government grant of £4 million in 1999 [17]. UCSF supports patent selection and validation, through pre- and post-patent POC and commercialization research and a close relationship with the regional innovation ecosystem.
- Working with the Oxford Innovation Society (OIS) a members-only "open innovation network" that brings business people and academics together and provides OIS members with 30 days advance notice on new technologies available for license.

- Managing the Oxford Invention Fund, a conduit for University donors interested in supporting UCSF-style activities [18]. Successful OIF investments provide a return to the fund. OIF-style funds, focused on early IP costs and POC experiments, could unload patent costs from universities and TTOs and be an attractive model for venture philanthropy.
- Creating the University of Oxford Isis Funds (UOIF), which provide financial resources to advance University technologies toward commercialization. UOIF is managed by Parkwalk Advisors, an independent investment firm that runs similar funds for the University of Cambridge and the University of Bristol [19]. The fund encourages investment by leveraging UK tax incentives that promote early-stage investing. Although the UOIF is primarily focused on early-stage spinouts, it is easy to imagine how such a fund could also be used to support the evaluation of invention disclosures, initial patent costs, and POC experiments to increase the attractiveness of new ventures to investors.

While this structure reflects conditions specific to the relationship between research funding and the academic community in the UK, in principle the Oxford approach could be adapted for tech transfer in the US. There's room to sympathize with US universities, which have been given an unfunded mandate to capture the value of the intellectual property they develop using Federal funds and are faced with the uncharted task of deciding how to best achieve this. Their initial activity in selecting what discoveries to patent has them performing essentially the same evaluations as would venture capital, but with far fewer resources. This is a fact, not an excuse, and given their utilization of public money for basic research, it should not release them from their obligation to the development ecosystem and to society, to do so in an efficient and effective manner.

We believe the TTO evaluation process needs to be better aligned with the needs of the entire drug development process, respecting the needs of inventors, entrepreneurs, Angel investors, pharmaceutical and biotech companies, and society as a whole. At its core, it will require university administrators to revise their expectations for TTO practice and outcomes and substantially increase TTO funding through traditional and non-traditional methods.

The first Translation Gap, *universities don't make what companies need*, is a major source of inefficiency, characterized by misaligned incentives, financial constraints, technical complexity, and uneven data collection. It inhibits iterative learning and prioritizes immediate goals over effective long-term planning. As with the British boat captain example cited earlier in the book, prioritization of short-term objectives may inappropriately redirect attention from clinically valuable but longer-term biotech translation objectives. We have described some alternate templates, already in existence, for performing and funding the process. These are only a sampling, certainly more or less appropriate depending on the regional ecosystem, but nevertheless models developed to address obvious weaknesses in the system.

Better outcomes would follow a more effective screening and development paradigm. To achieve them, universities need to make more reflective decisions about patenting, possibly protecting fewer inventions overall, but focusing on the ones most likely to fit these dual objectives: improving health through innovation, and serving as strong collateral for the investment thesis that determines survival in the VoD. As the system evolves, we need to collect better data on long-term TTO outcomes, to determine which new models are doing the best job.

The capacity of our drug development system is finite. Improved success will not come from simply increasing the number of patent applications and licenses, continuing adherence to the existing probability investing model. Effective technology transfer interlocks university creation of IP with the capabilities and capacities of the regional Angel investment and entrepreneurial networks. Failure to improve methods of converting IP into solid investment collateral will continue to impede the development of innovations likely to make a difference in people's lives, while wasting entrepreneurial resources and investor money.

We anticipate pushback on this from universities and TTOs. But it's worthwhile to keep in mind, when defending existing practices—which admittedly have elicited strong financial returns for some universities—that there's something even stronger than the supplier power universities hold by virtue of their control of IP. That something is the buyer power of investors, who may legitimately ask what has been done to validate the IP behind the company in which they are investing.

REFERENCES

[1] Makarechian H, Varner B, De La Peña W, Mendelson A, Hallett B. University of California: report of the working group on technology transfer. <http://regents.universityofcalifornia.edu/regmeet/nov12/f12attach.pdf>; 2012.
[2] Interview with author SD, February 17, 2016.
[3] Ballard A. New Business Intelligence Unit Aims to Improve UA Startup Successes. Published June 17, 2014. <https://uaatwork.arizona.edu/lqp/new-business-intelligence-unit-aims-improve-ua-startup-successes>; 2014.
[4] Tech Launch Arizona Annual report and roadmap update. Published October 15, 2016. <http://techlaunch.arizona.edu/sites/default/files/documents/2015/tech-launch-arizona-annual-report-2015-10-15.pdf>; 2015.
[5] Interview with author SD, January 13, 2016.
[6] Biotechnology Innovation Grant (BIG). <http://www.ncbiotech.org/research-grants/research-funding/biotech-innovation-grant>; [accessed 12.03.16].
[7] Technology Enhancement Grant (TEG). <http://www.ncbiotech.org/business-commercialization/business-loans-support/business-financing/technology-enhancement-grant>; [accessed 12.03.16].
[8] Herskowitz O. In house expertise. Nat Biotechnol 2015;33(8):801–4. http://dx.doi.org/10.1038/nbt.3302.

[9] CAP and UPSTART. <https://lsm.upenn.edu/innovation-entrepreneurship/cap-upstart>; 2016 [accessed 31.03.16].

[10] MIT Desphande Center for Technological Innovation. <https://deshpande.mit.edu/>; 2016 [accessed 31.03.16].

[11] Grdina M. Deshpande Center announces fall 2015 research grants. MIT News; 2015. Published October 6, 2015. <http://news.mit.edu/2015/mit-deshpande-center-announces-research-grants-1006>; [accessed 31.03.16].

[12] Email to author SD, March 22, 2016.

[13] SBIR:STTR. America's seed fund. <https://www.sbir.gov/>; 2016 [accessed 14.03.16].

[14] Small Business Administration. Small Business Technology Transfer (STTR) Program Policy Directive February 24, 2014. <https://www.sbir.gov/sites/default/files/sttr_pd_with_1-8-14_amendments_2-24-14.pdf >; 2014 [accessed 14.03.16].

[15] University of Oxford. Isis innovation. <http://innovation.ox.ac.uk/>; 2016.

[16] University hot desks. <http://innovation.ox.ac.uk/university-members/innovation-hotdesks/>; [accessed 14.03.16].

[17] Hockaday T. University proof of concept and seed funds. <http://innovation.ox.ac.uk/wp-content/uploads/2014/04/univ_proof_concept_seed_funds.pdf>; 2007 [accessed 14.03.16].

[18] Isis Innovation. Oxford Invention Fund. <http://www.isis-innovation.com/wp-content/uploads/2014/04/OxfordInventionFund.pdf>; 2014.

[19] <http://parkwalkadvisors.com/>; [accessed 14.03.16].

Good Innovation Is Not Always a Good Investment

Chapter 14

Due Diligence and Angel Incentives

After an invention has moved beyond the grants that supported its tenure in a university, and after the generosity of friends and family has been exhausted, the proximate source of funding is usually a group of people known as Angels. This is undoubtedly a nod to some notion of being guides to salvation, and it's true that there's an element of philanthropy attached—many people who have achieved success want to help others do the same—but the majority of Angels probably aren't involved solely for that reason.

In the Valley of Death (VoD), any new drug or device, while built on a technology platform, is in its early stages fundamentally an investment thesis, and investors want a return on their investment. The ultimate customer, the healthcare system or hospital, the doctor or the patient—is still a long way away. The immediate customer for an early-stage company is the investor, buying into a property for his or her portfolio. Once a technology manages its escape from the university, it must be packaged in an investment prospectus for consideration by Angel and other early-stage investors.

Don Drakeman has characterized biotechnology as the space "where money meets the molecule" [1]. Thus far we have considered what technology needs to accomplish in order to be ready for investors in the VoD, analyzing the process of invention finding its way out of the university. This is the push. Now we consider the pull end of the equation. Any technology has to meet certain basic criteria to be investable.

The culture clash between scientific founders and commercialization "facilitators" like technology transfer offices (TTOs), incubators, or accelerators, hits full speed when the inventors start pursuing Angel investors, because the science needs to be reconfigured as a credible proposition to support an entrepreneurial venture. The rigorous scientific review that accompanies a National Institutes of Health (NIH) application gives way to the ostensibly rigorous, but often inconsistent, process of Angel investing, where innovation, inspiration, and commitment meet the cold hard question of whether these already successful technology sponsors will open up their checkbooks.

Preserving the Promise. DOI: http://dx.doi.org/10.1016/B978-0-12-809216-3.00014-2

123

We have discussed how an invention is not significantly differentiated in the VoD by the nature of its technology but by the strength of its promise. In the VoD, inventions become collateral for financial instruments that are bought and sold as investments. The excitement of a drug or diagnostic is packaged to conform to a different set of aspirations. Angel investors may be in the game for intellectual and personal fulfillment, but their prime objective in *investing* isn't about advocating for a particular technology as much as it is about selecting a potentially lucrative investment for their portfolio.

Of course, for Angels it's not only about making money; there are lots of other investment alternatives with different risk and return profiles. These investors for the most part are people who have demonstrated an ability to make money by making effective decisions. So they may have a variety of motives, but cannot be expected to and generally will not invest in a company solely on the basis of scientific excitement or clinical gravitas, no matter how innovative the technology. The determination of an investable proposition is complicated and cumbersome, and the paths to a "no" decision are way more numerous than those to a "yes." Sometimes the reason for a "no" is a simple as *I just don't like the feel of this*, or the technology is in an area of little interest to a particular investor.

On the other hand, sometimes snap decisions are made without carefully explicated reasoning, to pursue perfunctory due diligence and then to ratify and invest in something that has already captured an investor's imagination. And this may be for a proposition that makes no greater sense or has no apparent greater worth than what was rejected in the previous breath. We've seen Angels literally demolish a proposition on logical grounds, then champion it with their own substantial investment. This isn't an indictment; it's simply a reflection of human decision making in the absence of perfect (or even close-to-perfect) information, and we all do it. (Of course, it's also true that much of what an Angel hears is laughably uninvestable … but we'll get to that later.)

One of the reasons investment decision making is so variable is that perceived value is a function of experience and perspective. Angels come from pretty much every background you can imagine. The authors of this book met years before we embarked on the project, through an investment advisor, when one Scott approached the other for money (and was turned down!). Interest was there on both sides, but the proposition was not well framed and the size of the request was determined without consideration of the other party's actual interests and needs.

With almost 300,000 Angel investors in the United States alone, potential investors aren't particularly hard to find [2]. Finding a good match and getting in front of them is another story, but Angel investment groups are actively seeking opportunities for investment, and they're liberally sprinkled throughout the start-up ecosystem.

Once an Angel or Angel group has been engaged, and an opportunity to pitch arranged, an interesting process of seduction occurs. It begins with a well-crafted pitch, an in-person presentation describing the technology, the team, and the business plan. If attraction occurs, the pitch inspires a further look called due diligence.

Most research projects originating within the university have a self-evident innovative spark, but few are actualized as potential commercial entities. At this point a technology may have been supported by an SBIR/STTR (Small Business Innovation Research/Small Business Technology Transfer) or NIH grant, or maybe some seed money from a regional development organization. The discussion to this point hasn't always been that focused, however, with respect to application of the science to the clinic, and whether it deserves investment from the standpoint of what problem is actually being solved. It's been a long time since technologies were investable on innovation alone, an "if you build it, they will come" basis. Rather, they may be ready to support an investment thesis if they have been validated experimentally, if they have a path to the clinic that involves clearly defined, investable milestones, and if they are supported by a team with the experience and time to make its potential a reality. But most of all, the investment thesis needs to appeal to the motives of, and make sense to, investors.

HOW ANGELS DECIDE

Inventor/founders enter the Angel arena with a patent or a provisional patent application and their great idea. They face a pressure test that will probably be repeated on dozens of occasions before their company achieves an exit. This is where the money meets the molecule, and it's an acid test—of the technology itself and of the management team's ability to generate and maintain forward motion.

Angels make preliminary investment decisions very quickly. The due diligence process that follows is generally methodical, but whether a start-up will be considered for an investment is akin to a job interview: the seeds will be planted, the tone set, and the decision on whether to proceed to the next steps determined within the first few minutes. It's painful to founders but unsurprising that a "no" can be sudden and final.

There is a huge disparity in risk for each of the parties. Everything is at stake for the inventor, who in most instances will make only a limited number of discoveries worthy of commercialization in a lifetime. Imagine the emotional indignity of being told your baby isn't pretty enough by people who are less interested in what the offspring will accomplish in its lifetime than in whether it can win next year's beauty contest. Never mind the fact that the baby has been the product of a dozen years of intense effort in the laboratory, may be authentically novel and creative, and may be able to solve an important health problem.

Considerably less is on the line for the TTO, which is continuously weeding through a cornucopia of ideas seeking investment traction. And, truth be told, very little is actually at stake for the Angel, who has sufficient liquid resources to enable a high-risk investment of tens or hundreds of thousands of dollars, and who has a similarly boundless supply of investment opportunities vying for his or her dollars.

As any beginning lecture on negotiation will tell you, leverage is *always* a function of who has more to lose. Therein lies the first fault line in the alignment of these parties' interests and priorities, the enormous buyer power that Angels hold and exert over the due diligence process, and therefore inventors' fate.

Angels are pretty astute, if not always with a wide bandwidth in the life sciences. They're experienced in business and commercialization in the same way that scientists are experienced in the nuance of empirical investigation. Beyond the impressions that drive next steps, they will require objective information that what they are considering is likely to have a positive return on investment. The process they use is due diligence.

DUE DILIGENCE—AN OVERVIEW

This is how it all works: Companies apply for funding consideration. An endorsement or referral from a known contact helps pave the way for the application. In reality, most of the groups in a region, from incubators to public funding sources to Angels, tend to see the same companies making the rounds. There's usually a domain-specific (e.g., healthcare, IT, and social media) screening committee that vets the applications and makes a recommendation to bring the company in to present, plus or minus a request for additional information. The entrepreneur is invited in for a 15 or 20 minute presentation followed by a question and answer session, and after they leave the room the investment group will decide whether to proceed with due diligence. Due diligence is typically led by the individual who brought the company in, and includes individuals with expertise in the company's domain. A recommendation to invest or decline typically takes 2–3 months and may be contingent on a co-investor. Angels often look for someone else to lead or coinvest in a round.

If this sounds a bit like a Dick-and-Jane primer, it's only fair counterpoint to the morass of jargon that usually accompanies the deal-making aspect of investing. One of the problems with the funding process, especially for new entrepreneurs, is that it feels unnecessarily mysterious. The reality is that it's rather straightforward, at least from an Angel's point of view. If the inventor makes a good impression, there's an apparent need in the marketplace, a relatively large population to serve, and a host of technical and operational skill behind the technology, it may be a good bet. If the founder makes an uninspiring pitch, there's no obvious customer need and/or a small target population, the invention lacks a cogent value proposition, or it isn't backed by capable people, it isn't a good investment.

DUE DILIGENCE—GETTING SPECIFIC

Due diligence is a nominally systematic but ultimately subjective process whereby success factors for a venture are evaluated to determine the advisability of investment. This entails questioning of not just the science, but of motives, competence, and ability to succeed given exogenous influences. Due diligence is a mutual process that involves basic questions about the viability of a company, its technology, and what it takes to survive. Its function is to explicate and reduce risk.

Whether conducted by Angels, greenhouse/incubators, venture capital, or private equity funds, the process is fairly similar—with most of the difference reflecting the domain expertise and priorities of the evaluators. The essential components of the due diligence analysis are listed below. Reduced to their essence, they simply confirm that the proposition being evaluated has a *reasonable probability of leading to an exit*, either to other investors with deeper pockets or to a strategic buyer. This is really the most basic concept in marketing. Unless the conditions exist for a transaction to occur—defined here as an event that returns investors' money—all the technology in the world, and all the money in the world behind it, will not guarantee a transaction.

The components of due diligence fall into three categories. The following covers most of the bases, though it is not necessarily an exhaustive list:

1. Exogenous factors
   - Unmet clinical or professional need
   - Size and growth of addressable market
   - Adaptability of the technology or product to clinical practice
   - Potential for sustainable competitive advantage
2. Mediators of development
   - Value of intellectual property (IP)
   - Attractiveness and plausibility of the technology
   - Likelihood that clinical proof of concept is achievable
   - Challenges of the regulatory environment
3. Fundamental requirements for the investment thesis
   - An attractive business model (enough customers, acquired quickly enough, to produce a rapid and sustainable return on development costs)
   - Financial viability including money already raised (imputed valuation), quality and perceived expertise of investors (implied endorsement), and reimbursement environment (ability to sell the thing)
   - Exit strategy, including deal terms, development timeline, proposed milestones, projected burn rate, and follow-on funding plan
   - Human resources, including track record and perceived capabilities of the management team, availability and access to development expertise and resources, availability and access to a substantive Advisory Board
   - Realistic contingency planning

It is not surprising that none of these factors will, by itself, justify an investment. The more interesting dynamic from the standpoint of "investability" is that serious problems with *any one* of these elements will cause most reasonable investors to require a proposed solution (e.g., "adult supervision" for a weak management team)—or keep their checkbooks in their pockets.

EXOGENOUS FACTORS

Unmet Clinical or Professional Need

It's always a bit stunning, despite the frequency with which this happens, to hear a pitch that fails to address exactly who is going to benefit from a technology and why they might be willing to adopt it. A recent example was a beautifully crafted and executed presentation one of the authors attended. It really was "pitch perfect," delivered by a founder who should have no trouble attracting funding partners based on intelligence, charisma, and a thorough grasp of the moving pieces involved in developing the technology. The company had done its homework in areas that are often neglected by start-ups, including market research on consumer interest and preference versus existing products. But wholly missing from the presentation, and a primary barrier to market acceptance, was the extent to which there is a genuine unmet need. The positioning was novel, intriguing and differentiating, and it seemed likely there would be customer interest, but it was unclear whether that would exist in a very small niche or among a significant population.

The most essential of Marketing 101 concepts, customer centricity, is so often lacking from pitches that it's no longer shocking, only disappointing. Why does this happen? Most often, the team focuses on how the technology is exciting and unique, on the presumption that differentiation of the technology is the same as meaningful differentiation in the marketplace. It is not.

This brings into question the inventor's credibility, and raises a barrier to investment interest that is difficult to overturn. The solution is often simple: instead of focusing on the scientific innovation itself, the investment pitch needs to describe what the product will mean to users, who's going to use it, and why. Which providers or patients will benefit, and in what ways? What therapy will it have to be appended to or displace, and to what extent is the current solution in the marketplace, and any competitive solutions also racing toward the clinic, insufficient? Are those limitations important enough to spur interest and adoption of the new technology, overcoming clinical inertia and financial barriers?

If I've got a better solution for a particular kind of solid tumor, let's say an immunotherapy alternative to chemotherapy, to what extent are patients, clinicians, insurers, and provider systems in need of that solution? Do they even recognize the need or am I going to have to educate them—a process that is invariably expensive, time consuming, and a barrier to adoption? Unmet need is the essential question underlying viability, and therefore the *first* issue that should be addressed before spending serious time on such due diligence questions as IP or development timing and cost.

Size and Growth of the Addressable Market

Most pitches begin with a statement regarding the size of the market. Too often this is stated in terms of aggregate dollars, or total patients with a particular condition, both of which are flawed. Dollars mean nothing for a variety of reasons: they're often estimates from syndicated or public data sources, which become "facts" by virtue of circular and self-referent citation. They almost never realistically (if at all) break out the costs of devices or drugs from the costs of services and facilities. They're usually gross estimates by global region, and may or may not include the societal cost of lost work productivity. Worst of all, they never seem to take into account the differential cost of competing methods to accomplish the same clinical effect. For example, I can take care of my hypertension through diet, a generic beta blocker, a much more expensive angiotensin receptor blocker, or repeated emergency room visits when things get out of control. What does that translate into when I talk about a "hypertension market" in dollars as an estimate of something big enough to warrant investment? A shortcut that new companies will often take is to suggest that the market is so big that if they can just capture a small market share, it's a whole lot of money. Thereby implicitly confirming to investors that they don't really have a commercial plan.

"Total patients" is a different kind of problem. The addressable market isn't the total number of people who have a condition, but you couldn't be blamed for assuming it is based on a typical investor pitch. There are 71,850 new cases of non-hodgkin lymphoma (NHL) per year in the United States, but that does not represent 71,850 opportunities to treat with your new therapy [3]. Why? NHL is a group of cancers of the white blood cells called lymphocytes. There are three different kinds of lymphocytes—B cells, T cells, and NK cells—that can give rise to NHL, and there are more than 30 different types of NHL. Some, like follicular lymphoma are slow-growing (indolent) but can change into a more aggressive type such as diffuse large B cell lymphoma. Furthermore, some patients are candidates for particular therapies based on proximity to tertiary care, insurance status, disease stage, and personal decisions about pursuing treatment—and others are not. A pitch for a new NHL therapeutic had better be clear on exactly whom it's going to treat, and how big that population actually is.

What is needed is an estimate of opportunities for use: potential occurrences of the target disease or procedure that can be addressed. The general formula is the total number of patients or number of procedures, adjusted by the factors that will mediate use, adjusted for realistic share based on your ability to penetrate the market. This figure then becomes the basis for a dollar calculation based on intended pricing, likely reimbursement status, and other factors. A range of potential value, called a sensitivity analysis, can be calculated based on different assumptions regarding pricing, overall market growth, and market penetration.

Markets are enthusiastically embraced when they include large numbers of patients, reflect a fairly unsatisfactory standard of care, and/or represent an easier path to approval and sale. Especially when there are few or no satisfactory alternatives, which opens the door to value-based pricing. The industry is regularly in the news for extreme pricing strategies applied even to older drugs without much competition, the most recent examples being EpiPen and insulin. For investors in early stage companies seeking acquisition by Big Pharma, the grail lately is to serve an underserved population with a *very* expensive drug.

We noted earlier the Senate Finance Committee investigation of Gilead for "revenue-driven" pricing of Sovaldi and Harvoni. At $84,000– 94,500 for a single course of treatment, US sales of these drugs totaled $20.6 billion in the 21 months following Solvadi's introduction: "Gilead pursued a calculated scheme for pricing and marketing its Hepatitis C drug based on one primary goal, maximizing revenue, regardless of the human consequences" [4]. That's not particularly creditable on the part of industry, but it's also not the point with respect to making an early investment determination. What if an early investor in a compound to treat Hepatitis C was looking at a syndicated market report, and basing his analysis on the size of the market before any of these drugs became available? He would be looking at dollars for symptomatic care, and miss the opportunity to get in on the ground floor of a $20 billion windfall.

If this seems farfetched, we might point out the failure *this week* of an investment group we know to support an important, effective second-generation diagnostic, primarily because of resistance from an investor who couldn't get past the size of the "total market" acquired thus far by a lousy first-generation product. There's been substantial distortion of the historical addressable market equation, as the pharma industry has increasingly adopted strategies to exploit high-value opportunities among small populations. Therapeutic areas formerly rejected as too small can now be embraced as cash-rich based on extreme pricing and carefully orchestrated reimbursement strategies. Orphan indications are a perfect confluence of opportunity represented by a small group of d esperate patients, for whom the Food and Drug Administration is inclined to expedite approvals. The formula is to serve a very narrow and previously ignored population, or a subset of a larger population—say, drug-resistant, nonsmall cell lung cancer with a specific mutation in the EGF receptor—with a very expensive drug.

The result: multibillion dollar drugs for populations in the thousands not millions, and half of new regulatory approvals going to orphan "specialty" drugs. Thus we have Soliris (eculizumab, Alexion), a great drug for the rare but potentially fatal disease called paroxysmal nocturnal hemoglobinuria, with a population of several thousand patients but sales over two billion dollars annually. Or Tagrisso (osimertinib, AstraZeneca), which at $13,000 per month could generate annual sales of $3 billion [5]. Certainly an investor pitch that resonates with a Solaris- or Tagrisso-like business model is likely to receive investor attention.

It's important to note that this makes some, but not all, orphan indications attractive financial opportunities. Let's say I developed something to reverse acromegaly, a severely disfiguring disease that is the result of too much growth hormone and usually leads to early death. There are so few patients in the world with acromegaly that any given endocrinologist may see 1–3 sufferers in the course of an entire career. This is not an exploitable opportunity, although it would be a very important cure for patients.

The bottom line is that in the orphan or "specialty" drug arena, we need to modify the addressable market equation, rebalancing the adoption question to account for patients who have no other options and therefore no price sensitivity (other than copays and inevitable restrictions on formulary access).

Adaptability of the Technology or Product to Clinical Practice

Clinical solutions do not administer themselves to patients. Drug therapies flow through pharmacies under the direction of physicians (except that insurers mandate substitution and penalize patients and doctors who insist on brands over generics), and are reimbursed by money that comes from third party payors and increasing patient copays. Who is going to give the drug to the patient, in what form, in what setting, and how that will be reimbursed are critical determinants of success. In the face of significant financial or other disincentives— e.g., requiring clinic versus at-home delivery of injectable therapies, or the time required for professional administration—the benefits of a new drug may not be enough to overcome the status quo of existing therapy. Reimbursement is a powerful lever and potently exercised determinant of who gets what.

Let's consider oncology as an example. The professional service revenues a medical practice can obtain for chemotherapy are higher for more efficient delivery; i.e., the amount of revenue that can be generated is greater for a drug that can be given over a shorter period relative to a drug that takes more time. Abraxane (nab-paclitaxel, Celgene), for example, is a nanoparticle reformulation of Taxol (paclitaxel, Bristol-Myers Squibb). Whether Abraxane is substantially better than Taxol with respect to outcomes is still open to debate for some cancers, but the reformulation has many advantages that lower the barrier to clinical use: it does not require premedication with high dose steroids, which makes patients uncomfortable, it can be given to patients who have mild liver dysfunction, and the neuropathy it induces tends to be less permanent than with Taxol. Furthermore, administering Abraxane is much more cost-efficient for oncology practice. Since Taxol is available as a generic, reimbursement limits are lower, and may not cover the "chair time" and nursing costs of the 3 hours needed for infusion. Abraxane can be given in just 30 min. In other words, the physician may lose money by administering Taxol instead of Abraxane. Because patients like it better, giving Abraxane whenever possible is a no-brainer. Estimated sales of Abraxane in 2014 topped $800 million [6].

A therapy that complicates life for physicians will need to meet a higher standard of clinical or financial outcomes to overcome the inertia of habit and be seriously considered for adoption. At the very least, it must not lose money for the physician. A classic case is the drug Bexxar (I 131 tositumomab, Corixa/GlaxoSmithKline), a radiolabeled monoclonal antibody that had demonstrated excellent outcomes in some cases of NHL [7]. Bexxar was not widely implemented, in part because medical oncologists had other therapies that they could give, which were of equivalent efficacy and generated more revenue for their practices. In addition, Medicare reimbursement for the drug could be thousands of dollars less than the physician or hospital would pay to obtain the drug. Thus, despite its efficacy, Bexxar fell in a hole created by a lack of practical and financial incentives for its use and was eventually discontinued.

Another example is Provenge (sipuleucel-T, Dendreon), a prostate cancer vaccine that offered patients a 4-month improvement in overall survival with relatively few adverse effects [8]. It entered the US market in 2010 accompanied by a positive recommendation from the not-for-profit National Comprehensive Cancer Network, (which produces the industry standard guidelines for cancer care), and had early acceptance at academic institutions. Provenge required a $93,000 upfront inventory investment from doctors, however, without any certainty about when they would be reimbursed. This, combined with patient copays that were typically 20% of the drug's cost, essentially killed Provenge as a therapeutic option in community oncology practices.

Dendreon's stock price collapsed into a black hole, eliminating two-thirds of its $3 billion market valuation in one day and eventually leading to bankruptcy: "[the company said] it could not deliver on promised sales of the high-priced drug because doctors weren't confident enough about getting reimbursed" [9]. Stock analysts complained about a "fundamental flaw" in the company's business model, which stemmed from limited efficacy, an idiosyncratic mechanism of action, a high price, and competition from easier-to-use medications.

There's another important element to consider. Providers are finding themselves financially responsible for a variety of costly patient management scenarios that were historically just added to the fee for service. Two examples are congestive heart failure inpatient stays, for which hospitals are now on the hook for readmissions within 30 days, and hospital-acquired infections, which must now be treated on the hospital's dime.

In dollars and sense, for the provider/hospital, the positive financial impact of global infection control measures or of opting for a more costly antibiotic must be weighed against the direct and indirect (e.g., public relations) costs of a higher rate of nosocomial infection. The competitive market basket of infection control alternatives thus includes not only those antibiotics, but also the cost of modifying institutional procedures regarding handwashing, surgical preparation, and patient interaction. One of the authors was involved a few years back in evaluating a new device for reducing disease transmission in healthcare settings. The economic basis of the analysis was a direct comparison of the incidence of nosocomial disease and the cost of negative outcomes versus the cost of acquiring and implementing the new technology.

For the drug developer as well, the calculation needs to take into account technological disruption, and not just competitors developing other antibiotics. *Clostridium difficile* is an increasingly intractable problem affecting over 500,000 hospitalized patients per year [10]. Many hospitals responded to the approval of the expensive *Clostridium difficile* drug, Dificid (fidaxomicin, Merck), by restricting the drug to prescription by infectious disease specialists only and by enhancing handwashing and hygiene programs for hospital staff. One might wonder how many competitive analyses estimating the marketplace for drugs to treat *C. difficile* infection included handwashing as a competitor? Doctors at the University of Pennsylvania recently described their success in using robots to shine UV light in hospital rooms in order to kill *C. difficile* spores [11]. This simple intervention reduced infection rates by 25% in cancer patients and saved the hospital an estimated $150,000/year. So, a very expensive drug may find itself competing for outcomes against a program to improve institutional hygiene, regardless of how much better the new agent is. The sustainability of the value proposition for a new drug is thus effectively tied to who is paying the bill.

Medical care financing is increasingly a zero-sum game with less and less autonomy for clinicians in determining what drugs to prescribe for their patients. Ultimate decision authority rests with third party payors (Medicaid, Medicare, and private health insurers), who require time-consuming pre-authorization for expensive therapies and may refuse to reimburse some drugs entirely. Efforts to improve the cost efficiency of healthcare delivery are inevitably driving the system toward valuing an intervention on the basis of dollars saved or dollars lost.

Any analysis of market opportunity needs to consider who will get the drug, who will give it to them, and why. It needs to incorporate assumptions about specific disease indications, the availability of competing alternatives, the practicality and economics of delivering a therapy in the clinic, and the motivations and requirements of the payors.

Potential for Sustainable Competitive Advantage

Sustainable competitive advantage is often viewed, especially early on, from the standpoint of intellectual property. IP is important, certainly. There's the question of whether a costly and time-consuming clinical development process can be easily undermined by a "just-enough" technically dissimilar effort, if the space is not sufficiently protected. There is the further consideration of the duration of exclusivity: Can costs be recovered and sufficient profitability be achieved within the patent window, since upon expiration the lion's share of margin migrates immediately to generics.

But for all the defenses against competition it provides, IP is no guarantee of market exclusivity. In its simplest form, and from an investment standpoint, sustainable competitive advantage really means staying power in the clinic. Markets that are characterized by longstanding clinical practice and underserved disease populations are ripe for innovation but may resist adopting new technology. Innovation causes disruption, which destabilizes practice, and new clinical approaches may themselves face the threat of rapid follower competition. Markets that are already in motion, or those that begin experimenting with new approaches, may resist stabilizing on a new therapy. Additionally, disruptions in the general environment—economic, regulatory, demographic legal, sociocultural—can have as much or more impact than changes in the competitive landscape. The problem is rendered even more acute in the healthcare space by the fact that almost all new life science technologies face a long development timeline, and must predict the environment they will face based on a best guess of what the market will look like in the distant future: as few as 3 years out for devices, or as many as 8–10 for drugs.

REFERENCES

[1] Interview with author SD. August 5, 2013.
[2] Sohl J. The Angel investor market in 2014: a market correction in deal size. Center for Venture Research, May 14, 2015. <https://paulcollege.unh.edu/sites/paulcollege.unh.edu/files/web-form/2014%20Analysis%20Report.pdf>; 2015.
[3] National Cancer Institute. SEER Stat Fact Sheets: Non-Hodgkin Lymphoma. <http://seer.cancer.gov/statfacts/html/nhl.html>; [accessed 25.02.16].
[4] United States Senate Committee on Finance. Wyden-Grassley Sovaldi Investigation Finds Revenue-Driven Pricing Strategy Behind $84,000 Hepatitis Drug. December 1, 2015. <http://www.finance.senate.gov/ranking-members-news/wyden-grassley-sovaldi-investigation-finds-revenue-driven-pricing-strategy-behind-84-000-hepatitis-drug>; 2015 [accessed 25.02.16].
[5] Dangi-Garimella S. Tagrisso approved, but can patients with EGFR-mutant NSCLC afford it? Published November 17, 2015. <http://www.ajmc.com/newsroom/tagrisso-approved-but-can-patients-with-egfr-mutant-nsclc-afford-it>; 2015 [accessed 28.02.16].
[6] Celgene. Celgene Corporation Announces 2015 and Long-Term Financial Outlook and Preliminary 2014 Results. Published January 12, 2015. <http://ir.celgene.com/releasedetail.cfm?releaseid=890827>; 2015 [accessed 25.02.16].
[7] Timmerman L. Why good drugs sometimes fail: the Bexxar story. Xconomy 2013 August 26, 2013. <http://www.xconomy.com/national/2013/08/26/why-good-drugs-sometimes-fail-in-the-market-the-bexxar-story/>.
[8] Jaroslawski S, Toumi M. Sipuleucel-T (Provenge(R))-autopsy of an innovative paradigm change in cancer treatment: why a single-product biotech company failed to capitalize on its breakthrough invention. BioDrugs 2015;29:301–7.
[9] Berkrot B. Dendreon plunges as Provenge prospects wither Reuters August 4, 2011. <http://www.reuters.com/article/2011/08/04/dendreon-idUSL3E7J43V720110804>; 2011.
[10] Centers for Disease Control. Clostridium difficile infection. Updated February 25, 2015. <http://www.cdc.gov/HAI/organisms/cdiff/Cdiff_infect.html>; 2015 [accessed 25.02.16].
[11] Penn Medicine News Release. UV Light Robots Cut C. Diff Transmissions by 25 Percent on Cancer Patient Floors, Penn Study Finds. October 9, 2015. <http://www.uphs.upenn.edu/news/News_Releases/2015/10/pegues/>; 2015.

Chapter 15

What Is Value?

Angel investor's due diligence is fundamentally a search for value—financial, scientific, personal, and social—and value becomes tangible when a start-up company defines its intellectual property. The term "intellectual property" in biotechnology is an assertion that an inventor, by intellectual pursuit, has produced a discovery the value of which requires protection. The goal of defining and protecting IP, via patent, is to prevent its unauthorized use by others, since the IP confers a prospective competitive advantage to the person who owns and practices it. This essentially creates a limited monopoly on the property, enabling the commercial value of the discovery to be fully realized without having to worry about anyone else trying to do exactly the same thing.

The premise of a company entering the Valley of Death (VoD) is that they can do something different, and better, than everyone else. Without this *impression* of exclusivity, it is hard to explain to an investor why one company has any better chance of surviving the VoD than any other, and a patent is central to that impression. Absent a submitted patent application or issued patent, a technology lacks a fundamental criterion for investability.

Patents have three essential requirements. In order to obtain a patent, an invention must be:

- Novel (unique compared with other inventions in the same patent space)
- Nonobvious (would not easily be created by a "person having ordinary skill in the art")
- Useful (clinically worthwhile)

The process of obtaining patent protection begins with a provisional filing, which provides a 12-month window to complete the patent filing. This is a relatively low-cost placeholder, and carries the weight, for purposes of the investment thesis, of implied qualification for protection. It's important to note that a provisional patent may not ultimately be filed, and even if filed, may not actually issue. If it does issue, it means only that the composition or design or intended use of this particular invention will be protected for a period of time—typically 20 years from the original filing (priority) date.

Preserving the Promise. DOI: http://dx.doi.org/10.1016/B978-0-12-809216-3.00015-4

But the implied exclusivity of a patent, however concrete in legal terms, is elusive in practical ones. Substitutes for existing technology and methods may be achieved by entirely different pharmacology or action. The market generally supports multiple solutions to a given medical problem, and they all represent potential competition. Exclusivity, therefore, should not be confused with a protection against competition because something else may provide a similar clinical benefit by an entirely different means. It is also easy to imagine the David and Goliath scenario that a start-up can face: irrespective of who is "right," an entrenched competitor with a franchise to protect will not stand idly by and wait for their market share to be eroded. They might buy the technology to extend their franchise, a positive outcome providing the sought-after exit. They might acquire the company and shelve the technology to protect their franchise. Or they could simply bury the erstwhile challenger in a (baseless) legal challenge until its funds dry up, or crush it with blunt force sales and marketing. And if all that's not bad enough, it's worth keeping in mind that even the strongest IP has an expiration date and therefore a finite ability to maintain its protective advantage. The important point to remember about intellectual property is that, while it may be prerequisite to investment, it's simply not enough by itself to create and sustain competitive advantage.

A solid IP position indicates that the technology occupies a unique position, but it does not follow that differentiation automatically provides an advantage that can be successfully leveraged in the marketplace. Stated in terms of VRINE, one of the models we teach to business students, IP may satisfy the attributes of (R)arity and (I)nimitability (prevents alternative technologies utilizing the same composition or methods), but provides no guarantee of perceived (V)alue, of (N)onsubstitutability, or of the company's ability to (E)xploit the opportunity. Even the best IP requires effective management and scientific support, and, more often than not, continued generation of additional IP.

Intellectual property is important for another reason, because it implies that the company has a right to practice the IP in its own efforts without infringing on others. This is "freedom to operate," an especially important starting point for a new company. Without this essential legal clarification there is a heightened risk that another company (or patent accumulator/troll) could tie up the new technology in costly legal action. A full patent database search is required to fully explore the potential for such IP conflicts, which is often outside the financial appetite and scope of start-ups and investors—so a pro forma analysis may be all that is done.

If a venture fails, selling the existing IP may enable some recovery of investment capital, but that's a closing-the-barn-door (after the horse has bolted) effect. For all of these reasons, the existence of a patent or patent application may be crucial to *perceived value* and therefore valuation, but IP does not confer an ironclad warranty of merchantability.

ATTRACTIVENESS AND PLAUSIBILITY OF THE TECHNOLOGY

Some inventions are fundamentally attractive to investors because they have the potential to impact a lot of people. Or someone close to home. For example: given that one in eight US women will be diagnosed with invasive breast cancer in their lifetimes, the odds of an investor having been personally affected by the disease (self, family, or friend) are quite high, and an emotional connection to the venture is easier to establish.

But there's more to it than addressable market or personal connection. Remember that early-stage investors, despite the capacity to be very venture capital-like in calculating the prospective financial value of an opportunity, are also in it for other reasons. The willingness to make what is effectively a high-risk donation has other drivers, including intrinsic appeal or the desire to "do good." One of the authors saw a pitch this week for lingerie that doesn't make the reconstructive surgery survivor feel like she's wearing a medical appliance. Everyone in the room was rooting for the inventor, despite the fact that her sales to date suggested a poorly conceived business plan. Some ventures are investable at an early stage because they matter, or because we really like the management team, or because they address a problem so "hot" and intractable that it's difficult to imagine that they wouldn't get market attention. And some are uninvestable, or have an inherently restricted pool of potential investors, simply because they fail to satisfy intellectual or emotional curiosity—elements of the investment equation we'll address later when we look at investor psychology.

All other things being equal (e.g., the size of opportunity, quality of the team and terms of the deal) one can imagine that it might be more difficult to attract early-stage money for a fecal bacteria transplant to treat *Clostridium difficile* than for an inhalation therapy that reduces flu symptoms. It's not accidental that the company developing the former is called Rebiotix instead of something more descriptive.

There are other factors at play as well, which make some investments inherently more attractive: credible new science for very valuable markets, development stage drugs that threaten incumbents and therefore represent enhanced exit opportunities through acquisition, tailored immunotherapies that are getting lots of attention in the popular press, categories with highly visible foundations supporting early-stage research (e.g., Michael J. Fox for Parkinson's disease), me-too ventures that follow huge commercial successes in the same therapeutic category, or science that is so intrinsically fascinating that it writes its own message in language accessible to those with less extensive healthcare domain expertise.

"Plausibility" means that the science is sound, that proof of concept is likely, and that preclinical and clinical milestones can be achieved. Data at an early stage are usually preclinical and focused on mechanisms, toxicology, and proof of concept (POC) animal experiments, so a significant leap of faith is necessary. These are precisely the reasons for so much emphasis on the scientific founder and management team, on a cogent explication of next steps, including a realistic development timeline and costs, and on the ability to "see" the future market by associative reference to successful comparator technologies. As we described earlier, one of the early biotech mega successes, Velcade for multiple myeloma, struggled with follow-on investment because the financial community had difficulty understanding how a molecule that prevented the breakdown of proteins in a cell would be useful for treating cancer.

LIKELIHOOD THAT CLINICAL PROOF OF CONCEPT IS ACHIEVABLE

This one is simple conceptually: does the new technology work, and how likely is it to fail? Key parameters here are:

- The size and scope of technological and experimental obstacles that need to be overcome
- Whether the science has been externally validated—preferably by a research center with substance and reputation
- The steps, timeline, and costs to establish feasibility as a safe and effective therapy or diagnostic

There are categories that resist investment because there have been too many prior failures, despite a great need and high levels of public research support. Consider, Alzheimer's disease (AD), the sixth-most common cause of death in the United States. AD currently affects an estimated 5 million people in this country, a number that will approach 14 million by 2050 as the baby boom generation ages [1]. The Alzheimer's Foundation of America estimates direct spending for AD (cost of care and the value of informal care) at approximately $203 billion annually, a level that could reach $1 trillion by 2050 [2]. The National Institutes of Health spends more than $500 million per year on AD research, with the amount projected to increase to $910 million in 2016 [3]. But the wind has been knocked out of private AD funding sails by a failure rate exceeding 99% in clinical trials for Alzheimer's disease, including discouraging data on such high-promise drugs as bapineuzumab (Pfizer, Johnson & Johnson) and solanezumab (Lilly) [4].

CHALLENGES OF THE REGULATORY ENVIRONMENT

The cost and complexity of clinical trials is a function of the rarity of the condition and associated difficulty of recruiting patients, the number of patients needed, and the duration of follow-up required to demonstrate effect. For example, a drug against an infection that is relatively common and has minimal effective treatments available will have a relatively straightforward clinical pathway, perhaps even gaining approval without randomized trial data. Similarly, a drug for a rare disease without effective therapies (an "orphan" disease) can use a nonrandomized study design and may achieve eligibility for fast-track approval by the Food and Drug Administration (FDA).

On the other hand, a drug for a disease in which there's a well-established standard of care is unlikely to be approved without rigorous Phase III data. Let's consider a new cancer therapy. If the increments in overall survival or progression-free survival are expected to be small in comparison to existing treatments, then the sample size of the clinical trial will need to be large and include a control group that receives the standard therapy—with an attendant high cost. In addition, so-called "registration trials" usually need to be multicenter, international trials, to reduce the potential for institution-specific bias effects. This is one of the economic drivers that have prompted pharma and biotech companies to focus on orphan diseases: they offer a straightforward or even accelerated clinical pathway, and because there are few or no alternatives for patients, drugs to treat them can command a very high market price.

In the early stages of building one of our companies, SD was convinced that AD was an ideal target for an monoclonal antibody (mAb) therapy. Using a novel antibody cloning method, his lab developed a mAb that may have been an ideal second-generation antibody therapeutic for AD [5]. Maybe we shouldn't have been surprised to discover that most investors considered the antibody to have no commercial value because of the difficulty performing clinical trials with AD patients and the hundreds of millions of dollars already wasted trying to develop AD immune therapies. Even if we'd had a cure for AD in hand, advancing the antibody to the clinic would have been nearly impossible in the context of generating early money for AD development. We then decided a better approach would be to repurpose the mAb as a treatment for amyloidosis, a rare disease with no good therapies. This would require a dramatically less expensive clinical plan, with easily measurable outcomes and an orphan drug designation.

ATTRACTIVENESS OF THE BUSINESS MODEL

The nature of the business model is domain-specific. In many respects this is a binary issue—it either makes sense to the investor or doesn't. There is no "right" answer other than the retrospective one that any investor brings to the review based on his or her past experience in the space. Generally speaking, the business model for drugs is to create pull-through by detailing clinicians, sampling, and advertising directly to consumers; to achieve formulary coverage by contracting with provider systems and Medicare; and to optimize pricing through wholesale and pharmacy distribution. The key development questions revolve around the selection of therapeutic target and disease population, as molecules and bioengineered compounds have effects that can be developed around multiple opportunities. The market opportunity factors include not only the addressable population and cost of therapy, but also the time and duration of development and the competitive and reimbursement environment likely to be in place at the time of launch.

If the new technology is a medical device, adoption is more complicated and anything with more than one potential application requires similar early selection of a target, for example, should a new orthopedic scaffolding material be initially focused on knees or the spine; and a series of subsequent decisions about marketing, partnering and distribution. If the subject is health IT, which is beyond the general purview of this book, the question is usually about whether to pursue a per-use or a subscription-based business model. In all instances, decisions about the "best" business model are never absolute, but a function of precedents, development and regulatory barriers, timeframes to milestones and follow-on funds, and the experience and worldview of the particular investors at the table.

FINANCIAL VIABILITY

Even at the earliest stages, investors need a path to revenue beyond the intrinsic interest or scientific value of a research investigation. Investigators with commercial ambitions should do their best to consider the realpolitik of drug development and marketing. Optimal selection of a target is a primary consideration. Founders are often faced with the conundrum of whether to accept opportunistic money from investors or industry partners who have a very different vision of where they would like to see a technology applied. The temptation to do so can be overwhelming in the face of dwindling funds to keep operating, but the consequences can range from favorable redirection to catastrophic misdirection—and this will only become apparent over time. There are only so many discoveries a scientist can make in a lifetime, and only a finite amount of time and resources for experiments. While an early shift in the scientific program is certainly less costly than a late one, it is in both the investor's and the inventor's interest to assure at least some correspondence in objectives.

Good science brings in money; when the horizon appears that signals the end of that money, founders need to go out and find more. In the early stages of a company, most scientists think in terms of the barriers to discovery, assuming that progress will lead to further money. It turns out, of course, that it is not scientific advancement per se, but *apparent progress toward a valuation inflection point* that attracts more money.

Unsurprisingly, success engenders success. A history of raising money brings credibility to the enterprise and points the way to more investment. For a development stage (i.e., pre-operational) management team this translates into a CEO who has raised money before. Good "jockeys" tend to raise more money from investors than do good scientists, and start-up CEOs are informally "graded" by the number of exits they have had and the sum total of money that they have raised over their years of experience. Similarly, a founder/inventor who is famous, works at a prominent university, or has a history of commercial development of ideas that have paid off for investors in the past will have a much easier time raising money than inventors without these associations.

Of course, it is also taken to be an expression of confidence if the scientist/founder has mortgaged his house, an indicator that he or she is likely to work very hard. This is completely rational and completely terrible at the same time. The common theme here is that well-sourced money leads to more money, and survival for any early-stage venture depends on not running out of money.

EXIT STRATEGY

Achieving an exit is never simple for an Angel, and even when it occurs, it may not have a significant upside. In soliciting an investment, it's important to craft an appeal that addresses the diverse range of investor interests. We'll talk more about incentives later, but for purposes of our discussion on due diligence, we'll focus on what investors want to hear, and what they don't. Clearly, a big part of the end game for anyone willing to write a check is about obtaining a maximum return in the shortest amount of time. All investors are predisposed to deal terms that favor their interests over those of other investors, that keep founders engaged despite continuous erosion of their equity, and that point to a reasonable probability of a high-multiple exit. But Angels are particularly sensitive to the fact that multiple rounds of fundraising may stand between their investment and an exit. The process of Angel investment is opportunistic, an attempt to simultaneously incentivize the company for short-term performance, while maintaining long-term influence over its decisions.

- Whatever terms early investors negotiate, they are ultimately only a defensive strategy against the reality of being diluted by later stage money. This can sound complicated when you start talking to lawyers and dealmakers, but it simplifies if you think of it this way: If I give you $100,000 now, and someone else offers you $10 million later, who do you think is going to have leverage in the subsequent deal terms?
- Keeping founders engaged and maintaining their passion is a delicate balancing act. The carrot is always that even though you, the originator of the technology, now own only a single-digit share of the thing you invented, that's a single-digit share of a very large pot of money vs. most or all of something that will never yield any revenue.
- There's an element of faith—or magical thinking—in all investment decisions. But on the subject of return, we both know a lot of investors whose behavior suggests they would rather bet on a very low probability, but very high return event, than a very high probability exit with a relatively modest return. It's an odd phenomenon.

HUMAN RESOURCES AND CONTINGENCY PLANNING

We've grouped these together because the ability to plan and execute around contingencies may be the most critical determinant of success and is the underlying premise of "bet on the jockey": the reliance of investors on the premise that lightning will strike twice in the same place, and the associated inference that past success of the management team is a key predictor of success. The most important quality of operational management is certainly adaptability, because it is a given, particularly in an early-stage environment, that everything—assumptions, interim goals, expected funding sources, experimental results, competitive environment—will change along the way. Experienced CEOs have a network of connections they can turn to for guidance, to build their team, and to create opportunities for collaboration and deal making.

REFLECTIONS ON DUE DILIGENCE

By now it should be pretty obvious why innovation can get lost in the financial pressure cooker of the VoD. Most of the criteria that determine whether a discovery receives support, the components of due diligence we've outlined here, have nothing to do with whether the invention will help people or not. By the time it's doing serious fundraising, the discovery will have come a long way from the "Eureka" moment in which it was created in the laboratory. It will have survived the filter of the university tech transfer office to get at least a patent application, and transitioned to a potentially investable proposition for the VoD. Now it hopes to achieve the backing of investors for the newly formed company and recruitment of management beyond the founding team. Whereupon the novelty and excitement of the discovery are reduced to a simple equation: does the investment proposition distinguish itself from all the other opportunities for investment, such that it can continue its journey?

The mechanics of the decision-making process among early stage investors reflects the fact that they are generally presented with far more opportunities than they can respond to, and undertaking the due diligence process consumes time without any immediate promise of return. A study of their investing process revealed that many Angels use an elimination-by-aspects (EBA) method to decide which opportunities merit additional study. In this method, prospects are first surveyed for a "fatal flaw," any feature that would rule out interest in an investment [6]. The study was performed by analyzing investor decision making in a reality TV show called *The Dragon's Den*, yet the lessons are clearly transferable to the VoD.

The EBA model, which emphasizes speed over accuracy, is intuitively understood by anyone who has participated in due diligence. The upside is a rapid and fairly rational screening process. The downside is the risk of rejecting an opportunity that might otherwise be supported by a more balanced decision model (in which strongly positive factors may be able to compensate for negative ones).

Examples of fatal flaws we have encountered in our work include (but are certainly not limited to) the following: a CEO who handles questions poorly, an inability to explain how an unusual drug will be administered, too many similar drugs in the marketplace, previous failures of a similar approach, weak IP protection, too much money spent too quickly (known as "burn rate"), and our particular grievance, an inability to characterize unmet need, estimate market size, or objectively assess the competition.

How much of this is going through the minds of the scientists who are pushing technologies out of their laboratories into the commercial sector? Scientific founders tend to assume that, if there is quality in the science and a true unmet medical need, there should be room in the VoD for their great idea to thrive. That's partly true, but the "if you build it they will come" paradigm disappeared from medical development a long time ago. Investors really do look for zealousness on the part of founders, but they want it tempered by concrete business thinking. They know that business strategy will change, many entrepreneurs are new to the process, and companies may pivot more than once on the road to commercialization. So the strategy doesn't need to be perfect, but if it reflects disorganized or wishful thinking rather than a coherent business strategy, that can easily become the fatal flaw.

It seems odd on the surface that an endlessly diverse group of innovation-driven companies are essentially interchangeable competitors for funding. Yet from an investor's standpoint, that is exactly the situation. The actual differences between technologies are only important to the extent that they support the essential investment thesis. Companies are judged on the basis of whether they will ultimately be able to exit at a multiple of the original investment. The due diligence process naturally homogenizes technologies into those likely to succeed in supporting the investment thesis and those likely to fail. It does not favor the disruptive over the mundane, or the transformational over the ordinary, especially when it seems that the disruptive and transformational project is less likely to work.

Profit motive is a desirable, necessary, and often destructive impulse. Certainly many early stage healthcare investors are driven by more than return on investment—perhaps philanthropy, the desire to make a difference, or personal exposure to illness and suffering. But profit-seeking alone isn't a formula for the whole system actually making sense. Investment objectives are not an effective mechanism for filtering the most innovative or clinically useful technologies.

Adam Smith argued centuries ago that the profit motive creates powerful incentives for investors to seek out and commercialize innovations that will produce the most value for consumers [7]. His arguments are the cornerstone of modern economic theory, and it may seem that economic incentives alone should guide the selection of the most important drugs for development in the VoD. This assumption ignores the fact, however, that the ultimate consumers of medical innovation, patients and doctors, are fairly distant from the decision-making processes that determine what is available for them to buy/use/ purchase/prescribe. They make choices on what drugs to give and receive in the clinic, but they have little influence over the range of options available, which are determined in large part by what Angels and follow-on investors can be convinced is a good idea. And in the VoD, short-term financial objectives blunt the influence doctors and patients can exert on the Angel decision-making process.

In the VoD marketplace, where financial instruments are bought and sold, the buyers are investors and the products are collateralized with biotechnology IP. The investor buys a piece of a company, in the hopes that he can sell it for more later, or provides a convertible note loan at a rate of interest that reflects the high risk involved. The value of the instrument is assessed, as for any investment, as a calculus of money in, time to exit, and predicted ROI, financial metrics that are often tangential to the value of the invention for human health.

Indirectly, Angels *are* the conduit for exerting the interest of medical consumer choice on the selection of technologies to develop in the VoD, but that's a tenuous connection supported only by the fact that Angels are people, often older ones at that, who are going to get sick someday. It would be facile to suggest that most Angels are primarily motivated by the idea that a given investment will lead to a drug they may ultimately need.

SO WHERE IS BIG PHARMA/BIG BIOTECH ON ALL THIS? A BREAKDOWN IN VALUE

We recognize that pharma is a business, and that business does not revolve around a primary mission of benevolence. When we look at early-stage companies in the context of eventual acquisition or licensing of their technology to pharma, it's clear that any venture needs ultimately to fulfill the needs of the industry, and therefore of the investors who mediate the transactions that occur between start-up and exit.

Behavior agnostic to clinical merit is exemplified by industry and investor behavior, which we've touched on earlier. Since the 1980s, if a drug isn't a potential blockbuster (annual sales >$1 billion), it has been hard to generate much commitment from top management. More recently, the landscape (but not the objective) has changed, and the pursuit of extraordinarily expensive specialty drugs has replaced the blockbuster equation of drugs that serve very large populations. "The average annual cost of therapy for widely used specialty drug products was $53,384 in 2013..., 18 times higher than the average annual price of therapy for brand name prescription drugs ... and 189 times higher than the average annual price of therapy for generic[s]" [8]. In this context, the traditional model of modestly differentiated drugs serving big populations is simply less interesting, and me-too drugs like the seventh or eighth angiotensin receptor blocker don't have the cachet they once did.

Large populations are also less relevant if they are in developing nations where selling prices are low, unless the business case also includes a population that can be charged a much higher price in an industrialized country. Thus, the industry routinely de-emphasizes the medical needs of the underserved and impoverished. For example, the Neglected Tropical Diseases (NTDs) are leading causes of chronic disability and poverty in developing countries, where they primarily affect children and women of reproductive age [9]. A survey of drug approvals from 2000 to 2011 identified only four new chemical entities (not reformulations or vaccines) approved for NTDs during the period, totaling only 1% of the 336 approved in the same time frame [10].

The power of money is not unique to the pharma industry, but the human consequences are. Annually, 20,000 people die in India due to rabies infection, even though a 100% effective therapy called rabies immune globulin exists to prevent the disease after a bite by an infected animal [11]. Why? Because there is no compelling financial incentive to make this $10–50 therapy universally available in India. In stark contrast, one of only 44 drugs approved by the FDA in 2014 was a topical therapy called Jublia, which for $539 assures that people with adequate prescription coverage don't have to suffer the humiliation of toenail fungus [12].

In another troubling turn, opportunistic marketers have lately developed a taste for buying the rights to inexpensive drugs in stable or low-growth markets, with no competitors, and repricing them at sometimes staggering multiples. Martin Shkreli, the ex-hedge fund manager and CEO of Turing Pharmaceuticals is the most notorious example, having hiked the price of the antiparasitic Daraprim by 5000% [13], but exploitative pricing is a business model being repeated in a raft of repurposed, reformulated, or repackaged drugs across the industry.

It may seem we're getting a bit off track here, but there's a point to looking at the industry in this way that isn't just about profit bashing. The pharma marketplace globally is suffering a breakdown in the connection between true value for human beings, the cost of producing medications to heal, and the desirability or undesirability of particular technologies based on investment criteria.

The VoD is corollary, operating in the shadow of, and in service to, the Big Pharma/Big Biotech industry. Neither industry nor the VoD market for technology is driven as much by value for clinicians and patients, as by value for investors. In the VoD, these forces work themselves out on a smaller scale, balancing the economic imperative of ROI with the desire to accomplish something meaningful. The VoD is deeply influenced by the direction of the flow of money in Pharma, and due diligence criteria are finely tuned to read and respond to changes in this movement.

Biotechnology investment trends from 2004 to 2013 show where the money is going, and where it is not: an increase in spending on metabolic diseases and ophthalmology, against substantial decreases in development spending on endocrinology (−60%), psychiatry (−56%), gastrointestinal disease (−49%), respiratory disease (−41%), and neurology (−39%) [14]. No one would propose that this reflects a decline in need or that we've eradicated disease across these categories. It's a question of investment for return, but it gets more complicated than that, because failure to invest means we lose ground at the same time demographics are expanding the problem. We end up with multiple drug resistant bacteria, runaway viruses, and a variety of other burgeoning public health crises.

The decision to start a company in a particular therapeutic area cannot help but be affected by the availability of follow-on funds and strategic partnerships in particular disease categories [14]. For example, in 2009–13, over $4 billion was raised by oncology companies, in contrast to just $491 million for respiratory diseases such as asthma, which are still the third-leading cause of death in the United States. One in six deaths in children 1 year of age and younger result from respiratory disease. Yet, limited development funding went to the category during this 5-year period, along with type 1 diabetes, Gram-negative infections, schizophrenia, arthritis, and other disease states affecting large numbers of people.

These spending figures reflect the combined activities of everyone in the drug development ecosystem, and strongly point to the conclusion that some diseases are intrinsically less investable, at least at present. As VC investor Joe Lovett, Managing Director of Louisiana Funds, told an audience of university technology transfer officials, "What we're really not interested in is something that is just a little better than something that is out there. What we as a fund are interested in … are technologies that can get into the clinic fairly rapidly, because the acid test is how this drug or medical device works in people. So we tend to shy away from technologies in the neuroscience area [such as] a new Alzheimer's drug; we tend to shy away from cardiac drugs that take a long time and very, very large…clinical studies to see if they work, like a drug for stroke" [15]. As the investment market determines what technologies will move forward, it also decides what will never be given a chance to help patients.

In a recent talk on translational medicine at the University of Pennsylvania, author Fishman gave cyclosporine as an example of transformational medicine, which captured enormous market value because it solved a huge problem and gave life to many thousands of transplant recipients [16]. The problem before cyclosporine wasn't so much technical—surgeons had long been connecting and disconnecting parts of organs—as immune rejection. Cyclosporine *enabled* successful organ transplantation. Fishman posed the question of whether cyclosporine would even have been developed in today's environment. Let's see: relatively small population, long and complicated development path, potentially high cost to develop, close regulatory scrutiny, high risk of failure, and a question as to the amount of room for extreme pricing given the already extraordinary cost of transplantation and the need for permanent chronic immunosuppressant therapy. Draw your own conclusion.

Selfishly, we would like to see funding track extremity of need. Below are the leading causes of disease-related death in the United States for 2013 (Fig 1) [17] and across the world for 2012 [18]:

United States

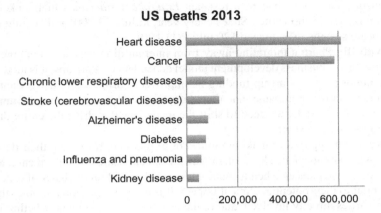

US Deaths 2013

World

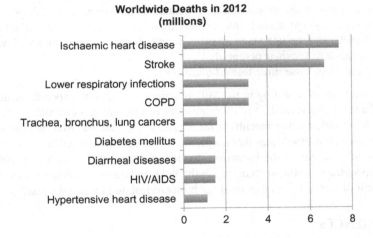

Should we attempt to adjust incentives in the pharmaceutical marketplace to more effectively support diverse clinical innovation in the VoD? The alternative is to continue the relentless pursuit of extreme-cost therapies for small populations, on a course away from drugs that help large numbers of patients, meanwhile ignoring vast areas of unmet medical need. Most of us will die of something other than cancer, but you wouldn't guess that if you were looking at the spectrum of biotechnology investments. Our commercialization priorities in medicine do not anticipate predictable threats to human health. The news is full of warnings we're potentially re-entering an era we thought had ended with the advent of broad-spectrum antibiotics, yet we're doing little about it. Failure to develop new antibiotics has us on a crisis course of increasingly resistant micro-organisms, such as carbapenem-resistant *Enterobacteriaceae*, which sicken 2 million people in the United States every year, killing 23,000, and costing the healthcare system an estimated $20 billion [19,20].

With Big Pharma migrating away from internal discovery as an engine of innovation to a business development model dependent on start-ups, it is increasingly important that start-up funding be improved. Furthermore, if we want to encourage start-up companies and their Angels to address the entire spectrum of unmet medical needs, we need to shift the incentives that drive the entire drug development ecosystem.

We're not opposed to making money, or to pharma prioritizing their development activity to create shareholder value. But healthcare is a special case, and there are consequences when technologies are advanced on the basis of criteria tangential to their potential clinical impact. It frankly doesn't matter, other than to the parties directly involved, and to the tastebuds of consumers, whether my fledgling soft drink company gets funded, but it may matter a great deal if an important new immunotherapy doesn't. Due diligence is rationally and appropriately focused on achieving ROI, but it's not necessary and perhaps not even advisable for it to do so agnostic of potential disease impact. If it does, great early companies will never be recognized, their technologies will never achieve critical POC, and the late-stage investment and pharma communities will never have a chance to see their potential.

We therefore raise three related questions:

1. Should Angel investing in the VoD remain agnostic to the specific features of a technology, relative to its value as an investment proposition?
2. Is it possible to alter incentives for Angels to increase the ROI on high-risk, high-value technologies that might otherwise fail due diligence?
3. Would changes in the incentive structure for late stage drug development impact the investment strategies in the VoD, and thereby encourage development of technologies that leverage both clinical and financial value?

REFERENCES

[1] Hebert LE, Weuve J, Scherr PA, Evans DA. Alzheimer disease in the United States (2010–2050) estimated using the 2010 census. Neurology 2013;80(19):1778–83.
[2] Alzheimer's Foundation of America. Cost of care: quantifying care-centered provisions of the "National Plan to Address Alzheimer's Disease." April 29, 2014. <https://www.alzfdn.org/documents/Quantifying-Care-Centered-Provisions-of-the-National-Plan-to-Address-Alzheimers-Disease.pdf>; 2014.
[3] NIH RePORT. Estimates of funding for various research, condition, and disease categories (RCDC). <http://report.nih.gov/categorical_spending.aspx>; 2016 [accessed 25.02.16].
[4] Cummings JL, Morstorf T, Zhong K. Alzheimer's disease drug-development pipeline: few candidates, frequent failures. Alzheimers Res Ther 2014;6(4):37. http://dx.doi.org/10.1186/alzrt269.

[5] Levites Y, O'Nuallain B, Puligedda RD, Ondrejcak T, Adekar SP, Chen C, et al. A human monoclonal IgG that binds abeta assemblies and diverse amyloids exhibits anti-amyloid activities in vitro and in vivo. J Neurosci 2015;35(16):6265–76.

[6] Maxwell AL, Jeffrey SA, Lévesque M. Business angel early stage decision making. J Business Ventur 2011;26:212–25.

[7] Smith A, Cannan E, editor. An inquiry into the nature and causes of the wealth of nations. Chicago: University of Chicago Press; 1976.

[8] Schondelmeyer SW, Purvis L. *Rx price watch report: brand name prescription drugs.* <http://www.aarp.org/content/dam/aarp/ppi/2014-11/rx-price-watch-report-AARP-ppi-health.pdf>; 2014.

[9] Hotez PJ, Pecoul B. "Manifesto" for advancing the control and elimination of neglected tropical diseases. PLoS Negl Trop Dis 2010;4(5):e718. http://dx.doi.org/10.1371/journal.pntd.0000718.

[10] Pedrique B, Strub-Wourgaft N, Some C, Olliaro P, Trouiller P, Ford N, et al. The drug and vaccine landscape for neglected diseases (2000–11): a systematic assessment. Lancet Glob Health 2013;1(6):e371–9. http://dx.doi.org/10.1016/S2214-109X(13)70078-0.

[11] Chakradhar S. Biting back: vaccine efforts redoubled as rabies deadline looms. Nat Med 2015;21(1):8–10. http://dx.doi.org/10.1038/nm0115-8.

[12] Graedon T. FDA approves jublia for fighting nail fungus, <http://www.peoplespharmacy.com/2014/07/17/fda-approves-new-topical-options-for-fighting-nail-fungus/>;2014[accessed 26.02.16].

[13] Carroll J. Why would Martin Shkreli hike an old drug price by 5000%? Only a 'moron' would ask. Fiercebiotech; 2015. September 20, 2015. <http://www.fiercebiotech.com/story/why-would-martin-shkreli-hike-old-drug-price-5000-only-moron-would-ask/2015-09-20>; [accessed 26.02.16].

[14] Thomas D, Wessel C. Venture funding of therapeutic innovation, a comprehensive look at a decade of venture funding of drug R&D. Washington, DC: Biotechnology Industry Organization; 2015. <https://www.bio.org/sites/default/files/BIO-Whitepaper-FINAL.PDF/>.

[15] Lovett J. AUTM 2015 Annual Meeting Venture Forum. <http://www.softconference.com/AUTM/sessionDetail.asp?SID=371165>; 2015.

[16] Moore D. Origin of drugs in current use: the cyclosporine story (contributed by Harriet Upton, 2001). Updated June 7, 2012. <http://www.davidmoore.org.uk/Sec04_01.htm>; 2012 [accessed 26.02.16].

[17] Centers for Disease Control. Deaths and mortality. Updated September 30, 2015. <http://www.cdc.gov/nchs/fastats/deaths.htm>; 2014 [accessed 26.02.16].

[18] World Health Organization. The top ten causes of death. Fact sheet N 310. Updated May, 2014. <http://www.who.int/mediacentre/factsheets/fs310/en/>; 2014 [accessed 26.02.16].

[19] McKenna M. Antibiotic resistance: the last resort. Nature 2013;499(7459):394–6. http://dx.doi.org/10.1038/499394a.

[20] Centers for disease control and prevention. Antibiotic resistance threats in the United States, 2013. <http://www.cdc.gov/drugresistance/pdf/ar-threats-2013-508.pdf>; 2013.

Chapter 16

Angels at the Crux of Invention

BAD STUFF GETS FUNDED AND GOOD STUFF DIES

I sat in a room full of smart, accomplished Life Sciences investors and entrepreneurs, watching a presentation by two inventors with questionable scientific credentials. The objet d'art was a purported absorbing and radiating device that harnessed the body's own energy and rechanneled it into pain relief. The following thoughts occurred to me as I digested this presentation:
1. Does anyone really believe this?
2. There's just as much potential to make money from gullible consumers in 2011 as there was selling electrical belts in 1911.
3. This would make a great infomercial.
4. Would anyone with a shred of clinical sense actually fund these people?

Naturally, the project was funded.

This true story is a classic example of Porter's risk of substitution at work in the Valley of Death (VoD). Here, substitution isn't the same as competition in the clinic, but instead revolves around selection of an alternative for investment. This might include funding *any* other opportunity, including questionable "medicine," rather than a company that might be developing a technology to address an important medical need. Nobody participating in the VoD is required to invest in biotechnology, yet we leave it to the discretion of those with investment-level resources to identify and support the inventions that will progress. We've noted that this isn't exactly a formula for choosing the inventions most likely to improve the health of individual patients or society at large. But it is the process by which technologies are anointed with the financial substance to progress. So an utterly idiotic, pseudo-scientific "invention" gets money that might otherwise be allocated to something useful, because it appears to be capable of generating investor-friendly returns.

Angels have to be accredited, which means they have more money than most people, and they want to do something both interesting and profitable with some of it. Their budget probably looks rather different than for the typical household: some of it goes to (second) houses, some of it to buy adult toys like cars and boats, and some to invest in a high-risk cure for an orphan disease that was discovered at a local university. This is all discretionary; no one making Angel

Preserving the Promise. DOI: http://dx.doi.org/10.1016/B978-0-12-809216-3.00016-6

investments is likely to be risking their livelihood or betting their future. The point is that Angels can spend some of this disposable income on a variety of stuff, including early-stage companies, for reasons that have nothing to do with the point of clinical discovery—which we idealistically suggest is to preserve and promote the fruits of our academic biomedical research enterprise so that they can do some good for patients.

Angels are not the National Institutes of Health, nor are they charities funneling the proceeds of everything from lemonade stands to sophisticated fundraising initiatives into specific areas of research. But because neither industry nor venture capital (VC) nor public funding adequately support early-stage biotechnology companies, we need Angels to take care of the next generation of cures—the "babies" of drug discovery—for us. They have inherited rather than consciously assumed the historical mantle of Big Pharma discovery. And because even the most dedicated philanthropists are motivated by What's In It For Them—gratification at some level of the needs hierarchy—if we want them to do the right thing for the future of clinical medicine, it needs to be in a way that makes sense for them. To support meaningful innovation, we need to improve the selection process, including due diligence, and adjust the financial incentives to better reward useful innovation and sustainable value.

If anything is going to change, there needs to be a convergence between the types of investments that society needs and Angels' own motivations, which include making money from their investments. This starts at the back end with incentives determined by clinical demand and payors, translates itself into the pharma and biotech development programs that serve those markets, is fed by the late-stage investment strategy of big capital, and ultimately arrives at the doorstep of Angels evaluating early-stage opportunities.

As stimuli to keep the money flowing, intellectual curiosity, forward thinking about the health of society, and individual interest in particular therapeutic domains only go so far. If we're writing a prescription to improve the investment climate, we need to be focused on improving the financial outcomes by enhancing the quality of the investment propositions. We need to keep Angels investing and we need to assure their investments are in the most promising, clinically useful, and transformative products of academic research. Otherwise, everybody loses. According to a 2016 survey conducted by the Angel Capital Association and Wharton Entrepreneurship, Angels invest in a median of 2 companies per year and a total of nearly 16 companies over a portfolio lifetime [1]. If someone new to investing does so a few times and never sees any gain, there's a good chance they may step back from the VoD ecosystem, or at least a particular segment such as healthcare, and put their money elsewhere.

The financial metric for investors is "wins" and rational losses—or at least ones that can be rationalized. If they win once, or lose in a way that makes them feel like they *could have won*, they'll play again. There's no sustainable business model where most of the customers continue to engage without hope or expectation of future gain. Well, perhaps there's one; it's called gambling.

The following is from a blog by Brad Feld, a very active investor in Internet companies, that describes the dynamics of an Angel investor drawdown he recently observed in his industry [2].

> *I have seen some of the more prolific Angels start to slow down because capital is not recycling as fast as they are putting it out ... The supply/demand imbalance is way off. While there is an increasing amount of seed capital/ seed investors, the number of companies seeking seed investment has grown much faster in the last 24 months ... Also, I think some Angels are just tired of the deal velocity. You have to work at it now ... and that makes Angels, especially semi-retired ones, tired ... If there is a big public market correction and Angels feel (a) less wealthy and (b) less liquid (or not liquid), you'll see a major pullback. Everyone is suddenly nervous.*

From the outside, it would appear there is plenty of money available for start-ups, since the news is full of biotech IPOs and breathless reports of a growing pool of investment cash. But the number of seed-stage companies is expanding as well, so the competitive dynamics of the VoD have not really changed. Absent an investment thesis that checks the right boxes, discoveries won't leave the universities, start-up companies won't survive the VoD long enough to achieve a VC investment or pharma partnership, pharma will be forced to throw increasing sums of money at a shrinking selection of viable companies, and the rate of introduction of new drugs to the clinic will stagnate. There's a compelling argument on multiple fronts to increase the success ratio for Angels in the VoD, generating healthier companies that divert less development time to chasing money. The result? More and more useful new drugs, a fundamentally "richer" development paradigm for both academia and pharma, and more choices for doctors and their patients.

This objective is one of the chief reasons why we undertook this analysis and have tried to develop prescriptions for making the process better. We know that simply making due diligence more rigorous will not solve the problem, because even good companies can fail for want of continuous support, and bad companies will continue to attract and consume money that could otherwise be used to support the good ones. Those reasons alone argue the need to improve the ecosystem, and this starts with bridging this second Translation Gap: *Good innovation is not always a good investment.*

The definition of success for inventors and investors may converge at some point on the horizon with prescribing a drug to a patient, with all its attendant financial and personal satisfactions. But from the beginning there is divergence between the drive for scientific innovation, which maintains a difficult inverse relationship with the risk of failure, and the monetary risk of an early-stage company that needs to sell investments in a hypercompetitive funding environment.

THE UNCERTAINTY OF SCIENTIFIC DUE DILIGENCE

In the VoD, financial instruments proffer investment theses supported by scientific experiments, and this is why it is so hard to find a corollary between due diligence on a VoD company and that company's long-term chances of success: the science is a wild card. Innovation is not always a good investment, and not only because markets are initially more resistant to disruptive change. It is simply impossible to predict whether a particular scientific program will work in the long term. Short-term is easier, since the target of the investment thesis is transfer of the financial obligation to the next investor. As we examined in the previous two chapters, the existence of a reasonable market proposition is a prerequisite that should be satisfied alongside the question of whether the technology actually works. Both are essential to a successful investment thesis in the VoD.

It is very difficult, however, to accurately calculate the risk of failure of an experimental program and incorporate that into the overall risk proposition. One problem is a lack of comparables. There are often precedents to analyze, in the same technology or clinical space, but by definition start-ups exist because they have, or propose to have, a novel way of solving a problem. This may include unique composition of matter, mechanism of action or implementation, or may derive from a differentiated approach to R&D (research and development). But direct comparisons to other companies can never be more than a surrogate, even if those competitors are trying to accomplish the same objective [3]. Furthermore, success will be influenced by the skills and influence of the scientific team, the substance and diversity of its supporting cast of advisors and consultants, the reputation and resources of the institutions with which they are affiliated, their relationships with industry ... and whether or not the product champions have the right crystal ball (otherwise known as good luck).

There are no financial markets for R&D per se. R&D does not inherently carry a valuation, even though it does drive a company's apparent worth. Within established industry, it's an expense on the balance sheet. For a start-up, it can be a major determinant of the company's burn rate, and because of milestone-based investing (see chapter: Ready for a Long-Term Relationship With a Science Experiment?), the primary predictor of continued funding. Its effect on company valuation is real, but can only be indirectly estimated as a corollary of the uncertainty it carries.

Certainly many of the technologies coming out of universities, especially those that have not been externally validated by someone else's research, simply cannot be counted on to work as promised. Absent external validation, the entire investment thesis is a sand sculpture: potentially elegant and beautiful, but subject to collapse with the tide of failed attempts to replicate the original findings. Even a well-supported research plan faces unpredictable obstacles as it moves from discovery through preclinical proof of concept, IND-enabling clinical work, manufacturing feasibility, regulatory guidance and other critical milestones. There is an outline for all this, but no one-size-fits-all formula that can be reduced to a predictive due diligence template. The sheer unpredictability of any early-stage venture, especially in the context of the very long development timeframe inherent in life sciences, means that *all assessments of viability are hypothetical* and based largely on the idiosyncrasies of investors' prior experience.

We believe the best model for the scientific component of due diligence explicitly recognizes that the risks of failure vary at different steps in the R&D plan, and relates critical *nodes of uncertainty* to funding milestones. Some research questions create profound vulnerabilities for companies because, if they cannot be resolved, an entire research program may implode. Others might be just as critical for a particular round of fundraising, but not devastating in the long run if a workaround can keep the project moving forward.

Companies with platform technologies—inventions that can generate a range of possibilities rather than a single molecule, device or diagnostic—are often jeopardized by potentially fatal nodes of uncertainty, and for this reason are unpopular with investors. Platform companies are founded on methods that provide a new way of discovering a drug. They are usually based on a novel understanding of a fundamental biological principle, are validated by the discovery of one or more proof of concept molecules that show the method can work—but are not yet suitable for clinical development. Everyone wants the *implications* of a platform, the possibility of transformative technology and the very desirable promise of a continued pipeline from the research. But, in one of the paradoxes of the early-stage funding world, great potential combines with the perception that platforms carry a lack of management focus, especially with respect to potential applications, and the fear that they just might not work. Absent a credible drug candidate for a specific therapeutic application, platforms have enormous difficulty attracting funding, and so the vicious cycle persists of transformative innovation being less attractive in the short term than incremental progress.

One example is a cell-free platform to identify molecules that can disrupt viral capsid assembly (such as Prosetta Biosciences) [4]. Typical of companies with platform discoveries, Prosetta has the potential to discover drugs to treat many different viruses, and published proof of concept data for a drug against rabies [5]. A molecule discovered with their method would provide a unique way of treating viral diseases that might have greater specificity for the virus, fewer side effects, and less chance of causing drug resistance. For a company like Prosetta, due diligence needs to assess the track record and credibility of the scientists, the results of early experiments, related research, and other factors potentially determinant of the (as yet nonexistent) drug's prospects. Questions might include: Does it exist in a drug library somewhere that can be accessed by the company or does a new library need to be created and screened? Can the proof of concept molecules be used as a lead to create a library that can be tested? How many molecules need to be screened to find enough credible hits, how much will that cost, and how long will it take? Positive answers to these questions would be presumed to reduce risk of failure, but they can't definitively predict success. It can be a long road to a VC investment or corporate partnership for a platform company.

A platform technology is on the cusp between something and nothing, one of those critical nodes of uncertainty. Once a few leads have been found, the risk proposition moderates for a time, while the molecules undergo testing that is important for the value of the company. This is not an easy task, but one focused on process rather than endpoint, and therefore less likely to stop everything in its tracks. For instance: measuring the kinetics and potency of the drug with its target, testing resistance mechanisms in vitro, and working out a manufacturing strategy are all significant obstacles. But the expertise to perform these functions is relatively easy to find, compared with the nonlinear leap that generates a new molecule.

New drug candidates face another challenge when they go into animal testing. Will they damage the liver, kidneys, lungs, or bone marrow at the effective dose? Every research plan has these nodes, and their number and potential intractability essentially create a discount factor for the value of the company. In other words, the potential value of a technology is adjusted by the risk of its failure. It is important to reinforce that value is measured here as the ability to support a funding strategy, not necessarily to reach the clinic. The research timeline and budget need to be calibrated to overcome nodes of uncertainty in the most efficient way possible.

Scientific due diligence is undermined by asymmetric information, especially when it comes to estimating how likely it is that an experimental program will fail or succeed. The inventor and scientific team know far more about the technology than the majority of early-stage investors. Yet it would be an extraordinary scientist who understands every nuance of commercialization, or can anticipate everything that needs to be known to make an R&D program successful. Even the most objective scientists are quite human in their ability to misconstrue their own work in the most favorable light, and there are enormous pressures in the VoD to balance financial objectivity—how long it will take and what it will really cost to execute a research program—with investors' natural desire to compress both. This is at the heart of the conundrum for the investment thesis. For investors, due diligence needs to connect a deep understanding of the science, which isn't necessarily their area of expertise, with what is: an understanding of funding strategies and typical development paths, knowing how to anticipate pitfalls that may arise, and having an intuitive sense of what questions to ask. Effective evaluation of the scientific plan requires a deep background of expertise across multiple domains.

INVESTING TO THE NEXT MONEY

Reflecting on the scientific uncertainty, it becomes clear why trying to "de-risk" a technology by performing due diligence is problematic. First, the timeline for development of a drug is so long that it is virtually impossible to predict future fundraising prospects at the beginning. Second, it is impossible to predict the market structure of a therapeutic category in 7–10 years, estimate the threat of new entrants and scientific paradigm shifts that may render current projects obsolete, and envision how increasing exertion of buyer power (resulting from pressures to reduce healthcare spending) will change the reimbursement model for new drugs.

Think about this for a minute. An early-stage company has not started making money, is still navigating the treacherous path of product development, is still subject to the political vagaries and practical dysfunction of regulatory authorities, still has to prove clinical superiority in complicated and expensive clinical trials before it can even try to file for approval; and even if it does manage to do all those things, finally, immutably faces the merciless landscape of competition and reimbursement. *This entity, this early-stage company, is somehow "valued" at a multiple that reflects a chain of what-ifs.* The size of the number is a multiple of the money already invested, and has a relation to commercial sales and profit potential that is strained to incredulity. It is also, in the absence of revenue, an infinite multiple of current sales.

In fact, much of the outcome of due diligence revolves around the fundamental question: How likely is it that the company will reach a value inflection point before the current funding runs out? The exercise of due diligence focuses on the usual suspects of unmet need, IP, market value of the technology, and market potential, but what it comes down to is a determination of the probability that the entity can survive further due diligence so that more money can come in. Will there be someone else down the road who will relieve the original investors of their debt, capture their equity at a profit, or at least support the venture (and all the other money that's been invested in it) until an exit can occur? If potential follow-on investors disagree on what the value of a company is, or should be, then the calculus of investing in the VoD breaks down.

REFERENCES

[1] Angel Capital Association. Angel Investors Maintain Diverse Portfoloios, with Median Check Size of $25,000, According to the Early Results of "The American Angel" Campaign. <http://www.prnewswire.com/news-releases/angel-investors-maintain-diverse-portfolios-with-median-check-size-of-25000-according-to-early-results-of-the-american-angel-campaign-300291949.html>; 2016.

[2] Feld B. Are individual Angel investors starting to get tapped out? <http://www.feld.com/archives/2015/09/individual-angel-investors-starting-get-tapped.html>; Published September 10, 2015.

[3] Aboody D, Lev B. Information asymmetry, R&D, and insider gains. J Finance LV 2000(6):2747–66.

[4] Prosetta. Home page. <http://www.prosetta.com>; 2016.

[5] Lingappa UF, Wu X, Macieik A, Yu SF, Atuegbu A, Corpuz M, et al. Host–rabies virus protein–protein interactions as druggable antiviral targets. Proc Natl Acad Sci USA 2013;110(10):E861–8.

Chapter 17

Investment: A Nuanced Decision

Making a decision about which biotechnology start-up to support requires extraordinary powers of discernment, practical experience in business development and scientific R&D (research and development), and weeks or months of intense study. *Prima facie*, it may be surprising that investments occur at all. Yet there's a dynamic and extremely active community of early-stage investors, which feeds into a dramatically larger (in terms of capital) network of venture capitalists (VCs), private equity firms and Big Pharma. Angels invest, companies receive funding and the process of converting a discovery into something of enduring significance begins, all in the face of lousy odds of success. Why? Much of this is driven by the persistent notion that playing the odds is effective—that making enough investments will result in a few wins that are large enough to offset all of the ones that fail. This is certainly true if you look at aggregate published statistics, but as with any average the data are subject to enormous variance as a function of expertise and good fortune: high-profile successes of magnet Angel groups with access to the best deals are exciting, but not projectable to the early investing universe.

Early-stage investing operates on the assumption of a limited "determinable probability distribution" for the outcome. In other words, there is an entire practice of investment built around a presumed constant ratio of positive outcomes to the number of investments made. That ratio rests on a casino mentality that, while sophisticated on its surface, in fact reflects ingrained habit, averages that aren't always relevant to the individual circumstances, and the unfortunate presumption that the particular technology doesn't matter so much as long as you make enough bets. Even "near-misses" are processed as near-successes that invigorate more risk-taking, instead of providing negative reinforcement. Among investors we both know, this is rationalized to the acceptability of "base hits" (modest exits) instead of "home runs," and seen as validation of investors' own ability to pick the best horse. Successful investors presuppose, based on the empirical evidence of their own prior successes, that they are good at personal control and not just lucky—after all, these are financially successful people.

Preserving the Promise. DOI: http://dx.doi.org/10.1016/B978-0-12-809216-3.00017-8

There's also an implicit assumption that investors can influence outcomes through an astute rendering of the future, which essentially involves creating one's own luck. Many investors have made their fortunes working in fields similar to the ones they are investing in, so they enter with a sense of particular expertise not only in the art of the deal, but in applying their experience, analytical skills, and savvy to the particular technology domain they're supporting. They also expect that their personal involvement in the venture, at minimum as an advisor, and if the investment is large enough, perhaps as a board member, will enhance the likelihood of success.

Investors' motives are generally aspirational, in one way or another. The obvious answer to the question of why anyone would make an early-stage investment is the same one SF once got from a former Goldman Sachs executive explaining why they ignored their corporate values for a guy who grew a portfolio 40-fold: for the money. But that's insufficient.

For all of its trappings of rational and carefully orchestrated analysis, early-stage investing is based in no small measure on emotion and risk tolerance, rather than a direct line from calculating odds to realizing outcomes. Angels fully recognize they are dealing with a high-risk activity, and they are doing so with money they can afford to lose.

> *...assume you are going to lose all your money...don't do it unless you are worth at least $1 million or earn at least $200,000 per year...[and] limit the size of your overall bet. (Andy Rachleff, CEO of Wealthfront and faculty at Stanford Graduate School of Business) [1]*

All of the people we know who indulge in this very expensive book club seem to have three motives, loosely connected by a somewhat paradoxical mix of similar, though variously flavored, DNA:

- The first is *intellectual curiosity*, manifested as a desire to be present at the gestation of new ideas.
- The second is the *desire to make something happen*, which drove us all to succeed in the first place, and has now transmogrified into facilitating the process rather than driving it ourselves—an all-consuming process familiar to founders, which almost all of us have already been.
- The third is the *need for the rush*, which is a complicated subject that deals with pain and pleasure centers in the brain and is scientifically explored as reward theory.

The last point revolves around the fundamental question of why, given the low probability of success, anyone would make an early-stage Angel investment. Those in our acquaintance are smart, successful people, few of whom grew up with a silver spoon in their mouth. Rather, most built their instincts into the ability to capitalize on a market opportunity that others couldn't see. They are often socially conscious, yet fulfilling a social mission doesn't fully explain them. Rationally, they know that they are betting on propositions that have a relatively small probability of success, in an environment where there is a high probability that the early guy will be crushed by the later, bigger money. What is the explanation for this expensive, high-risk activity?

Absent a Warren Buffet-like rigor in keeping emotion out of any investment decision, continued participation in the funding circus by people who presumably know better can be explained by findings from neuroscience and social psychology. These are, not incidentally, exactly the same factors that explain why people play all sorts of games of chance.

There's some interesting evidence about "activation" of risk-taking neural circuits and how it applies to investment decisions. Kuhnen and Knutson, for example, used event-related fMRI to examine brain activity in subjects making optimal versus suboptimal choices in financial decision making, on the basis of whether they deviated from a "risk-neutral" strategy. The authors found that brain activity experienced as "excitement" by the subjects preceded making high-risk choices and correlated with activation of the nucleus accumbens (NAcc) and medial prefrontal cortex, important sites in the brain for learning by reinforcement and addiction [2]. This pattern was distinct from activation of another part of the brain, the anterior insula, which occurred when low-risk choices were made. The authors hypothesized that different neural circuits promote high risk or low-risk choices, and that "excessive activation of these circuits may lead to investing mistakes."

In a follow-on behavioral study, these authors studied a group of 75 adults from San Francisco area [3]. They used a series of decision-making games to determine whether their subjects learned more from losses (risk aversion) or gains (loss aversion) and assessed how their measured decision-making preferences correlated with their financial status. They found that "those who learned rapidly about gains had more assets, while those who learned rapidly about losses had less debt." One can infer from this that Angels, typically successful people with a history of favorable higher-stakes economic choices, may be drawn toward high-risk investments—exactly the sort of behavior associated with investing in the Valley of Death (VoD)—as a function of a conditioned neurological response.

These observations emphasize the role of operant conditioning (learned response) on subsequent investment behavior. Wins and near-wins condition investors to greater risk-taking. So does endorsement from presumed investment "thought leaders." There's a very strong human tendency to follow rather than lead as a means of mitigating apparent risk: in social psychology, the concept of diffusion of responsibility works both to diminish individual responsibility for the consequences of one's actions and to encourage pack behavior. It's not difficult to find rooms full of intelligent, sophisticated investors who have been successful entrepreneurs or business people themselves, conditioning their investment decisions on a favorable evaluation (and willingness to invest) by someone else.

It's unlikely that anything we say, or any empirical findings, are going to affect any change in neurocognitive wiring. Nor is there anything intrinsically wrong with Angels supporting any technology they desire. But when the product of the entire research enterprise needs to pass through a filter of Angel due diligence, it's important to look at the mechanism we use to adjust for unreasonable risk. Like watching a casino gambler peel off hundred-dollar bills at the craps table, it is painful to see investors incurring unnecessary losses as money flows to companies that have no chance of survival.

There's a reason Angels are called Angels. They mind the first tollgate for the "gates of heaven" to which founders aspire. As the burden of early-stage funding migrates even further to the arms of Angels, they would perhaps do better to stop emulating a traditional VC investment model and explicitly recognize the more complicated rewards structure that drives them. Angels are, after all, complicated, and driven by a wide range of motives. But rationalization of purpose demands that investors calculate time and planning horizons in a framework of milestones that necessarily ignore huge and unpredictable external forces. Otherwise, who in their right mind would ever invest in a company, or create a start-up that has no hope of generating any revenue for a minimum of 7–10 years, especially when they hope to achieve a return on investment in less than half that time?

It's worth taking a moment to look at some of the intangibles that influence Angels. The first of these is social networks and local ecosystems. Angels tend to invest locally, and the existence of a direct social relationship with an entrepreneur, or with someone who is willing to vouch for the entrepreneur, helps allay uncertainty. Formal or informal social connections may encourage both investors and entrepreneurs to engage in a more collaborative way, perhaps to behave in a more equitable fashion, while providing both parties with better insight regarding each other's capabilities and limitations. A study of investing trends among Silicon Valley and Boston Angel groups showed that direct personal relationships strongly facilitated investments, although these effects were less important for entrepreneurs who had a reputation for building successful companies (and therefore built-in credibility) [4].

The next intangible is the influence of nonverbal cues. It's clear when observing any pitch session that investors are highly attuned to the impression created by the presenter. Body language, inflection, and projection of confidence are basics of communication theory, but it's not always clear to founders what they are conveying, or failing to convey, through their use of verbal and nonverbal language in a fundraising context. Angels who rate high on the scale for social perceptiveness and extraversion are more likely to respond favorably to founders' overt enthusiasm and apparent emotional commitment to the enterprise. Those with a more analytical cognitive style may be attuned to how rigorously entrepreneurs have supported their technological case or how well they have prepared their presentations [5].

Companies must strike the right balance: expressing enthusiasm without overstating the stage of development, promoting innovation without exceeding credibility, and practically contextualizing alternative technologies without ignoring the seriousness of competitive development efforts [6]. You'll hear the term "secret sauce" bandied about if you spend any time in the fundraising world, and while it refers to unique competitive advantage, it's not a bad metaphor for the balance that needs to be achieved in a pitch: just the right amount of Sriracha, neither too mild to generate interest nor too hot for investors' palates. Everyone *says* they want the hot sauce, but too little innovation will fall flat, and too extreme a departure from current practice can be equally detrimental. A company without significant innovation is unlikely to receive funding, but a company that overemphasizes its innovative stance may appear too radical for investment. Self-awareness is desirable, yet treads a fine line with self-deprecation that conveys a lack of confidence. Realistic assessment of gaps in capability or resources, or of challenging market conditions, conveys comprehension and honesty, but excessive focus on potential barriers increases perceived risk. Passion and persistence are prerequisites, but they need to match the temperament of the audience and overtly reflect a willingness to accept input.

Everyone brings their own armamentarium to a fight. For investors and inventors, these include shared beliefs about the intrinsic value of healthcare innovation and independent attitudes about the best way to get there from here. In the context of evaluating an opportunity, it includes perspectives both rational and irrational, bound only by the mutual desire to reduce relative risk. So each party seeks to answer the questions that their past experience has shown to be the most important, the most predictive of a positive outcome, and most consistent with their interests and personality styles. We speak of scientists and Angels as though they are archetypes, but of course neither is homogeneous; each approaches the investment thesis in his/her own way.

Because no one is an expert in every domain, the diversity of technologies and opportunities that start-ups represent lead to necessary short-cuts and inductive leaps in reasoning, with a heavy emphasis on instinct and personal connection. There needs to be a plausible scientific plan, a good management team, motivation and energy—and the absence of any fatal flaws that could derail the investment. Because what really matters, in the face of biotech's inherently long development timeline, is the ability to agree on a valuation that guarantees a forward path. Since valuation is a negotiated number, this house of optimism also depends on everybody drinking the same valuation Kool-Aid. That valuation, which must over the course of development stay ahead of the money that has already been invested, is the intersection of all of these elements—scientific plan, management acumen, and ability to solve potentially fatal flaws—into a comparative risk profile that favors one investment over another.

This algorithm for selecting which technologies will have a chance at commercialization in the VoD is the core of the second Translation Gap: *Good innovation is not always a good investment.* Most of what our academic institutions produce will not be commercialized because we do not have endless resources. Even if the ecosystem could support everything that is truly innovative, there are so many variables at work that most new ventures would still fail. To invest in the face of these dreadful prospects, if they have any hope of achieving a satisfactory return Angels need to select inventions that best fit their investment paradigm. The process of information sharing that is due diligence needs to connect the dots between innovation and investment.

Inventions that are so innovative, so distant from familiar archetypes that they cannot be explained to investors, won't have a chance for investment (we described such a situation earlier with bortezomib). Nor will discoveries that cannot be neatly molded into a milestone-based investment thesis. Technologies that are championed by entrepreneurs and inventors inexpert at managing the challenges of communication and commercialization in the VoD will likewise go unsupported.

The VoD, as a market for financial instruments rather than technology, is plagued by a focus on deal terms and lack of iterative learning. Most inventors and entrepreneurs can start only a small number of companies in their lifetimes. The timelines for each one may extend to 10 years or more. The reasons for failure are so diverse that they may have little to do with the quality of the team or the transformative potential of their technology. But if they do, how will anyone know? When someone who has been there before jumps back in to the VoD, is it reasonable to think they have learned enough from prior experience to significantly reduce the odds of failure?

The VoD ecosystem is deeply affected by macroeconomic and regulatory forces that have nothing to do with the quality of its technology but bear heavily on the risk proposition of the financial instruments it trades. Will the lessons learned in 2015, in the midst of a biotech IPO surge, be applicable in 2016 if the disasters of Valeant, Tetraphase, and Cara close the initial public offering (IPO) opportunity? Even so, is it meaningful, or even measurable, if the odds of failure improve from 95% to 85%? What makes it even more challenging is that the system operates in an information vacuum because most of the early investment activity is private and therefore unpublished.

Incentives driving the parties involved in investment and commercialization are not aligned. This is partly because technologies coming out of universities are too early to enable effective scientific due diligence. We addressed some of this problem in the first Translation Gap: *Universities do not make what industry needs*. But the lack of alignment also occurs because low risk, base-hit projects are better investments, in a probability model, than swinging for the seats. The primary way for an Angel to make money in the VoD is by attracting subsequent investors and ultimately an acquirer. Angels shy away, in fact, from companies that want to commercialize their technologies themselves rather than finding and/or exiting to a commercialization partner.

So this is how we select the discoveries that will have a chance at commercialization: Angel investors looking at innovation in terms of whether it can support an investment thesis, which they want to buy into and get out from under early. In this context, biotech isn't on the priority list of investments, since it demands a continuous series of debt transactions, collateralized by a high-risk scientific proposition and with a development timeline that may extend for 10 years or more. Our overconfidence in the free market dynamics in the VoD and the pharmaceutical marketplace has led us to passively accept this model as a filter for what deserves to be supported, for what will even have a chance to help patients.

REFERENCES

[1] Rachleff A. Why Angel investors don't make money…and advice for people who are going to become angels anyway. TechCrunch; 2012. published September 30, 2012. <http://techcrunch.com/2012/09/30/why-angel-investors-dont-make-money-and-advice-for-people-who-are-going-to-become-angels-anyway/>; [accessed 26.02.16].

[2] Kuhnen CM, Knutson B. The neural basis of financial risk taking. Neuron 2005;47:763–70. http://dx.doi.org/10.1016/j.neuron.2005.08.008.

[3] Knutson B, Samanez-Larkin GR, Kuhnen CM. Gain and loss learning differentially contribute to life financial outcomes. PLoS ONE 2011;6(9):e24390. http://dx.doi.org/10.1371/journal.pone.0024390.

[4] Shane S, Cable D. Network ties, reputation, and the financing of new ventures. Manage Sci 2002;48(3):364–81.

[5] Mitteness CR, Cardon MS, Sudek R. The importance angels place on passion when making investment decisions: why does it matter to some and not all angels? Front Entrepreneurship Res 2010;30(2):2. <http://digitalknowledge.babson.edu/fer/vol30/iss2/2/>.

[6] Parhankangas A, Ehrlich M. How entrepreneurs seduce business angels: an impression management approach. J Bus Venturing 2014;29(4):543–64.

Chapter 18

Ready for a Long-Term Relationship With a Science Experiment?

Once the wedding and honeymoon are over, and an investment in a company has been made, the relationship of an investor to the company moves to a different level. They have acquired interest in a financial instrument that has uncertain prospects and limited liquidity for an indefinite period of time. In the Valley of Death (VoD), this could be for more than a few years.

Until the point of execution, investors occupy the comfortable position of almost total leverage; due to enormous buyer power in the VoD, prospective investors can always walk away and pursue the next opportunity. After the investment, they are joined at the financial hip to an entity that is no longer actively seeking their approbation, but instead has turned its attention to meeting requirements for the next round of funding, foremost among which is keeping its valuation ahead of the amount already invested. This is a relationship, for both parties, which has no easy exit.

Not all due diligence questions can be answered realistically by a new company, and given the ambiguities surrounding an early-stage venture, it's inevitable that some answers will be accepted as reasonable rather than definitive. Remember that the objective of due diligence is to expose fatal flaws, not only in the plan but in the founder's thinking. Oddly, due diligence is more rigorous, and an investment more easily derailed, when the start-up is further along because it's easier to find specific flaws in a more developed business. So it's neither inconceivable nor infrequent that issues which *could* prove fatal are deferred on faith in the fundamentals of the opportunity: uncertainties about IP, the competitive landscape, and of course the actual versus hoped-for performance for the new technology.

Less attractive answers to these questions may emerge between this investment and the next round. Circumstances change; individual investors have different priorities and perspectives, and each fundraise will be different in both expectation and due diligence process. For example, one of the "star" presenters at a conference one of the authors attended was selling an entirely different proposition than in his last fundraising round. This wasn't in itself objectionable, but the founder had to turn down an offer of $150,000 because the new

Preserving the Promise. DOI: http://dx.doi.org/10.1016/B978-0-12-809216-3.00018-X

investor demanded a reduced valuation. The previous valuation may have been unrealistically high, but this nevertheless would expose prior investors to something called a down round, explicitly reducing the value of their investment.

The same conference showcased some terrific, and some positively awful presenters. Some completely failed to articulate such basic business plan elements as their value proposition or even what it was they were proposing to develop, and most, including some of the good ones, failed to realistically quantify their target audience. Such omissions don't eliminate the possibility of getting funding—we saw two companies get on-the-spot commitments from some pretty sophisticated investors, of $200,000 and $350,000, respectively, despite a lack of precision around their target markets. But it does reveal the mercurial aspect of funding, in this case the indirect influence of a shark-tank setup and an audience of 800 investors.

So getting money from one set of investors does carry a certain pheromonal quality, but it doesn't mean the company will seduce anyone in the next round. We would be more likely to recommend presenting a well-drawn Guy Kawasaki deck [1] than an overblown business plan, for the simple reason that too much precision very early on is both unreliable and possibly restrictive. Yet we can't help noting the number of start-ups that have failed to exercise the discipline required to formulate a credible investment thesis. Any written business plan will of course evolve as the market changes, the science progresses, and the company moves forward. But given the almost endless number of challenges that start-ups need to overcome, the absence of rigorous thinking and contingency planning is likely to prove fatal, even if the first investor has fallen hopelessly in love.

Assuming that due diligence reaches a satisfactory denouement, the newly joined partners have a mutual interest in success, which is neither the same thing for both of them, nor the same thing as having aligned interests (beyond a positive financial outcome). This morning SF spoke with a young CEO on her second start-up. The first one was a moderately successful and fairly quick exit, but one that occurred only because she vigorously fought for taking the company in a direction other than the one the investors wanted. Financial success doesn't necessarily mean alignment on technologic or clinical goals, but rather the successful positioning of the company to bring in more money with a valuation that stays ahead of the amount already in.

The excitement of the scientific founder at being able to further advance the research becomes secondary to performing experiments that will support the investment thesis. An Angel investment is not an R01[1] grant, the objective of which revolves around the broader societal mission of the National Institutes of Health (NIH). There may be a conflict between innovation and financial

---

1. "The Research Project Grant (R01) is the original and historically oldest grant mechanism used by NIH. The R01 provides support for health-related research and development based on the mission of the NIH" [2].

objectives, as the value of the company rests on executing the research plan, even if the budget and timeline demand a detour from the founder's original intent. How much money is available for research that optimizes the long-term value of the invention, compared to how much should be spent on milestone-focused research that supports the next round of fundraising? It is very easy for opportunistic money to become the enemy of scientific or clinical objectives.

DUE DILIGENCE VERSUS DE-RISKING

For an Angel or other early-stage investor the underlying question is always, "What do I get for my money?" and the follow-up question is just as inevitably, "What are the terms of the deal?" There is a fundamental divergence between founders, who undertake the intrinsic risk of progressing an invention, and investors, who take a financial risk associated with supporting that technology. The technological development risk rests on inventors' confidence in the merit of the science, the financial risk on investors' confidence that they can determine which investments will yield the best return. Yet the paradigm for investors is maintaining a 10:1 or better ratio of investments to expected successes, which if you think about it fundamentally undermines the premise that they're really good at making the right "picks." For the founder/inventor, it's all or nothing—they're generally not involved in multiple ventures at once, hoping to rely on probabilities to generate success.

Even though they have confidence in the companies in which they invest, Angels choose to participate in a process that incurs a high failure rate, can ruin even the best companies in the VoD, and depends upon imperfect and asymmetric information. The decision whether to invest may be driven by due diligence, but the decision about how much to invest, and on what terms, is driven by a different set of criteria. In simple terms, having made the decision that an investment might be a good idea, investors try to minimize the risk of that investment by reducing their potential losses if the venture runs into financial difficulty, while maximizing their gains in the event of success.

This is codified, as with any irrationally hopeful behavior, into a model that suggests it is possible to enhance personal control in the face of daunting odds by apparently improving those odds. This is what actors in the VoD call de-risking, which is just an investor's tool for *shifting rather than eliminating* the burden of risk. This process should not be confused with due diligence—although the two are often conflated.

De-risking is often described in the context of waiting until later in the process, when achievement of additional milestones, e.g., proof-of-concept, safety, or toxicity studies, have reduced the apparent risk of failure. Applied to the terms of a VoD investment, however, de-risking may include following rather than leading a round so that the risk is underwritten by a larger, lead investor; leveraging foundation or government grants that are not dilutive of equity; engineering deal terms to preserve their priority of repayment if the company runs into trouble and to limit exposure in a down round; or enabling the exercise of a conversion preference at the next round of funding. Savvy investors taking substantial equity will also try to preemptively maintain control and retain influence on future fund raises. These details are first laid out in a "term sheet," an elaborate scaffold of legalese that is the opening move in obtaining control over the enterprise.

The language of deals—convertible debt, discounts, warrants, valuation caps, liquidation preferences, restructuring, pro-rata rights, and so forth—is sufficiently opaque that it requires financial expertise to navigate and legal counsel to execute. Inventor/founders, typically inexperienced at such transactions, are explicitly disadvantaged in the process. We won't describe here how to construct a term sheet, but we want to examine the philosophy and dynamic created by the process. The term sheet is most often developed by the prospective investors, and the deal terms are adjusted so that the risk of being an early investor is rewarded—typically by discounts or warrants that improve future returns. This is done in part to mitigate the expected dilution from subsequent funding rounds, since reduction in the value of early investors' stake is a key mechanism by which later-stage investors optimize their return.

We recently sat in on a fundraising round that explicitly demonstrated this problem. An Angel group was negotiating terms of a prospective investment. Because there was already money in the company in the form of a debt instrument called convertible notes, which enable investors to convert their holdings to equity at a discount, the new investors sought additional protection of their position. Instead of accepting that there's only so much one can do to assess the probability a given company will succeed, they wanted to dictate contract terms that: (1) put them in a higher priority position to get paid back at a subsequent financing round, acquisition or dissolution and (2) prevent their shares from being diluted. This isn't wrong, it's simply the investors' idea of mitigating risk. But of course it has nothing to do with mitigating risk at a macro level, it just means they have repayment priority if things go badly. And the subtext is a lack of confidence in the investment.

For a scientific founder of a company, taking money from an investor feels very different from an NIH or foundation grant to their academic laboratory. Founders are often surprised to find themselves working for their investors, as the locus of control follows the money. Founders see Angels as partners, but the fundamental transaction is that the Angel is buying a part of the scientist's past and future intellectual efforts. From the beginning, the seat of power in the relationship is evident. Founders' shares are typically designated "common shares," with no special protections, whereas shares purchased upon conversion are "preferred shares," with valuable liquidation preferences that are exercised at the founder's expense. This aspect of de-risking enhances the prospective value of an investment *by transferring value from the founder to the investors.* The primary counter to this is, frankly, the desire to maintain goodwill between the parties, and the very practical impetus to not alienate scientific founders while they are still critical to the process. This diminishes as the financial and operations management, and control over follow-on investment rounds, supersede the preeminence of the original discovery as a driver of development.

Terms that favor later investors dilute more than the pocketbook of the people who created the technology, or the Angels who financed the early stages of development. They impose financial burdens on the company that require the technology to advance rapidly in order to support the investment thesis. If the founders were under any misapprehension about the dominance of buyer power in the VoD, the term sheet and the funding agreement that follows—over which all but a few superstar start-ups have very little influence—make the relationship perfectly clear. The price of money is autonomy.[2] Everybody is working for the investors now, despite disavowals from investors that they don't so much want to take control of a company as "support it" so that it can "succeed."

It should be obvious that no compilation of terms, no matter how unilaterally favorable toward the investor's interests, can intrinsically take the risk out of a high-risk activity like early-stage investing. There's simply enormous uncertainty intrinsic to scientific progress, and in the VoD it is combined with financing risk, regulatory risk, market risk, and other factors. Even at late stage, superstar-driven companies like Verastem, with an apparently "de-risked" cancer drug (defactinib) that looked good in Phase II testing, can implode near the finish line if clinical trial results are disappointing [3].

De-risking drives an increase in company valuation, on the questionable premise that achievement of milestones reduces the likelihood that the venture will fail. More accurately, what it does is *reduce the number of ways* in which the venture might fail. This has superficial legitimacy. It makes sense of course to reduce risk, but the reality is that de-risking, as it is commonly applied, is just an investment tool for shifting the timing and burden of risk to a different stakeholder. De-risking is like putting up guardrails or getting insurance on a race car, so that the people whose money is on the line reduce their financial risk … but the driver can still crash and burn, even on the last lap. When FierceBiotech editor John Carroll reflected on the collapse of Celladon ($CLDN), upon failure of their clinical trial for a gene therapy in heart disease, he wrote "When a lead drug at a biotech goes under, it can be an extinction-level event" [4].

FINANCING THE BIOTECHNOLOGY START-UP

For the past decade or so, it has been common practice to structure seed-stage biotechnology investments as convertible debt. Convertible debt is one of the most common financial instruments traded in the VoD, across a broad range of technologies. The company borrows money, at a set rate of interest, which

---

2. For example, if a new company were valued at $1 million, a raise of $500 K would require that founders turn over half of their company, depending on the stage and cost of development, a few months' to a year's operating expenses.

converts into stock at the time, valuation and associated share price of a specific funding event. This might, for example, be at the time of a Series A Venture Capital investment. Most convertible debt also includes a discount, so that the money already in can be converted to shares at a lower price than the new investors are paying. For example, assume that a company raises $500K in convertible debt with 8% interest and a 25% discount. After a year, a VC (venture capital) fund invests $2 million on a valuation of $4 million, setting a share price of $1. The original Angel investor would receive 720K shares, purchased at a price of $0.75 each and a total cost (including interest) of $540K. This is 180 more shares than he would have received if he had invested at the same time as the VC. The discount on conversion compensates for the increased earlier stage risk by offsetting the dilution that will naturally occur when the valuation increases at the next round.

One of the advantages of convertible debt is that it provides an alternative to pricing a round, since the valuation of a company just starting out is pretty much a negotiated guess. Founders will overestimate the value of their companies to protect their equity. Investors will tend to underestimate its value to maximize their shares for a given level of investment and protect themselves from a future down round, although the smartest investors we know urge an effective balance, and may actually push conservative founders to think higher. Nonetheless, as entrepreneur-turned-VC Mark Suster blogged, "There is no rational explanation for valuations of A round companies by ANY objective financial measure. It's simply what a market is willing to pay based on a future belief that your company will grow [at] a non-linear rate and be worth much more in the future" [5].

Convertible debt also gets around the "friends and family" problem, in which nonprofessional investors put money into a company at an artificially high valuation, only to see themselves taking a "haircut"—investor-speak for the loss of investment value in a down round—when the next round is more appropriately priced.

The shares sought by investors upon conversion of debt into equity are *preferred* shares, meaning they carry liquidation preferences that give their holders priority over founder's shares and common stock held by other investors. Convertible debt incentivizes entrepreneurs to focus on increasing valuation so that, when the debt is converted into shares, they are able to retain a meaningful share of the company.

This sounds pretty good for both investors and inventors, right? Well, not necessarily. We'll discuss some of the potential problems later, but some key considerations around convertible debt include:

1. Convertible debt is often seen as a comfortable "middle ground" for entrepreneurs between debt financing and equity financing. But it's really no different from a loan on terms that are largely favorable to the lender, including loan repayment on a fixed schedule and interest well beyond typical lending rates (because the collateral may turn out to be worthless). Of course, if

everything goes well, it would seem a better deal than the loss of control associated with the sale of stock.

2. Convertible debt is usually set to convert at a subsequent financing event, but can be triggered by a revenue threshold, a financing threshold, or another business milestone. These are all speculative at the time of issue. If the conversion event doesn't occur, the initial investment remains in the air and is subject to discretionary conversion, which is unlikely to serve the founder's interests.

3. The conversion discount or bonus requires financing background and finesse, and therefore favors the experienced investor. Too low a discount will be a barrier for early investors; too high a discount, without a cap, or too much time elapsed before the next round, will decrease the valuation.

4. Investors like convertible debt because they (hopefully) get a good deal early, they don't have to haggle with the entrepreneur much about terms, as they would in a priced round, and if they have pro-rata rights they get to piggy-back on a VC or other lead investor setting the terms later (typically for Series A preferred stock). In addition, the convertible debt investors obtain a discount to the Series A price, since they invested their money earlier, when the company was a higher-risk proposition.

5. Some convertible debt terms grant investors liquidation preferences that may enable them to achieve a disproportionate return if the company achieves an exit that exceeds expectations [6]. We'll cover this in more detail later in this chapter, but the upshot is that a big Series A round can give note holders a much higher multiple of return than they actually paid for, on the sale of the company, at the founder's expense [6].

BUYING AND SELLING IN THE VoD

Convertible debt has become an extremely common form of seed-stage financing, but it is by no means the only one. Angels and entrepreneurs alike may prefer an equity investment, in which they agree on a share price and transact a portion of the company outright as equity for money. Whether by convertible note, some other form of debt, or equity financing, investors "buy" financial instruments in the VoD in order to ultimately "sell" them—preferably at a substantial multiple, with the probability and size of sale a function of the company's scientific and business progress. So, apart from a credible technology and management team, investability depends on the potential to increase the value of the assets that are used as collateral for the investment.

Angel investors rarely take early-stage healthcare companies all the way to commercialization. Their objective is to maintain or increase their interest, through a series of subsequent investment transactions, but only until an exit to an institutional investor or strategic partner at an attractive multiple. Think of it this way, using a real estate analogy: mortgage originators are not investing for the payoff of the mortgage by the borrower, but to transfer the obligation as a financial instrument to institutional investors. The ability to achieve the desired return is dependent upon the ability to attract the next investor or partner, and thereby transfer ownership of the financial instrument at an attractive multiple of the original investment.

As no early-stage investor can reliably guess the timing and size of return at some unspecified future date, what everyone really is betting on is whether the company will be able to raise money to keep operating until it reaches the exit. This doesn't look binary, since there are multiple transactions along the way—seed rounds, Series A, B, C, and so forth—but at some point it is. The alternative to successfully achieving the next capital raise is that the company runs out of money and goes out of business. This is the essence of de-risking: increasing the probability that a continuous stream of money can be raised until the investors can cash out. Will others help support the venture until an exit can occur? Will someone down the road have the interest to buy out the original investors? Notably absent is the question of whether the new drug actually reaches the clinic.

So what happens as the company wends its way through the VoD? Accumulation of debt and parceling off the company in equity pieces to investors. In the prerevenue years, companies incur financial obligations to investors to keep operations going. At the same time, the interests of the companies become subverted to the needs of an investment strategy based on the *transfer of these financial obligations*. While any service or sales revenue the company can generate along the way is a valuation enhancer, the investment strategy is not necessarily connected to the generation of revenue. Everybody who has money in eventually wants to get out at some optimal point, where the ratio of valuation to money in is at its maximum achievable multiple. Even the most novel and transformative technologies are morphed into chits in this high-risk game. This is the essence of *exit-based investing*.

The majority of exits in exit-based investing involve convincing someone else to assume financial interests in a company, preferably at a greater price than was originally paid for them. In the VoD for biotech, buyers may be VCs increasing the ante with substantial funding, investment groups (e.g., private equity), or Big Pharma, which have access to the tens or hundreds of millions of dollars required to take a drug through clinical testing. Fundamental to this process is that the companies must sustain a continued increase in their valuation with every investment round, so that they are eligible for increasingly larger investments (and ultimately acquisition). Use of proceeds is always a key element of any funding pitch, but tends to ignore the fact that, while much of it is used for development and operations, a substantial portion supports the time entrepreneurs need to spend on ongoing business development—which in this context means generating the next round of investment.

Both the revenue-driven market for the products pharmaceutical companies provide and the VoD are driven by the pursuit of return on investment, but in the clinical market revenue is generated by the purchase of drugs or devices and is "paid back" to investors through dividends and stock appreciation. In the VoD, the product is the investment proposition and the operating income is provided by investors with the expectation of a payout through a liquidity event. Because clinical medicine is the product in pharma, the amount of money that is spent on drugs by patients, insurers and providers corresponds roughly to its value to those constituencies (although this is being increasingly unbalanced by extreme pricing for biologics and other specialty/orphan drugs).

In contrast, the VoD market is one in which promises are exchanged for what are essentially very high interest loans. The collateral for these loans are the companies themselves, based on their estimated valuation—which is determined by how much investors are willing to pay vs. what they think the technology ought to be worth. Most companies in the VoD are prerevenue, or at least deriving most of their operating income from investments, and they do not compete for product customers but rather for investors who will front them loans.

It is poorly understood, as the media tout the next big scientific breakthrough, that the clinical marketplace for drugs is only tenuously connected to, and at the terminal end of, the process of biotechnology innovation. This wasn't always the case, as Big Pharma was historically the primary driver of discovery, but the migration of its business model from investing in discovery to buying the product of other people's discovery has changed the paradigm. The VoD exists in parallel to the clinical market, and does advance drugs forward, but as a discovery and development resource it is dependent on investment transactions rather than drug sales.

If you step back, the "normal" of investment appears even more circular considering that VCs and other sources of the "big" money ultimately required for crossing and enabling an exit from the VoD are spending someone else's money, that they in turn have borrowed on the promise of an investment return. This is distinct from the money that is transacted at an exit to Big Pharma, but which is also ultimately an investment of pharma shareholder money—just in external rather than internal drug discovery. From start to finish, the VoD is primarily a competitive marketplace for borrowing money.

THE PERILS OF CONVERTIBLE DEBT

We have alluded to the fact that convertible debt can potentially be harmful to a company. To understand the problem, we need to look more closely at how the protective provisions and advantages an investor demands can spin out of control, to the detriment of the company, founders and investors. Discounts provide an incentive for investors to support a company in its embryonic stages. This is not a problem unless and until, as often happens, there is an unanticipated delay in reaching milestones, which extends the timeline for obtaining a Series A round and causes a shortfall in operating income. As the company's coffers empty, additional funds are required. Angels may elect to "pay to play" (a forced choice between putting more money in or losing the value of their prior investment), if their confidence in the science and the management team is sufficiently intact. At the same time, most seed-stage companies are continuously seeking new Angel investors, and new investors may be coming in at this time. But on what terms, and with what impact on the earlier players?

A 20% discount may give way to a 25% discount. Shares may be diluted by a decline in valuation. Discounts and preferences may need to be extended for new investors. Bridge financing is likely to carry a heavy interest burden. The numbers of VC-based exits and Pharma partnerships are proportionately few, since there are lots of VoD companies with compelling scientific stories, reasonably good management, and comprehensible value propositions. So it is not inconceivable that Angels may be invested in even an outstanding VoD company over 5 or more years with multiple rounds of financing. As the amount of debt increases, and each borrowed dollar accumulates compounded interest, the sum of money eligible for discounts balloons and the valuation has an increasingly difficult time staying ahead of the level of investment. A potential Series A investor may find that, for any reasonable estimate of valuation, a company owes its Angels more than the company is actually worth.

We recently met an old colleague who had taken over the reins of a biotech company working in the infectious disease area and supported by a single Angel. The company had just completed a management overhaul after spending $24 million yet failing to achieve the golden "one year to an IND" stage. A back-of-the-envelope calculation suggests that their company has spent more than six times their net valuation, and with an annual burn of over $5 million annually, will likely continue to spend more every year than its market valuation. There is no way this company will be able to move forward without someone, most likely the early investors, "writing off" the accumulated debt in a down round.

Companies are in a similar position when convertible debt notes expire, either at a fixed point in time or attendant on a qualified financing event. Artificial maturity dates on financial instruments may demand restructuring at arbitrary points in time, that may not relate to a particular technical milestone or increase in valuation. Nevertheless, the company is required to renegotiate its debt and in the worst case, may have to repay other investors who have preferred shares from the proceeds of the next round. Once again, the company has virtually no leverage to counterbalance the buyer power of the investors, who may again demand additional consideration for their risk. A company without money in the bank, pushing up against IP deadlines, and behind on technical or fundraising milestones is a prime target for a down round—if additional funds can be raised at all. And granting additional consideration to investors almost inevitably means transferring value from the founders.

A common feature of convertible debt, with the potential to decimate a founder's holdings even in the event that a company is successful, is a liquidation preference. Debt is converted into "preferred stock," which can have whatever privileges the parties negotiate, and have priority over the "common stock" held by the company's founders. A liquidation preference means that, when the company is eventually sold, the holders of preferred stock will receive their investment dollars back first, and only then will the rest of the proceeds be distributed among other shareholders.

Angel investments can contain a valuation cap. The valuation cap sets an upper limit for the valuation of the company at which Angel investments can be converted to stock in a Series A round, which may be the first time a share price is set for the company. This preserves Angels' proportional ownership in the company if the Series A investment comes in at a much higher valuation than was expected, but it can have disproportionate effects on the founders' compensation in a liquidity event, especially if the company's valuation at the Series A round is significantly higher than the cap [7]. For example, if Angel investors have notes based on a valuation cap of $2.5 million, and a Series A round is based on a pre-money valuation of $10 million, the Angel shares will still convert as though the Series A was based on the $2.5 million number—so the Angels are essentially buying shares at one-quarter of the price paid by the new Series A investors. Upon a buyout of the company, they will receive a liquidation preference based on the share price set at the $10 million valuation, which is 4× (four times) the price at which their shares converted and far more than they originally invested. All of this money would be siphoned from the pockets of common stock holders, including the founders. A simple contractual fix that limits the liquidation preference on convertible debt can prevent this complication [6].

All of these potential pitfalls derive from the fact that investors continue to exert their buyer power over a company after they have invested, especially if the company will need them to invest more. This leverage continues to flow not to the company, but to those with the deepest pockets who ultimately control the deal terms. Entrepreneurs and founders, sometimes naïve to the vagaries of financing, are ripe for a ride down the apparently attractive path of convertible note financing. Convertible notes are not necessarily all vanilla flavored, and even well-intentioned Angels may contribute to a latticework of debt obligations that can hurt both founders and investors in the end. The structural features of the financing and its reimbursement obligations conjoin with extended timelines to disenfranchise founders, burden the company with debt that can swamp the true value of the company, and even in some cases make a Series A financially unworkable. At their most extreme, badly designed terms can leave Angels without a potential exit unless they agree to give up previously negotiated privileges and discounts. When the old money runs out, the new money gets to make the rules.

Maybe this would all be theoretical if the risk of failing to meet scientific and fundraising objectives were not so high. But bumps in the road, unexpected crashes, and/or changes in course are inevitable for every company in the VoD. The costs of accommodating these challenges are amplified because convertible debt is enormously expensive money for any company carrying the risk proposition of participants in the VoD.

REFERENCES

[1] Kawasaki G. The only 10 slides you need in a pitch. <http://guykawasaki.com/the-only-10-slides-you-need-in-your-pitch/>; 2015 [accessed 26.02.16].

[2] National Institutes of Health. NIH research project grant program (R01), Updated December 15, 2015. <http://grants.nih.gov/grants/funding/r01.htm>; 2015.

[3] Weisman R. Verastem shares plunge as drug trial fails: cancer therapy's results spur a 67% loss in stock's value. Boston Globe 2015 September 28, 2015. <https://www.bostonglobe.com/business/2015/09/28/verastem-shares-plunge-after-company-halts-cancer-drug-trial/trHend-PQ0ewSqLm2pixltJ/story.html/>.

[4] Carroll J. The top 10 biopharma pipeline disasters of 2015: Mydicar–Celladon. FierceBiotech. 2015 October 29, 2015. <http://www.fiercebiotech.com/special-reports/top-10-biopharma-pipeline-disasters-2015/>.

[5] Suster M. Bad notes on venture capital. Posted September 17, 2014. <http://www.bothsidesofthetable.com/2014/09/17/bad-notes-on-venture-capital/>; 2014 [accessed 27.02.16].

[6] Suster M. One simple paragraph every entrepreneur should add to their convertible notes. Posted May 30, 2015. <http://www.bothsidesofthetable.com/2015/05/30/one-simple-paragraph-every-entrepreneur-should-add-to-their-convertible-notes/>; 2014 [accessed 27.02.16].

[7] Ancer J. The problem in everyone's capped convertible notes. Posted April 29, 2015. <http://siliconhillslawyer.com/2015/04/29/capped-convertible-notes-liquidation-overhang/>; 2015 [accessed 27.02.16].

Chapter 19

Investing in Hockey Sticks

THE HOCKEY STICK—A MATTER OF INFLECTION

The fuel that supports the high-stakes wrestling match between Angels and founders, the reason why they are willing to burden themselves, their companies, and the technologies they support with so much debt, is the hope of a spectacular exit. Angels' financial hopes for their investments in the healthcare Valley of Death (VoD) are subject to the irreducible fact of scale: their investment can move a technology in the right direction but will never be enough to get a new drug to the clinic. The factors underlying their investment interest are the terms of the deal, the number of fundraises required for clinical approval, and the "hockey stick" revenue projection that drives valuation.

Hockey sticks have a long handle that turns abruptly upward into a steep angle. In a hockey stick graph, the number of customers acquired, units sold, or dollar revenues are plotted over time (see Fig. 19.1). In the VoD, the *promise* of a hockey stick supports the investment thesis by projecting the ultimate commercial potential of the technology—which is distinct from but ultimately correlated with the return an early stage investor obtains on his investment. Two things change over time: perceived risk, which is mediated by progress on scientific and clinical milestones, and perceived valuation, which is driven by (1) de-risking and (2) the clarity imposed on financial projections by performance in clinical testing. By clarity, we mean the size and inferred impact on the patient population of the developmental compound.

The negotiated valuation of the company increases relatively slowly as the company establishes itself and its IP portfolio, and then more rapidly as the company progresses through clinical development and builds strategic collaborations. The hockey stick attached to most fundraising pitches, on the other hand, almost always includes an abrupt change in slope that assumes a geometric rather than incremental increase in revenue, quickly following launch. It's the promise that makes multiples of 5×, 10× or even 20× seem achievable, and sometimes achieved. We can point to examples. Sovaldi (sofosbuvir, Gilead) for Hepatitis C saw first year sales of $10.3 billion, the perfect hockey stick [1].

Preserving the Promise. DOI: http://dx.doi.org/10.1016/B978-0-12-809216-3.00019-1

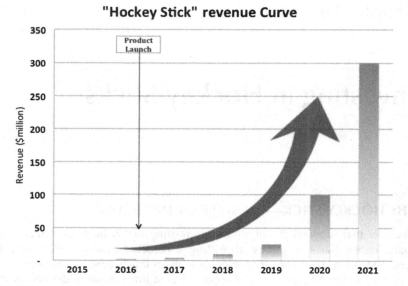

FIGURE 19.1   Hockey stick value curve.

Impressive as that is, it is a rare occurrence relative to the number of biotech compounds under development.

Yet most pitches, whether for biotech, small molecules, devices or diagnostics, make conceptually similar projections to buttress the investment proposition. The corollary point in development that prompts an exponential shift in valuation is the ultimate de-risking event: Food and Drug Administration (FDA) approvable status or approval.

Anyone who is involved in this space sees a lot of business plans that surge and project hundreds of millions of dollars, or more, within a few years on the market. However, the "home run" market opportunity for a given new technology is only occasionally realized, and most early stage investors are skeptical even if excited about this type of projection. What this is, in the early stages, is implicitly and mutually understood hyperbole, a biomarker of "investability."

Prospective deals need to look like they have the potential to become a hockey stick so that they can attract initial investment, and so that they (actually, the VoD financial instrument they represent) can be acquired or transferred at a significant premium to the amount already invested. If a prospective drug doesn't work well enough, or isn't useful for a sufficiently large population at a price point the market will tolerate (if not be happy about), it won't be able to attract the investment needed for clinical testing. If it cannot undergo clinical testing, then Angels' investment in preclinical work will never be paid back. It's not that anyone can reliably calculate market adoption at an early stage. But the hypothetical uptick does need to be dramatic enough to rationalize an investment that *a priori* has a 90% or greater chance of failing entirely.

It's clear why founders and investors want to buy into the hockey stick premise. The notion of a revenue curve making its abrupt upward transition buttresses the concept of a milestone-driven inflection point that is accompanied by a dramatic increase in valuation. In essence, it's the ultimate proof of concept: Not only does the technology work, but here's why people will want to buy it. Associating valuation with significant revenue potential reinforces scalability and enables sale of the technology or company; but it's also useful prospectively because earlier stage investors want—no, make that *need*—to believe in the ability of the technology to achieve a hockey stick trajectory.This, of course, generates a continuing quest for the needle-in-a-haystack development opportunity that is fully explicated, not more than a year or two from submission to FDA, and targets a growing need among either a very large or very desperate patient population. There's nothing wrong with that as a business target; in fact, it makes perfect sense from an investment perspective to pursue the opportunity with already reduced development risk and a shorter time to investment return.

Angels are well aware that their money may be hundreds of times less than what will eventually be required to get a drug to the clinic, and that their hopes for a big payday are dependent upon massive additional funding. They strive to preserve and increase the value of their early investments as drug development proceeds, so that they hold a meaningful interest in the company as it realizes the hockey stick promise.

MILESTONE DRIVEN INVESTMENTS

Every early-stage biotech investment is so high risk that, from a purely objective point of view, it's a bit fantastical, like investing $100,000 on a space launch. It's an essential prerequisite to moving forward, but not enough money in itself to cause real change or even affect the probability of success. Every successful company in the VoD will eventually transition from Angel support to institutional support provided by venture capitalists (VCs), investment banks, or Big Pharma, in which the new money and leverage dwarf the old. With each round of fundraising, the new investors will seek to enhance their prospective return at the expense of the earlier investors—for example, by negotiating a lower valuation for the company, downgrading preferred stock shares to common, and stripping warrants, discounts or other protections. As we've already noted, their leverage is most extreme when the company is running low on cash.

The point is that the rules of the game are prescribed by the money. The enormous power that later stage investors like VCs wield is exemplified by the aggressive, even predatory, term sheets that accompany their investments in companies they support. SF attended an investor fair sponsored by a local law firm with a prominent IP business. A panel participated in a mock term sheet negotiation. The terms were extreme by design, seeking downside protection for the investor on half a dozen counts that put together would never be acceded to by even the most desperate inventor. But the intent and tenor of the negotiations was absolutely on point. Essentially, the scientist/founder was to cede the following to the investor: a preferred equity position with a guaranteed 1.5 multiple no matter what, additional warrant coverage based on performance, board control, employment compensation control, forfeiture of founder's stock in the event of walkaway, liquidation preferences, and full ratchet antidilution to protect the investor while unilaterally diluting the existing equity. The panelists, early-stage VCs themselves, were unrelenting and unrepentant in their demands that investor risk be mitigated at the inventor's expense.

Unreasonable? Probably not; all negotiations are ultimately an accommodation to effect a transaction, and that accommodation is invariably tilted in favor of the party with less to lose. As a company courts an institutional investor, they need to negotiate the best terms they can get under the circumstances, which include technical and clinical progress, management acumen, cash reserves, an evolving competitive landscape, and the relative demand for their investment proposition based on a network of investor interest.

In the march toward the hockey stick inflection point, where the new money takes priority over the old, investors and founders try to counteract the funder's increasing leverage by keeping the company strong. Every fundraise is tagged to a specific set of objectives, "milestones" that, when met, will clearly increase the value of the company and its attractiveness to subsequent investors. Having more potential "buyers" puts the company in a stronger position. The amount of money invested at any point needs to allow the company to reach a valuation where new money can be brought in. The ideal is a company so attractive that both existing and new investors would be loathe to walk away from the deal.

Milestones can be scientific or commercial, but the science is usually planned in tandem with a commercial objective, a robust proof of concept that leads to a Big Pharma partnership. Examples include: creation of an optimized lead molecule at the laboratory stage, demonstration of efficacy and safety in animal models, proof of concept in medical device prototypes, and early success in limited human trials for small molecules and biologics. Each of these is explicitly associated with an inflection point, at which the "pre-money" valuation[1] increases to a level where the assumption of a higher level of financial obligation is justified by a commensurately de-risked value proposition.

The leverage of new investors to set terms depends on how soon the milestones are reached and how much money the company has left when the milestone has been achieved—essentially whether it has sufficient time to raise new money on the basis of the increased valuation. Even before the current financing

---

1. The amount that the company is worth at that stage, even though no revenues may have been generated.

documents are signed, every company in the VoD recognizes the imperative to be thinking about the next money. At the same time, the principals' time is being spread between engaging potential pharma partners, applying for research grants, networking among investors, supporting the IP portfolio, deepening market understanding and business planning, expanding the technical and management bench, and filling in the unanswered questions remaining from the due diligence process. Not to mention, of course, executing the scientific plan that supports the investment thesis.

That plan has a complicated charter that prioritizes responsiveness to the needs of potential partners and the stated concerns of advisors and potential investors. It needs to focus on reducing uncertainty by overcoming technical barriers. It must, at each fundraise, make an ever-stronger case that the pathway to the clinic is feasible.

Achieving milestones signifies that: (1) the venture has been capable of managing itself under the existing leadership and (2) it is likely to overcome the next hurdle, assuming sufficient capital investment. Assumption of additional financial obligations to and by investors becomes rational, on the basis of increased probability that development will lead to a drug candidate Big Pharma will want to buy.

Since most investors are thinking about a timeline to return that is shorter than the discovery-to-market timeline for a new drug, they'll generally want to exit well before the drug reaches the market. Therefore, milestones are critically important for investors as *inflection points that represent opportunities for another transaction*. Even though milestones are directly tied to progress in the development of a therapeutic, it is clear that development from laboratory to clinic is focally a process of investment, and not just one of guided research sponsorship. The relationship between scientific progress and the amount of investment is the fundamental driver of the equation.

The finesse of biotech investing is the risk–reward balance. Experienced investors are essentially determining entry (investment) at the juncture of reduced risk of failure relative to the amount of cash needed. There's alignment between founders and investors at this point: the goal of the company is to achieve funding sufficient to reach the next milestone, and the goal of the investor is to invest enough money so that a new milestone can be reached that will allow the raising of additional funds. Ideally, the value of the company will have increased enough to accommodate a much larger investment. For survival in the VoD, the valuation of the company must continue to increase at a rate greater than the amount previously invested.

If this sounds like a Ponzi scheme, in a sense it is, and it is important to emphasize again that valuation is a *negotiated number*. Everyone does well as long as the company continues to achieve milestones that all parties agree are value-enhancing. Debt is assumed and transferred or converted into equity without actually generating anything of objectively quantifiable value. If a disagreement arises on valuation, or if a milestone is missed, there is the danger of a down round, or no round at all, leading to the semi-desperation of a bridge loan—which is simply the financial manifestation of a loss of confidence or momentum.

THE PERFECT DEAL

The logic of the milestone-driven investment strategy seems safe and reasonable, threatened primarily by the risk of scientific or management failure and the uncertainties of continued fundraising. Yet, the outcomes of the milestone-driven investment strategy in the VoD are significantly challenged by unbalanced market forces that can drive not only unfavorable terms for founders, but mutually destructive decision making. In a negotiation for a funding agreement, it may be assumed that the forces active during the negotiation reliably result in an equitable and successful collaboration. But investors' disproportionate buyer power controls the amount to be invested and increases the cost of that money, as defined by the terms.

To increase the potential profit from an investment, buyers have a natural incentive to negotiate the most favorable deal: they're investing for the optimal ratio of investment to return, calibrated by preset milestones and the corollary projected increase in valuation at subsequent transactions. At the same time, company founders' natural desire to present the most favorable picture of the odds for success, and to tailor their development plan to the expectations and budget of investors, will encourage them to underestimate the funds required to meet a planned milestone, especially when available cash is running low. Scientist/founders tend to be optimistic and will attempt to manage on whatever money is available, especially when the alternative is to go out of business.

Surrounding all this is a level of uncertainty that tends to follow a natural history of time and money requirements expanding beyond initial projections. This isn't necessarily bad planning. Scientific development reflects a series of experiments around hypotheses, some of which pan out while others do not, with limited predictability. The amount of money needed to de-risk an entire development program can only be estimated based on prior experience with comparable, but never identical development programs, and the number is ultimately very difficult to estimate. Thus, the eventual financing agreement will reflect the unbalanced buyer power inherent in the investor–inventor equation, as it molds the parties' accommodation to uncertainty and risk. The result is a pretty good chance of underfunding development and/or diverting it to short-term and opportunistic interests rather than long-term value.

Limited funding inevitably affects decision making, as the goal of creating a clinically relevant technology becomes subordinate to collecting enough money to reach the next milestone and stay alive in the process. A company that is undercapitalized or cannot achieve long-term funding stability will be unable to invest in infrastructure, address unforeseen challenges, effectively shift focus or revisit a key experiment as necessary, or attract and retain a skilled workforce.

The "perfect storm" occurs pretty frequently in the VoD: a company that has depleted its reserves and/or missed a milestone loses all negotiating leverage for the next fundraise, and may be reduced to begging for a bridge loan on unfavorable terms, shedding equity for less than its previous share price, or cutting back operations to survive. Prior investors may face a "pay to play" proposition, where investing additional funds is the only alternative to losing their principal sooner, in the hopes that they won't lose it later. This isn't any different from doubling down on a gambling bet, and it is a philosophical departure from de-risking that entails even more commitment to a high-risk investment. A round highly leveraged to the benefit of the next investor almost certainly means significant dilution of the original investors' shares. So does taking in additional money at or below the prior valuation, the definition of a down round.

We've both attended far too many "progress" sessions where the focus of the discussion was entirely on whether the company had achieved its milestones; if not, why not; how they would do better in the future; and the amount of runway they had left until they required an infusion of cash to keep trying. A company on life support is a terrible outcome. That this happens too often can be traced to unbalanced competitive forces within the VoD, combined with mutually reinforcing technological and financial risks. It's an outcome that is destructive to all of the parties involved: nascent companies, investors, and the clinicians and patients who might ultimately have benefitted from their efforts.

ROI VERSUS INNOVATION

It's expensive to develop a new therapeutic, diagnostic, or medical device. Even in the enveloping arms of Big Pharma, failed programs are the norm rather than the exception, and the cost, complexity and low probability of success result in aggregate development expenses that dwarf those of other industries. Large sums have to be mobilized to support late-stage potential for return. This, combined with the hunt for very large multiples which are only possible with "blockbusters," has shaped the strategy of biotechnology investors. Like Big Pharma before them, many institutional investors have restricted their focus to later stage properties, making it clear that they have little interest in technologies that are too early in development, or whose exit prospects are constrained by market potential under the "billion dollar threshold." This is for the entirely cogent reasons that: (1) the time and money and opportunity costs are similar for investments in a $100 million and a $1 billion drug and (2) given the ability to invest large sums, the exit horizon is shorter and yields a better return on investment for a late-stage than an early-stage opportunity. One needs only to follow the succession of very big biotech exits over the past 2 years for proof. The potential for outsized returns in the face of massive risk has calibrated the entire biotechnology investment thesis toward the late play with a spectacular payday.

We previously discussed how we have shifted much of the overhead burden of research into medical innovation from Big Pharma to the VoD. When we consider the cost of supporting the nation's R&D (research and development) infrastructure using borrowed money, on terms calibrated to accommodate the inherent failure rate of drug development, it's clear that even the companies destined to succeed must incur enormous levels of financial obligation. The risk investors take in providing those funds needs to be compensated, as preferred shares, warrants or discounts, liquidation preferences, and repayment of interest, at every transaction. Without the opportunity for a spectacular payday that has been driving biotech exits the past 2–3 years, it would be difficult to find anyone, at either an early or a late stage, who would support drug development. This is precisely the calculus that is behind Big Pharma shedding its R&D overhead and chasing financial windfalls at the expense of broader clinical objectives.

It's hardly surprising that investor prioritization of shorter time frames and greater ROI (return on investment) supersede other interests and are *the* dominant forces in the VoD. Or that this has been responsible for migration of institutional investors to projects in later stages of development. Nor is this unique to Venture Capital. Even Angel investors have moved to reposition themselves at later points along the timeline, to get closer to the "hockey stick" inflection point.

The hockey stick represents for investors the confidence that this management team, with this technology, facing a particular set of market forces, and in the context of the current regulatory and reimbursement environment, can succeed where dozens or hundreds of other similar technologies have failed. That confidence is both a contributor to and the result of magical thinking. Having subscribed to the premise, investors—savvy people who know better than to base their decision on emotion—suffer the same cognitive dissonance as everyone else. Therefore, the universe to which they have subscribed also needs to look like a hockey stick, and thus validate their thinking. If you are at the horseracing track, and you've put a lot of money down on Wow Baby, the reward circuitry in your brain wants ratification: the substantiation of a sharp upward spike in betting (corollary to the hockey stick spike on a prospective investment) on "sure thing" Wow Baby. The possibility that Wow Baby may stumble and break his leg and/or the jockey's neck at any time only lends flavor to the experience.

True "hockey sticks"—products whose revenues suddenly head for the stratosphere after years of slogging in development and modest initial customer capture—are relatively rare, the result of a unique confluence of vision, technology, timing, unmet or unrecognized need, and yes, luck. Furthermore, trend lines do not extend upward to infinity, and they are more often than not discontinuous in their upward (or downward) progression. Every product or service offering that has ever been conceived, every industry that has emerged to replace another, will inevitably follow some variant of the product lifecycle "S-curve" you can find in any business textbook.

All of this leads to the conclusion that exit-based investing perhaps isn't the best way to assure important new breakthroughs make their way to the clinic.

It's not that this doesn't happen in the present system, or that profit motive hasn't always driven drug development in Big Pharma; it's that the intrinsic merit of healthcare technologies isn't the primary driver here. Large elements of idiosyncratic interest, short-term thinking and the quest for outsize returns drive decisions that should be tempered by other considerations. Whereas the process starts with an inventor introducing a technology to the commercial world for advancement, when the technology arrives in the VoD it becomes the subject of a complex betting game.

This is the essence of the culture clash within the VoD. There is a *fulcrum of tension* between the value of a discovery to society, which is spiritually in sync with the aspirational drive of the inventor, and the largely if not exclusively financial motives of late-stage investors, who are the people with the power to make drugs happen. The irony is that those making the highest-risk bets yielding the lowest absolute return on investment, Angels, are being increasingly relied on to support healthcare innovation until it has advanced to the stage where late-stage investors (VCs, pharma, or a strategic partner) want to assume the risk. Likely outcomes for Angels taking these early-stage risks include:

- Higher absolute failure rates compared with later stage investments
- Getting squashed (diluted) by later stage investors
- Lack of milestone progress resulting in delayed exits, and therefore holding shares much longer than anticipated
- Timelines to market that keep expanding for reasons beyond prediction or control
- Premarket revenues from partnering or licensing that might be enough to keep the company going but aren't going to put a return in anyone's pocket.

Even if you've made a good bet and a portfolio company has a continuous string of up rounds, there's a pretty good chance that later stage money's ability to dictate share value will mean that your money hasn't multiplied since you wrote the check X years ago. The Angel Capital Education Foundation, an entrepreneurship think-tank and advocacy organization, analyzed data from 538 Angels, covering 3097 investments, 1137 exits and closures [2]. 73% of these investments were seed-stage or startups, 55% of them prerevenue. Over half of them returned under 1×, a loss of principal. An overall multiple of 2.6 with an IRR of 27% was driven by the small minority of investments yielding a return between 5× and 30×, but most especially by the tiny fraction with a greater than 30× exit. This is the basis and rationale for investing on probability ratios; the rule of thumb is that 1 of 10 exits pays for all the failed investments plus a profit. It may work financially—except in an economic downturn when exits are elusive—but is hardly the formula for filtering the most important new medicines from the most lucrative ones.

In the VoD, technology is too often a pawn, and progress is primarily tied to investment rather than innovation. The result is that an uncountable number of promising technologies will never be realized, taking with them to an early grave the aspirations of founders and the prospects for saving human lives. In the market for capital that is the VoD, innovation for its own sake, or for the sake of a higher purpose, is no longer affordable.

The technologies that fuel the investment thesis in the VoD are discovered with public and charitable money, carrying with them society's best intentions. But getting to the clinic requires that they somehow survive a financial gauntlet of obligations to private investors, who wield tremendous power over the companies they support and the work to be done. We are not opposed to investors making very large bets, or making lots of money on those high-risk bets, but we are concerned about the power of capital to misdirect or destroy that which it is supposed to nurture.

We believe in better aligning the interests of founders, investors, and society through a shared process that respects both financial and medical objectives. A rationalization of the flow of money within the VoD would reduce the risk for late-stage investors, while preserving value for, and the motivation of early stage investors. It would ultimately improve the return from investment in the research enterprise, enhancing both human and investment return.

REFERENCES

[1]   Pollack A. Sales of sovaldi, new Gilead hepatitis C drug, soar to $10.3 billion. New York Times February 3, 2015. <http://www.nytimes.com/2015/02/04/business/sales-of-sovaldi-new-gilead-hepatitis-c-drug-soar-to-10-3-billion.html?ref=topics&_r=0>; [accessed 27.02.16].

[2]   Angel Capital Education Foundation. Returns to Angel investors in groups. <http://www.angelcapitalassociation.org/data/Documents/Resources/AngelGroupResarch/1d%20-%20Resources%20-%20Research/ACEF%20Angel%20Performance%20Project%2004.28.09.pdf>; Published April 28, 2009 [accessed 27.02.16].

Chapter 20

Harps for Angels

The world is often unkind to new talent, new creations. The new needs friends.
(From the movie Ratatouille, Pixar Animation Studios) [1]

Many of our greatest biomedical innovations begin within the academic research enterprise. Some discoveries, arguably the ones with the greatest clinical and/or commercial potential, are licensed early on to established companies that have the resources to move them forward. Others receive institutional support in the form of sponsored research agreements or other limited funding arrangements. A few proceed through an abbreviated round of public and private funding before an acquisition by one of those same strategic partners.

It's clear, however, that the amount of creative biomedical output from academic research dwarfs the capacity of public and private funding sources to take those technologies all the way to the clinic. Consequently, most discoveries enter the Valley of Death (VoD) without the benefit of institutional support, in a more or less precarious and embryonic state. Most venture capitalists (VCs) aren't interested yet—the common refrain from founders is that they've been told they're "too early"—and friends and family money runs out pretty quickly in the context of biomedical development. So most new technologies require the seed financing that only Angels and very-early-stage VCs can provide. It's imperative for continued biomedical innovation that Angels keep investing, and that requires both monetary and less tangible incentives.

Angels are the catalysts that enable billions of dollars in funding to be channeled into the VoD. These early-stage investors purchase high-risk financial instruments, supporting scientific inquiry that might someday impact the way patients are treated, with the hope of receiving a substantial return on their investment (ROI). Preserving their interests is essential, and this must happen within the context of the whole early-stage biotechnology ecosystem. This means making the VoD marketplace for technology-based financial instruments as attractive as possible, ensuring that de-risking means something beyond defensive deal terms, and embedding a management team capable of ushering the technology to value-creating milestones. We believe strongly that success ratios can be enhanced, that it's not necessary to play a game of historically conditioned probabilities that 1 out of 10 investments will pay off *and* compensate for the

Preserving the Promise. DOI: http://dx.doi.org/10.1016/B978-0-12-809216-3.00020-8

189

other 9 failures, and that a better aligned and better informed process can yield a higher ratio of successful exits *and* successful drugs. The most successful companies, for principals, employees and investors, are the ones that premise their actions on long-term sustainable value rather than short-term return. Long-term sustainable value in the context of biomedical innovation means supporting the right investments, but the key to better yield is defining and actualizing those investments with the potential to change the lives of patients. Portfolios full of healthy companies with cogent, sustainable technologies and development programs will achieve more and better exits and provide a greater return to Angels. The better their returns, the more they will invest, and thus the system will expand to the benefit of all parties.

The financial strain on the system, stoked by imbalanced market forces, has led to the tacit acceptance of a funding process that is intermittently profitable but in many ways destructive to participants' interests. We've analyzed the pressures operative within the VoD as a competitive marketplace for financing. We've discussed how the forces that incentivize investors in the short-term also de-incentivize founders and increase the financial burdens that companies must assume to fund their operations. Aggressive terms favoring investor over founder interests discourage the latter, and may even compromise follow-on investments with a valuation that is too high or burdensome warrants that reduce returns for later investors. Overly optimistic budget projections that appear to enhance the investment may result in underfunding of milestones, eventually making companies so unhealthy that no exit is possible. The expected failure rate of VoD investments is so high that it may be difficult in the short term to distinguish the causes of failure, some of which may be attributable to current trends in seed-stage financing. These include an emphasis on convertible debt as an alternative to a priced round, warrants, discounts, and valuation caps, all of which became prevalent after the 2008 biotechnology bust—without rigorous assessment of their effectiveness. Greater rationalization of the flow of money within the entire VoD ecosystem would provide the best companies more opportunity to set and reach value-enhancing milestones, while reducing the waste engendered by poorly conceived and executed initiatives.

Of course, we are writing from our individual perspectives as an Angel investor and a biotech company founder, but our aim is more holistic. Improving the process by which investments are raised and spent should be a collaborative effort; one that involves technology transfer offices, founders and their companies, and investors, and one that we propose would be enhanced by *playing the long game together*. The essential consideration, we've noted, is whether the proposed technology and development program will support a sustained series of financial transactions reflecting ever-increasing valuation. It's the classic short-term versus long-term question. Intuitively, it shouldn't just be about getting to the next fundraise, which is the founder's survival objective, or just getting to a liquidity event, which is the investor's financial one. By holistic, we mean a focus on the ability to attract a definitive institutional investment that can carry the scientific discovery to the clinic—if it proves to be medically sound. This, we believe, is what should describe a cogent investment thesis.

The authors have participated in many discussions with academic researchers and research groups in which excellent ideas are floated, each with a potential for changing medicine, often in exciting ways. But it's not the clinical proposition per se that will support an investment; each of these ideas needs to be filtered through the lens of an investment thesis that will enable navigation of the VoD. The scientists need to work out a plan with tech transfer, business advisors, and investors. They need to deconstruct the technical path, identify the critical nodes of uncertainty, determine the shape of the team, and collaborate to determine whether it makes sense to move forward. Not every innovation can be converted into an investable strategy, especially when one factors in the length of time required to reach the clinical trials pathway and the potential for market acceptance. Even great ideas are not necessarily investable.

The VoD is the conduit that is supposed to bring therapeutics from academia to market. Angels' essential and early role in the biotechnology ecosystem means that they are the gatekeepers who determine which technologies will be supported. They carry the weight of vetting early technologies, presumably so that the ones which progress to market are the most effective *and* the most profitable. They naturally do so within a broad context that includes factors tangential to the science itself. The technologies that are the most novel, that open up completely new pathways for medical discoveries, that pile on the speculative risk that accompanies a paradigm shift, may be less investable than an incremental twist on a commonly understood path to the clinic. Philosophically, this is in conflict with what society purports to value: the best solution for unmet medical needs isn't necessarily the most expedient or lucrative path to the clinic.

We've noted that the distribution of money within the VoD is only loosely correlated with the quality or innovation of the technology. The closer correlation is between the allocation of money and an estimate of risk versus potential ROI. As an investment venue that presents incredible financial uncertainty in an often undercapitalized market (notwithstanding the currently high flow rate of institutional cash to late stage ventures), the VoD rewards the selection of drugs most likely to fulfill the investment thesis. Those may or may not be the drugs most likely to have the greatest impact in the clinic. This isn't a new or surprising phenomenon, and in many ways it parallels the internal competition for budget and development priorities when Big Pharma is the engine behind discovery. A recent article about Ibrance, an important new treatment for advanced breast cancer, makes this crystal clear [2]: On the one hand, the head of oncology development at Pfizer is on record regarding the company's "moral obligation" to help breast cancer patients, noting that "it is our responsibility to get [the drug] to them." On the other, despite the new compound having been born of Nobel prize-winning research [3] and a prototype drug found to be active in breast cancer at the National Institutes of Health in the early 1990s [4], "Pfizer wasn't going to fund further clinical testing and other development costs if it couldn't anticipate good financial returns from a resulting drug." After three years of analysis into how to best ensure they wouldn't leave any money on the table, Pfizer finally set the price for Ibrance at $9850 a month [5].

We're past the dry spell occasioned by the 2008–11 recession, and right now there is plenty of money available—for late-stage properties. It is perhaps incumbent on us as a society, and certainly on the players within the VoD, to direct that money to the most valuable initiatives in the VoD. Because the VoD is a marketplace for investments, we consider this as a process of refining the investment thesis to encourage the greatest probability of both clinical and financial returns.

So what we're talking about is aligning incentives, not when the deal terms are negotiated, but in the creation of an investment proposition that addresses clinical and societal benefit—not simply as rationale for financial projections, but as foundational to the *long-term, sustainable value of the venture*. This is also likely to rebalance the scale in favor of transformation over incremental change, innovation over me-too efforts. Innovation, of course, is tossed around as the *raison d'etre* of discovery and development, and therefore of the VoD, but it's notoriously difficult to prospectively quantify. Visionaries get it; that's what makes them visionaries. The rest of us sometimes claim to know what is innovative, but almost by definition genuine innovation won't make sense to many of the first people to hear of it.

It's an old saw, but if you asked people in 1910 what they thought would transform transportation, they would probably have suggested a better horse, not a smoke-belching, oil-consuming, noisy and dangerous mechanical buggy. What we know from experience (and therefore after the fact) is that the most innovative ideas, even if not entirely fantastical, are nevertheless laden with risk. Reducing the risk straining the drug development ecosystem, and improving ROI in the process, is likely to help more of the Velcades of the future make it through. Steps to improve the value proposition of the riskiest, most innovative inventions should logically increase their success rate as well. An improved, desirable, and valuable model would better align the interests of founders, investors, and society's interests through a shared process that respects both financial and medical objectives.

CONSIDERATION OF THE MACRO ENVIRONMENT

We have examined the decision-making process from the standpoint of the Angel investor, the inventor, the company, and the investment thesis they share. Moving forward from the perspective of the Angel investing process is just one starting point, in order to build a common understanding and to demonstrate the forces that can be modulated for better outcomes. We hold that protecting Angels should be congruent with improving the success rate of getting drugs to the clinic, which requires an alignment of outcomes. We could as easily focus on healthy outcomes for founding scientists, but they are already intrinsically motivated to move their technologies forward and the key is to avoid financial machinations that demotivate them. We could highlight companies, but it is clear that survival in the VoD is an interconnected issue. We focus on Angels here because they are the VoD's gatekeepers, and their decisions can make or break the prospects for a given invention.

The failure rate of Angel investments in the VoD is so high that solutions must account for systemic causes for failure, such as exogenous conditions that affect the absolute amount of money available for investment in a particular domain and geography. Although rarely measured with any specificity, the dollars available in any region are finite, and can only support a finite number of companies. Angels often invest locally, so regional numbers are probably more important than national ones. Beyond touted, published commitments of regional development organizations, there's no tracking system for these private, local financing transactions. And in any event, there is no *a priori* correlation between the productivity of a region's academic research institutions and the financial capacity, interest, and investing habits of the local Angel community. Regardless of the quality of a company, succeeding with one investment round is not predictive of success with the next, especially if local Angel investors with an interest in a particular area are temporarily tapped out.

A market can be saturated with investment opportunities, to the point where adding additional companies to the mix diminishes rather than increases funding prospects, due to either a concentration of dollars in a few prominent investments or diffusion of resources across too many. The immense buyer power of Angels and the failure rate of companies suggest either that markets are oversaturated or that too few viable opportunities are available. The questions revolve not around a particular investment opportunity but its regional and temporal context: How many other companies are marketing similar financial instruments to the same buyers at the same time, how much money do the companies need, and how much money is available from early-stage investors? The core of the investment equation is how many of these investments can realistically be expected to exit within a reasonable investment horizon? The long-term success of companies and their investors requires a dispassionate accounting with respect to these questions.

REGIONAL, ECONOMIC, AND CULTURAL INFLUENCES

Success also depends on intangible regional factors, such as the entrepreneurial culture, access to intellectual capital, and proximity to university and industry resources, as well as to public and private initiatives such as incubator facilities, accelerators, greenhouse and other economic development funds and research tax incentives. Communities such as Boston and the San Francisco Bay Area have enormous interdependent networks of expertise, personal relationships that provide information and trust, world-class universities and research institutions, and long-standing initiatives for economic development and infrastructure.

Their results are much better than average, catalyzed by the vast sums of capital they attract for both seed and later-stage companies. This is both a source of, and stimulant for, even more investment.

Every budding innovation center may want to copy Cambridge or Palo Alto, but emulating structural components ignores the influence of culture, in much the way that legacy businesses are unable to replicate the success of competitors fundamentally differentiated by worldview. Think of the classic business case of legacy air carriers versus Southwest Airlines. The culture and nature of constituent participation are fundamentally different, such that adoption of Southwest "features" by the legacy carriers (such as boarding protocols or route selection) will never replicate the latter's key to success. It's not just about infrastructure, or industrial age of the community, or even local experience in a given domain. On the surface, Philadelphia (for example) should be able to muster the same resources, capabilities, energy and, to a degree, money; and the region has had some high-profile successes. But the culture of risk-taking is different, and that represents a different proposition for a VoD investment in Philadelphia than for one in Cambridge.

It is worth having a look at which of these factors make a causal difference and which are simply correlations driven by success breeding success. There's a general consensus about the importance of strong advisory guidance, for example, but limited formal analysis of how specific skill sets and characteristics influence company success. Are there different success rates for seasoned individual Angels as opposed to Angel groups? To what extent is domain expertise predictive, and should that red flag otherwise smart investments for an Angel without any background in a particular area? There are management and leadership qualities that point to an investable entrepreneur, but are there specific personality types that point to a successful Angel? One of the authors is a highly selective investor directed by his domain knowledge and a conservative disposition with respect to assuming other people's risk, but has had a high success ratio with a limited number of investments. As a template, is this strategy superior to following the rule of probabilities with respect to high-risk investment?

We both know investors with deep experience in finance; does that presage more or less success compared with outcomes guided by the expertise of a former biotech executive, a professor of immunology, or a good business lawyer? Beyond the financial requirements for accreditation, are there academic or professional qualifications associated with higher rates of return? If you look at 20,000 Angels investing in healthcare, what are the behavioral characteristics of the most successful Angels? These questions may seem unanswerable because they are largely idiosyncratic to the opportunity and circumstances, but that doesn't make them less relevant or impossible to study.

We know relatively little about the early-stage investment sector as a whole, or regionally, since so many deals involve terms and outcomes that are not publicly disclosed and for which the only source of information is the investors.

Again, this may in some respects be intractable, but it is hard to understand why an investment marketplace of such enormous economic and societal impact is so poorly quantified. A recent survey cosponsored by the Angel Capital Association and Wharton Entrepreneurship seeks to redress this, at least in part (results of the survey will be available later in 2016) [6].

In the absence of better data correlating characteristics of VoD investments and returns, deals will continue to be struck on the idiosyncratic experience of the parties in each deal, rather than analytical guidance. There is significant potential to improve due diligence based on precedent, and to highlight (and therefore fund) those initiatives, public and private, most likely to have a positive impact. More needs to be done to measure VoD practices, outcomes, and the effectiveness of economic development initiatives with respect to investor returns and technology outcomes.

REFERENCES

[1] Lewis B. (Producer), Bird B. (Director). Ratatouille. United States: Pixar Animation Studio/ Walt Disney Pictures; 2007.

[2] Rockoff JD. How Pfizer set the cost of its new drug at $9,850 a month. Wall Street J 2015 December 9, 2015. <http://www.wsj.com/articles/the-art-of-setting-a-drug-price-1449628081/>; [accessed 27.02.16].

[3] Nobel Media A.B. The Nobel Prize in Physiology or Medicine 2001. Nobelprize.org. <http://www.nobelprize.org/nobel_prizes/medicine/laureates/2001/>; 2014 [accessed 27.02.16].

[4] Carlson BA, Dubay MM, Sausville EA, Brizuela L, Worland PJ. Flavopiridol induces G1 arrest with inhibition of cyclin-dependent kinase (CDK) 2 and CDK4 in human breast carcinoma cells. Cancer Res 1996;56(13):2973–8.

[5] Dangi-Garimella S. Tagrisso approved, but can patients with EGFR-mutant NSCLC afford it? November 17, 2015. <http://www.ajmc.com/newsroom/tagrisso-approved-but-can-patients-with-egfr-mutant-nsclc-afford-it>; 2015.

[6] Angel Capital Association. Angel Investors Maintain Diverse Portfoloios, with Median Check Size of $25,000, According to the Early Results of "The American Angel" Campaign. <http://www.prnewswire.com/news-releases/angel-investors-maintain-diverse-portfolios-with-median-check-size-of-25000-according-to-early-results-of-the-american-angel-campaign-300291949.html>; 2016.

Chapter 21

Connecting Innovation to Investment

Public and philanthropic initiatives that increase the likelihood of success for a Valley of Death (VoD) company can be powerful incentives that de-risk, and thereby encourage investment in, innovation toward important unmet medical needs. Regional economic development programs play an important role in the VoD through non-dilutive grants and loans or matched coinvestment. These programs are part of the ecosystem that influences what Angels choose to invest in, and they provide infrastructure, resources, and expertise to help those investments succeed. They possess a deep bench of scientific and financial expertise, and collaborative relationships with investors, universities, incubators and others in the start-up ecosystem, that extend and buttress due diligence by private parties and effectively bolster confidence in these intrinsically high-risk investments. This may be the very best definition of de-risking.

The North Carolina Biotechnology Center (NCBiotech) in Research Triangle Park, for example, directly supports development of the state's biotechnology sector by providing research and business loans. From 1989 to 2012, NCBiotech made 239 loans to 168 early-stage companies, of which 95 were still active when the Battelle Technology Partnership Practice reported on the program in 2014 [1]. At that time, the 95 companies had a total of 2188 employees in 2014 and revenues estimated at $1.9 billion.

Kenneth Tindall, PhD, Senior VP at NCBiotech, described the process for selecting companies for support: "Ultimately the decision making is made by our board, which includes venture capitalists (VCs), attorneys, people with experience in this area. The level of due diligence is very good—that kind of quality provides a Good Housekeeping Seal of Approval. We've been told by the Angels as well as the local VCs, 'when you put that loan out, I went back to my pile of business plans.' It's that important" [2].

Regional funds can also be critical connectors between academic institutions and the investment community. As we envision technology transfer offices (TTOs) adopting a more selective and entrepreneurial culture in the future, their natural partners will be publicly funded initiatives, which will facilitate the evaluation and promotion of new discoveries. Ongoing information sharing

Preserving the Promise. DOI: http://dx.doi.org/10.1016/B978-0-12-809216-3.00021-X

197

coordinated by the regional funds, regarding what a university has in the innovation pipeline, what the VoD and clinical marketplaces are looking for, and what Angels are actively seeking, can lower the barriers to matching the best technologies with the right financial supporters. Although it may not be primary to their charters, public development funds should play an activist role as connectors, breaking through the information silos that can inhibit investors and universities from working together to select the best technologies.

Venture philanthropy (VP) is uniquely positioned to de-risk the most innovative technologies in the VoD. More often than not, investment activity in the healthcare VoD is agnostic to the particular disease being addressed, as well as the objectives of clinicians and patients. The notable exception is disease-specific philanthropic organizations, which provide research support and thereby connect what is needed in the clinic with what captures money in the VoD. With their personal connection to the disease they are advocating, they have a passionate interest in the needs of patients. They are maximally motivated to support innovation, and are acutely aware of the market forces that can pull a treatment forward to the clinic. By throwing their experiential weight, credibility, and cash into an early-stage company, they can focus on innovation and support the objectives of the companies—and their private investors.

This VP model *embraces* risk because its disease-specific focus balances the imperative of financial return. As former Chief Business Officer of Experimed Bioscience, Peter Heinecke, notes "A VP fund has a double bottom line: one line is still return, but the other line is the social good that you are advancing" [3].

The first and best known VP was the National Foundation for Infantile Paralysis, later the March of Dimes, which supported the development and clinical testing of Jonas Salk's inactivated polio virus vaccine [4]. The Cystic Fibrosis Foundation (CFF) has been one of the most successful in pioneering the VP model in the present era. Frustrated by the slow pace of translation of genetic research they had sponsored into drugs for CF patients, the CFF invested $40 million in 2000 in a start-up biotech company, Aurora Biosciences (subsequently Vertex Pharmaceuticals). Building on a broad coalition of doctors, patients, industry, and academia, they eventually directed $150 million to development and clinical testing of ivacaftor (Kalydeco, Vertex Pharmaceuticals), a drug that eases the symptoms of patients who express a defective form of the CF protein and was approved by the FDA in 2012. A follow-on drug, lumacaftor/ivacaftor (Orkambi, Vertex Pharmaceuticals), which treats an additional population of CF patients, was approved in 2015.

Philanthropic organizations act as accelerators of development by proactively modifying investment priorities in the VoD. "Maybe if we had been patient, some other drug companies would have come along. I am spending $75 million with Vertex for something that they would maybe develop in 3–4 years, but my $75 million will accelerate it by 2–3 years. If we really want to drive our destiny, we can't take the chance that someone else might not pick up the project," explained Bob Beall, CEO of CFF [5].

VP thus plays an activist role, especially for disease states that do not fulfill the typical criteria for investment because of too small a patient population or too intimidating a history of failed research efforts. Well-known entities fulfilling this function include the Michael J. Fox Foundation for Parkinson's Research, The Leukemia & Lymphoma Society (LLS), the Multiple Myeloma Research Foundation, the National Multiple Sclerosis Society, and the Juvenile Diabetes Research Foundation (JDRF). The JDRF, for example, supports a wide range of companies working in very high-risk research areas, including pancreatic beta cell regeneration and a Type 1 diabetes vaccine [6]; and the LLS initiated the Therapy Acceleration Program, which supports both preclinical and clinical studies in leukemia and lymphoma [7].

Funding from the National Institutes of Health (NIH) targeted at start-up companies, through the Small Business Innovation Research (SBIR) and Small Business Technology Transfer (STTR) grants, is an essential mechanism for encouraging investment in innovation and a source of non-dilutive funding for companies in the VoD. The SBIR grant is for small companies, whereas the STTR grant supports formal collaborations between companies and academic institutions. "The program allows new and small businesses to use government funding to develop early-stage technologies to the point that they can be evaluated and supported by private capital markets," according to Scott Shane, Professor of Economics at Case Western Reserve University [8].

SBIR and STTR grant applications undergo rigorous scientific evaluation by NIH study sections, with the stated goal to "stimulate technological innovation" [9]. By providing an informed endorsement that assesses both scientific innovation and commercialization potential, then backing up that assessment with non-dilutive funding, SBIR and STTR grants are the critical link between the creative values of the NIH research program, clinical/societal objectives, and the investment decisions made in the VoD. As with philanthropic support, NIH grants help enhance the survival of transformative technologies whose risk profile may be too high for earlier stage investors. Increasing the number, scope, and periods of support for these early-stage grants as a matter of public policy would be a powerful means to support the highly innovative technologies that most deserve commercialization in the VoD.

The NIH also supports translational research through its Therapeutics for Rare and Neglected Diseases (TRND) and Bridging Interventional Developmental Gaps (BrIDGs) programs [10,11]. Neither program actually provides funding, but they do tap into NIH expertise and provide preclinical testing to support IND applications for work coming out of academic labs, start-up companies, or established Pharma. The model is collaborative, heavily milestone-based and validating for subsequent private investment in the VoD. Many of the drugs that have passed through the TRND and BrIDGs programs have achieved Series A VC funding or found a private sector partner. Although the number of drugs in these programs is relatively small, companies with molecules in TRND or BrIDGs programs have achieved strong validation of their societal value and potential for clinical success [12]. The fact that nonfinancial criteria are used to select projects for the TRND and BrIDGs programs—e.g., the severity of the unmet medical need—may enable survival to subsequent private investment for discoveries that are not initially attractive VoD investment theses.

REDUCING THE RISK OF SCIENTIFIC FAILURE

What everyone fears most in the VoD, after running out of money, is a technology that doesn't work, or for any reason fails to conform to the research plan. We've talked about critical nodes of uncertainty in the development process. Think about a stream running over a roadway after a rainstorm: it's either easily traversable or above your car doors, but it is impossible to discern which one in advance. The obstacle is unplanned, unnerving, and failure to cross over it has the potential to upend both scientific and commercial development. Even the most promising technologies, shepherded by the most qualified scientific teams, *will* encounter unexpected obstacles and may miss milestones. When these coincide with the transition to the next funding cycle, the results can be fatal.

The unique vulnerability of companies in the VoD arises because fundraising is tied to achieving technical milestones. In the exit-based investing paradigm, money is based on a calculated return which is, in turn, based on valuation. Each investment round is predicated on accomplishment of a milestone, after which the presumptive value of the company will increase. In the VoD market for financial instruments, each round of investment needs to create enough additional value so that more investment can be obtained. A fundraise when a milestone is missed is a recipe for a down round. The science and the company are essentially the same, but the company has spent whatever was previously borrowed, the inferred risk is higher, and the deal terms will be less attractive.

The failure of a critical scientific experiment can be devastating to a company on many levels. At the very least, the experiment/task will need to be repeated, or an alternate solution to the problem worked out, both of which consume resources. Disagreements may emerge among team members over the reasons for and solutions to the problem. Scientific staff will question why so much money is raised, but so little spent, on science. Managers and investors, powerless to affect the progress of critical scientific experiments, may push an opportunistic view over long-term strategy as the immediate question becomes how to raise the next round of money, and thereby salvage an investment, on bad news. Fatal flaws kill programs and wipe out investments.

It may seem that the best way to reduce the risk of scientific failure is a fundamentally good idea, validated by thorough examination of process and prospects through a qualified scientific advisory panel. Assuming expert guidance and a talented scientist/founder, the experiment itself would not seem to be a modifiable source of inefficiency. But we have already established that the amount of money in the VoD is insufficient to advance every worthy innovation, so some technologies will die for lack of funding even though they are technically viable or exciting. Furthermore, there is a direct relationship between the terms of an investment and the ability of a given company to meet technological milestones.

The enormous buyer power held by investors means that early stage companies are often only able to raise enough capital to support them through the next technical milestone, and not beyond—say 6 to 12 months. There may be no alternative to this funding reality, and scientist/entrepreneurs will generally take whatever they can get, but operating on the norm of short-term funding tranches is intuitively counteractive to long-term thinking. The focus of technology development becomes subverted by the need to raise more money, and this may not be in the best long-term interests of the technology or the company. Underfunded companies will not have the wherewithal to adapt their research program to overcome unexpected pitfalls and shifts in strategy, nor will they be able to invest in infrastructure or retain skilled employees. Even if the science is working, and a milestone is met, short-term funding horizons may not provide enough time for a company to raise new money on the basis of the newly increased valuation, leading to a down round for the prior investors.

There is no stage of technological development that does not carry a significant risk of scientific failure. This is particularly the case for the most innovative technologies. During term sheet negotiations, it may seem that the interests of the investor and company are at least partially aligned. But the paramount risk of scientific failure inherent in the VoD means that everyone's interests need to be aligned approaching *and following* the conclusion of the deal. It's a basic tenet of negotiation that the real test of the relationship begins after the paper is signed.

Companies and Angels need to have the same conversation, setting milestones and timelines to achieve a valuation that can bring in the next money on better terms and with an objective sense of progress and de-risking. The issue of financial return should be explicitly on the table, forcing inventors to think about it in other than pie-in-the-sky terms. What can realistically be attempted or achieved with the available cash, and what if the plan goes awry? It's equally important that the inventor's aspirations be on the table, forcing investors to at least consider factors other than financial expectations. In essence, everyone needs to stop thinking that the other party is a rube for their differing worldviews: investors aren't simply one-dimensional financial mavens oblivious to clinical value, and founders aren't just laboratory tinkerers naïve to commercial realities.

The fundamentals of negotiation aren't about to change; some people are inherently adversarial, others temperamentally predisposed to be conciliatory. But there's an awful lot of evidence to suggest that integrative negotiation (which focuses on satisfying at least some of everyone's needs) produces a better outcome than distributive negotiation (which satisfies one party at the other's expense). This is intuitively and particularly the case where the objective, a combination of scientific, clinical and financial progress, relies upon mutual success.

We believe that companies should try to raise money in longer increments, say enough to run for 18–24 months. This would give some breathing room to achieve each value-generating milestone, at least somewhat free of ongoing fundraising demands, and time to raise new money that reflects the value of the progress the company has achieved. Technological ambition and potential should be explicitly matched to the VoD marketplace, taking into account the realities of funding, scientific progress, and survival. Cautious investors can divide rounds into tranches that reward interim progress, and keep everyone moving forward. We recognize this timeframe as an optimistic goal, but think it as a worthwhile one that helps answer how the company will merit its next fundraise and where the money will come from. Innovation that cannot capture anyone's imagination probably should not proceed.

A financially healthy company that can confidently march toward a technical milestone, one that represents an authentic increase in value is a much better bet than a weak company in which the investor has a favorable liquidation preference or participating preferred shares. To quote a banker with deep experience in biotechnology investing, "The pref is schmuck insurance and we don't want a bad deal." We need to seek deals that are good for everyone: investors, companies, and technologies. In the end, when a VC comes on the scene, the new money will dictate the terms of the deal. If the company is weak, the preferences and discounts the Angels have fought for so earnestly will all have been illusory anyway.

REWARDING THE LONG GAME

If you look at the entire development lifecycle, Angels contribute a relatively small amount of the cash to the progression of any medical innovation. Their contributions are made to embryonic companies, when risk is enormous, and at a point when the prospects of an invention are anything but obvious: like searching a group of children in an elementary school playground to find the future brain surgeon. Ideally, an Angel investment will establish strong proof-of-concept, preferably animal safety and efficacy studies that show a clear path to the clinic, so that the company can proceed in the direction of an exit. A sale of the company or an initial public offering (IPO) would provide excellent investor returns, but our nascent brain surgeon still has to learn her anatomy and there's a pretty good chance she'll fall off the swings a few times along the way. The majority of seed-stage drug, device, and diagnostic companies are years and multiple fundraising rounds from a liquidity event and need to aim their sights at an institutional (VC) investment round that will support the company on its way to an exit.

If a VC round is achieved, what happens to the Angels? The focus of this book has been the transition of a technology from the university to early private investment rounds, but the transition between Angel and large-scale institutional funding is an equally critical juncture for companies—and for the health of the VoD ecosystem as a whole. Angels who come in early and do not participate in follow-on investments are especially vulnerable to dilution, which affects the upside of participation in a liquidity event. After entering into an investment on the strength of their own buyer power, Angels become subject themselves to the buyer power of the VCs. New money dictates the terms, and every new fundraise exerts pressure to downgrade the value of the existing investments because that enhances the multiple for subsequent investors. For example, existing shares may be forcibly converted to common shares, stripping the Angels of their liquidation preference. It only takes one down round (investors buying into a company at a lower valuation than the previous round) to wipe out Angels' prospect of a strong return on investment.

Because of this vulnerability, Angels can lose even if they pick a winning technology. A cynical view is that they de-risk technologies for VCs, who can step in to pay the college tuition when the budding brain surgeon has a 4.0 GPA and scores 800 on her math SAT. Angels naturally try through initial deal terms to maintain their position through future fundraises, but few have the wherewithal to maintain a pro rata contribution as the investment rounds grow from hundreds of thousands to tens of millions of dollars. The reason Angels are always looking for the hockey stick inflection is that it satisfies their time horizon and predicts a *possible* exit at a point where the multiples are high. One of the authors recently participated, with a group of Angel investors, in a high multiple exit to Big Pharma in under 3 years, but the timeline here was clearly the exception to the general case. The core drivers behind the initial investment and two follow-on rounds were a large patient population, a powerful scientific team, and an R&D process in which in vitro results would predict in vivo activity. These factors substantially shortened the time to exit, so that the Angel investors were able to participate in a rapidly accelerating valuation as the investment achieved important milestones and approached exit. This single investment was a notable win for the region, with an exceptional return, and it is hoped it will energize further life sciences investment among the local Angel community.

In the more typical long-term scenario, the question remains: how to increase the value of an investment to an Angel, providing participation in the hockey stick inflection without complicating follow-on investment? Angels frequently have pro rata rights granted in their notes, but VCs generally exclude all but major investors from exercising these rights in their rounds because the hassles of communication, legal fees, and paperwork outweigh the benefit of bringing in small amounts of follow-on investment. The challenge is to create a vehicle for coinvestment that would not complicate future fundraising.

One solution could be for Angels and Angel groups who had previously supported a company to join together to form a new LP, which would stand as an independent entity for all future transactions with the company and investors. This entity would be able to purchase participating preferred shares at the new price, but without voting rights or board involvement that would complicate the picture for VCs. In contrast to pro rata rights, which are intended to keep the proportional interest in a company the same, these coinvestment rights would be limited, perhaps to the amount of the original Angels' investment in real dollars (i.e., excluding warrants and interest). To keep legal and practical complications for the new investors to a minimum, all communication with the company would happen through a single designated member.

This template provides Angels with access to a relatively de-risked investment in which they have contributed to the de-risking, and the opportunity to coinvest with experienced institutional investors whose examination of the opportunity builds on the early stage due diligence. Further, it enables them to invest in a round closer to the hockey stick inflection point provided by clinical proof of concept, where an exit by IPO or acquisition is possible.

The model for this proposal comes from the coinvestment participation rights that many TTOs include in their patent licenses and transfer to other investors who join in when an A-list VC group leads a funding round. Incentives that would reduce the burden on fundraises could include limiting participation rights to fundraising totals below a certain threshold or offering common shares rather than preferred. The only way this would work is if the opportunity were entirely discretionary to the new investors at every fundraise. The terms would need to be such that there is no motivation to strip them.

Why would VCs go along with this? Well, maybe they wouldn't, but it's worth considering the upside: It de-risks their own investment and perhaps expands their net for finding "hidden gems" in the future. Angels are intimately familiar with their portfolio companies, so a decision to coinvest rather than to walk away and hope for the best is a strong endorsement of the science and the management team. Angels as a group include talent at least as diverse and broad as VCs, so building relationships between Angels and VCs is a way to strengthen the biotech ecosystem, further aligning the investment and technology objectives of the two groups in selecting the best companies to support in the future.

Considering the huge bundle of cash the CFF obtained from its royalty arrangement with Vertex, it seems inevitable that royalty payout clauses will find their way into Angel investment term sheets. There is a growing belief among those funding research that they should eligible for royalty income that arises from entities and/or technologies in which they have invested. For example, the American Heart Association (AHA) stipulates that grant recipients "agree to the AHA's right to participate in revenue from Inventions that are the subject of licensing or other revenue-generating agreements, regardless of whether the Invention is patented or copyrighted" [13]—and this is for funds provided to not-for-profit organizations. Angels are giving essentially the same benefits to for-profit organizations, explicitly supporting an investment thesis from which others will reap the rewards, so why shouldn't they be entitled to royalties? Their buyer power would inhibit companies from objecting, although we recognize that such rights could become a poison pill for future investments.

We actually think there is a rationale for allowing Angels access to royalty payments, i.e., payment drawn from net sales of a drug in the clinical market-place, rather than from liquidity events. Royalties reward the long game, betting on companies and technologies likely to have sustained potential, rewarding critical self-evaluation and honest communication. They may also push deal flow toward innovation. Whereas low-risk, me-too technologies might do better in the classic investment thesis model of the VoD, true paradigm shifts are likely to make more money in the long run.

The creation of an Angel LP for the purposes of coinvestment also makes a royalty plan workable. The LP could be eligible for a "nibble" royalty, sufficient to substantially reward Angels without significantly affecting the overall investment thesis and becoming a target for elimination by VCs. The key would be a *capped ROI* based on original dollars invested. Angel investor John Landry has proposed a 3× – 5× royalty return for IT investments [14]. Without intending to set definitive standards for this, a 3× return on $2.5 million would draw only $7.5 million from sales, and this could be taken over time from an 0.25% nibble royalty, netting the full payment in 3–5 years for a drug that climbs to blockbuster status.

At the end of the day, the numbers should take their place in the context of aligning Angel interests with our needs as a society: to nurture and promote the most valuable and innovative products of our research enterprise. Both sets of interests need to be satisfied, because if the Angels are not there, then nothing happens. At the same time, it's critically important to support an investment paradigm that keeps the drug development engine moving forward for a wider, rather than narrower, range of diseases and therapeutics.

REFERENCES

[1] Battelle Technology Partnership Practice. 2014 Evidence and opportunity: impacts of life sciences in North Carolina. <http://www.ncbiotech.org/sites/default/files/pages/2014%20Battelle%20Report_Full.pdf>; 2014.

[2] Interview with author SD, January 13, 2016.

[3] Hanson S, Nadig L, Altevogt B. Venture philanthropy strategies to support translational research: workshop summary forum on neuroscience and nervous system disorders. Washington, DC: Institute of Medicine; 2009. <http://www.nap.edu/catalog/12558.html>.

[4] Rose D. The history of the March of Dimes. August 26, 2010. <http://www.marchofdimes.org/mission/a-history-of-the-march-of-dimes.aspx#>; 2010 [accessed 27.02.16].

[5] Fielding S. Nonprofit disease foundation investments in biotechnology companies: an evaluation of venture philanthropy. M.A. Thesis: Harvard University—MIT Division of Health Sciences and Technology; 2011. <http://dspace.mit.edu/handle/1721.1/68463>.

[6] Juvenile Diabetes Research Foundation. Current partnerships. <http://grantcenter.jdrf.org/grant-center/industry-partnerships/>; 2016 [accessed 27.02.16].

[7] Leukemia and Lymphoma Society. Therapy acceleration program. <https://www.cff.org/Our-Research/Our-Research-Approach/Venture-Philanthropy/>; 2016.

[8]   Shane, S. Why the SBIR program is worth funding. January 2, 2015. <http://www.entrepre-neur.com/article/241290>; 2015 [accessed 27.02.16].

[9]   Small Business Administration. SBIR-STTR: America's seed fund. <https://www.sbir.gov/>; 2016 [accessed 27.02.16].

[10]   National Center for Advancing Translational Sciences. About TRND. Updated September 1, 2015. <https://ncats.nih.gov/trnd/about>; 2015 [accessed 27.02.16].

[11]   National Center for Advancing Translational Sciences. About BrIDGs. Updated September 9, 2015. <https://ncats.nih.gov/bridgs/about>; 2015 [accessed 27.02.16].

[12]   Fagnan DE, Yang NN, McKew JC, Lo AW. Financing translation: analysis of the NCATS rare-diseases portfolio. Sci Transl Med 2015;7(276):273–6. http://dx.doi.org/10.1126/sci-translmed.aaa2360.

[13]   American Heart Association. Award agreement terms and conditions. <http://my.americanheart.org/professional/ResearchPrograms/AwardsPolicies/UCM_475340_Awards.jsp>; 2016 [accessed 27.02.16].

[14]   Moore G. John Landry's fix for angel capital: get rid of the exit. Boston Bus J 2010 December 10, 2010. <http://www.bizjournals.com/boston/blog/mass-high-tech/2010/12/john-landrys-fix-for-angel-capital-get-rid.html/>; [accessed 27.02.16].

Translation Gap 3

Technology Transfer Wastes Money and Innovation

Chapter 22

Mitigating Supplier Power

HOW IT'S NOT SUPPOSED TO WORK

The power of technology transfer offices (TTOs) over the interests of their inventor/scientists and technological innovation itself was illustrated by a case that involved a US East Coast medical school and a Midwestern university. Scientists at the two institutions had collaborated on the discovery of novel molecular structure that could lead to a new way to reduce disease progression in a chronic disease that affects the elderly. A biotechnology company conducting development work in the space wanted an option agreement that would give them a period of time to evaluate the molecule, and submitted a proposal to the university with option and license terms.

The university TTO informed the medical school TTO that they were satisfied with the terms and eager to execute the option agreement. They wanted the agreement in place before they committed to paying the fees associated with converting the provisional application into a utility application. The biotech company also felt that the matter was urgent: "A fast turn-around is advisable, if we want to prevent this technology from falling by the wayside" [1].

The university invited the medical school to be a party to the executed option/license agreement, offering to share the revenue from the option and license. The medical school TTO refused the invitation, replying that "since we did not agree with the terms in the executed option agreement, we decline to execute the letter agreement" [2]. Instead, they insisted that the company execute a separate agreement with them. The biotech balked at this idea, feeling that it had already received approval of its terms and, as a cash-strapped start-up itself, wasn't eager to incur additional costs to the license.

The result was a standoff, with the company refusing to pursue a separate option, the university TTO trying to bring the medical school along with their agreement, and the medical school TTO refusing to option their rights through any means other than a separate agreement with the company. The company set an end-of-year deadline, at which time it would cancel its option with the university. The medical school TTO went silent for 4 months, refusing to respond to emails and phone messages. When the deadline passed, the company kept its promise and terminated the option agreement. The university TTO, in turn, abandoned the patent application.

Preserving the Promise. DOI: http://dx.doi.org/10.1016/B978-0-12-809216-3.00022-1

The opportunity to commercialize the invention was lost. The inventors were outraged by this behavior, because their molecule was a nonintuitive discovery that had resulted from years of effort and they had been excited to have a company license the idea and try and move it forward.

We have kept some of the details to ourselves; the events occurred some time ago and the individuals involved have moved on. In any event, we include it not to take the institutions to task, but as a useful starting point to unravel the complicated incentives and disincentives that contribute to Translation Gap 3: *Technology transfer wastes money and innovation.*

THE REAL COSTS OF SUPPLIER POWER

It is hard to justify letting a promising technology die, especially when there is a company willing to assume patent costs and reasonable fees. In the case we've described, an agreement had already been negotiated, to which the second TTO could have easily become a party with minimal out-of-pocket expenses. Why would one TTO let the technology die instead of signing on to an apparently reasonable agreement *already executed by another TTO*? Why would they walk away from both an upfront payment and a large potential upside? And, from a broader perspective, what is the rationale for a medical school standing in the way of another institution commercializing an important clinical discovery?

This behavior is the result of conflicting demands. TTOs receive licensing and other fees, but they obtain most of their funding from, and are subject to the goals and expectations of, university administrations. Because longer term royalty income is uncertain and budgets are annual, most TTOs are cost centers rather than profit centers, and are measured by short-term metrics. This means they are focused on generating a series of deals to fulfill expectations of the university administration, and their fallback is to negotiate terms based on presumed "best practices."

In the instance we've described, although we can't be sure what was in the tech transfer officer's head, it was more than likely a problem of optics and precedent: what are the types of deals our TTO makes and what are the terms? The terms of the proposed agreement were not as lucrative as the medical school TTO was accustomed to receiving and the potential value of the deal was significantly reduced by the need to split the option already negotiated by the other TTO. Within the context of the medical school, agreeing to an option and license that didn't fit its standard financial criteria was unacceptable, since it was embarrassingly low and possibly precedent-setting, and would suggest that the TTO was not effectively performing its job. It was certainly also an issue of prioritizing internal resources. To negotiate with the university TTO might take as much time and expense as negotiating a separate license with the company itself, or working on one of the many other deals waiting for the attention of the medical school TTO. So it was better for the medical school to kill the technology than to approve an agreement they didn't like.

This is a classic example of misaligned incentives getting in the way of clinical development. A key player in the technology commercialization process is incentivized in ways that oppose supporting innovation. Whether a technology gets a chance at commercialization in the Valley of Death (VoD) depends on a negotiated option or license that is consistent with the expectations and habits of a particular TTO. If the TTO cannot be satisfied, the innovation is sidelined or dies.

Porter maintains that supplier power is most extreme when "the supplier group does not depend heavily on the industry for its revenues" [3]. TTOs are suppliers of the underlying collateral for funding in the VoD. Most TTOs spend more money than they take in and most of what is licensed will never achieve substantial revenue. As noted by Louis Berneman of Osage Venture Partners at the AUTM conference in 2015, "99% of start-ups are not going to get venture capital. And after all the due diligence and everything else we do, three out of four venture capital companies fail. 30–40% of them run through our money without any positive outcome, 70–80% of them don't hit their financial targets" [4].

It follows that most technology licenses have little or no real value in the beginning, and while there is clearly prioritization, it is impossible to predict which of those licenses will be the "home run" that drives enormous royalties back into the university. Thus, a TTO is not highly dependent on the sale of any particular technology for its long-term revenue. (We acknowledge that certain paradigm-setting technologies, such as siRNA, CRISPR Cas9, and Chimeric Antigen Receptor T cells have a clearer path to venture capital (VC) funding and potential IPOs (initial public offerings).)

Instead, the technology transfer business model is based on assembling a portfolio of promising deals that meets the expectations of a university administration and is in accord with industry standards. This is a probability model, not unlike investing by Angels or VCs, based on making more "shots on goal." Technologies are vetted based on apparent scientific promise, faculty prioritization, the particular expertise and connections of technology transfer officers, and the opportunistic availability of a buyer. The likelihood of any one technology reaping a tremendous reward is so low that when it happens, it makes regional or national news. In this context, dropping one licensing opportunity is like the difference between buying 99 versus 100 lottery tickets. In our story, what was a catastrophe for the inventor and their technology was, for the medical school TTO, a minor shift in the risk: benefit position of their portfolio.

REDUCING THE COSTS OF TECHNOLOGY TRANSFER

This dynamic is expensive to the VoD ecosystem. As Porter observes, "Suppliers serving many industries will not hesitate to extract maximum profits from each one." In other words, when suppliers sell to many different companies, and no individual company contributes disproportionately to its profits, TTOs will demand as much from each transaction as possible—for the simple reason that they can always move on to the next transaction. Given annualized budgets, this translates into an overemphasis on upfront payments and unilateral terms. Their monopoly power is further enhanced in an individual case because the offer is a highly differentiated product available from a single source. Inventors are only in a position to commercialize their own discoveries, but they don't have the rights to do so; everything they invent is owned by the universities that employ them. In the VoD, this means that TTOs are in the driver's seat with respect to terms: they can always walk away, regardless of the protests of the entrepreneurs and investors on the other side of the table.

The connection between supplier power and its burden on the VoD is best appreciated when one considers the structure of technology license agreements. A typical license demands an execution fee, annual maintenance fees, milestone fees, commercialization fees, materials transfer fees, and, of course, royalties. Nobody would argue against reasonable fees to cover the considerable costs of technology protection and management by universities. Or against their receiving royalties from commercialization of a technology that originated in their labs. But it should be equally clear that fees charged before a technology is generating revenue, while it is still being used as collateral to borrow money from investors, is a diversion of money that could be used to support development and overhead.

Milestone fees are the best example of fees that don't make a lot of sense, yet are routinely charged by TTOs. They are assessed when an outlicensed technology achieves a specific technical or clinical objective. For example, one actual license for a university platform technology was a 35-page document stipulating a $75,000 fee for enrollment of a patient in a Phase I clinical trial and twice that amount for enrollment of the first patient in a Phase II trial. This license was in tandem to another, also required for the use of the technology, which stipulated a $150,000 payment on completion of a Phase II trial. Thus, *without incurring any risk or expending any additional effort*, the licensors charged $375,000 before any revenue was generated by their IP.

Let's look at the impact of these fees on the cost of development. Clinical trials can easily reach $2–5 million for a Phase I study (the earliest phase of human trials). Because the money taken out for the milestone payments originated as a transaction in the VoD, that trial is funded by money that has been borrowed or collateralized with equity. The cost of that money is interest on the debt or the value of the equity given up by the company that licensed the IP—which may include preferred shares, discounts, liquidation preferences—and also carries the expectation of a substantial multiple of return on the investment. As a result, the obligation incurred to pay milestone fees could ultimately be several times the payment itself. This situation exists every time that a university imposes a fee on a pre-revenue technology.

This situation testifies to the potent supplier power held by universities licensing their technology. How many industries are able to charge a success fee if their products pass a lab test years before they are available for purchase? It is like a restaurant demanding an additional $5 if a cheeseburger looks especially delicious on the plate, before anyone has taken a bite. What is most disturbing about a milestone fee is that the university has done little or nothing beyond the initial development effort to earn it; meeting the milestone was primarily the result of the start-up company's efforts supported with investors' money. Furthermore, these efforts were expended on improving something the university already owns and from which they will achieve a revenue-driven payday if those efforts are successful and result in a royalty stream. It would actually make more sense for a university to *reduce* its fees charged to any company that advanced its technology, as a reward for the company's efforts on the university's behalf. That would require risk-sharing, however, which is in conflict with the short-term metrics that incentivize TTOs.

Of course this is a bit of heresy with respect to the traditional US TTO model. And even if we were all to agree that non-royalty fees are a drain on the system and counterproductive to long-term success, the reality of the Bayh–Dole Act remains. TTOs are financially constrained arms of not-for-profit institutions, operating on annual not long-term budgets, with a mandate to effectively manage the university's IP. The cost of a technology license reflects the fact that the TTO setting the terms needs to balance its budget, and one obvious way to do that is with upfront fees. Such fees are financially practical and actually rather logical from the standpoint of making sure the licensee has skin in the game, and the university isn't "giving away" valuable technology. It's equally true that they are a de facto *tax on innovation.*

There's a clear short-term benefit for TTOs to maximize their upfront revenue. From the perspectives of clinical benefit, volume of useful technology transfers, and investor return, however, it is in everyone's long-term interest to minimize the expense of licensing. TTOs require a safe and practical way to turn inventions over to inventors and companies that positions them to maximize the long-term value of their IP. Nontraditional models, already in existence at selected institutions, move away from upfront and milestone fees that siphon money out of the VoD, and take a longer view that shares both risk and reward.

This starts with developing practices that streamline the handling of IP. Logical changes to improve the impact of investments in the VoD can be envisioned, and the process of technology transfer can be simplified. For example, it's almost never a bad idea to reduce unnecessary legal process in favor of standardized agreements. License fees don't need a protracted negotiation in every instance, and we believe there's a strong argument for rebalancing short- and long-term payments, especially things like milestone payments that aren't driven by ongoing contribution of the TTO.

Movement has begun in this direction with the creation of an "express license." The Carolina Express Exclusive License Agreement [5] is a draft license with standardized annual fees that depend on the type of invention and the business model. We especially like that the document is publicly available, and therefore can serve as a touchstone for other inventors and TTOs. The terms do not include scientific or clinical milestones. They do impose a fee at a sale or IPO of 0.75% of the entire transaction, which replaces the upfront with capped participation in a liquidity event; and there are standard royalty fees. The 0.75%

still fits our definition of a tax on innovation, but it's paid at a more appropriate time. It's a carried charge that doesn't consume early investment dollars, and it's realized when everyone is potentially doing pretty well because of the company's success.

The question, of course, is whether it is possible to backload license fees, shifting that cost burden away from early-stage investors in the pre-revenue period. Darren Fast is the Director of Technology Transfer at the University of Manitoba, Winnipeg. He faced a local industry unwilling to work with the university because of onerous licensing/IP costs [6]. Building on his experience as a life sciences VC, he attacked the problem by drastically altering his university's licensing practices. Their licensing agreements now include only basic fees (e.g., patent filing) and a royalty—no milestone payments. While this has reduced revenues in the near-term, especially during this operational transition, Fast calculates that he will bring in more revenue over the long haul because the real money comes with getting a product to market. Fast's approach is having a positive effect on research in the university because it lowers the barrier to companies supporting work being done in their labs. He estimates that in its first year, his policy enabled an additional CAN$1 million in research support.

Because Canadian faculty own 50% of the inventorship rights, they are not required to work with the university on commercialization. Fast created a business model that encourages faculty to work with his TTO. To maximize the amount of money available for development, his licensing fee is "a trivial amount, just enough so that they have to write a check" [6]. He also avoids equity, which due to institutional policy would have to be divested as soon as shares are issued, and thus eliminates the issue of institutional conflict of interest.

Fast also wants to encourage ongoing working relationships between founder/scientist's university labs and their new companies, through sponsored research agreements that build on the licensed IP: "We want to be flexible and find a solution that works for everybody...We assign [new IP] to them right off the bat, on the same terms. We want them to continue inventing. That's what they're good at." Fast has found that, despite having the ability to opt out, the vast majority of his inventors choose to work with the university TTO. The value proposition is the ability to work with an experienced guide, actively seeking to streamline the costs of start-up company formation. This is intended to attract, rather than force, faculty engagement, a significant contrast with the imposed control of a typical TTO.

ASSIGNMENT OF AN INVENTION: WHAT IF WE GIVE IT AWAY?

Given our observations in the first part of this chapter, it is easy to imagine throwing out Bayh–Dole altogether as part of the solution. Subscribers to this point of view would grant inventors the so-called "Professor's Privilege" of owning rights to their own inventions. Or, as proposed by Robert Litan and Lesa Mitchell of the Kauffman Foundation, allowing inventors the right to choose their own licensing agents if they are unhappy with the TTOs at their institutions [7]. By creating a competitive market for licensing services, faculty would have access to the best tech transfer expertise, and agencies which would compete in classic market terms for the best customers by providing the best services and outcomes.

We don't support this proposal as an across-the-board solution. Who would be excited to start a for-profit company that performed the duties of a TTO, including assumption of substantial upfront costs in patenting and legal fees— when the customers for their licenses are themselves cash-strapped start-up companies with indeterminate prospects for success, years away from VC funding, let alone an exit. To make this business model work in the short term would require even higher, nonsubsidized license fees, and that would increase, not decrease, the costs of technology transfer and require passing those costs on to early-stage investors. This is exactly the opposite of what's needed to overcome the third Translation Gap. It seems to us the better route is to preserve and expand the advantages of the current system, while recasting the incentives that lead to undesirable outcomes.

Ideally, TTOs are integrated into the culture and operations of any university that sees its mission as both creating and commercializing technology. For many faculty, interactions with tech transfer officers are the first step in commercializing their technologies, a process that requires learning and collaboration over an extended period of time, pre- and post-licensing. The technology transfer officers we have known range from impassioned novices to Jedi Masters, but their effectiveness in implementing the opportunity of Bayh–Dole is undeniable. The fact that TTO operations can be inefficient or compromised by misaligned incentives should not overshadow the critical role they play, and the substantial value that they add to biotech commercialization.

But Litan and Mitchell make an important point. The value of the technologies produced by a university has no *a priori* connection with the expertise, resources and effort—patenting, legal fees, finding a licensee or funding a business advisor—that will be required to support it. In a very real sense, Bayh–Dole traps innovation within universities because absolute supplier power gives it only one way out: to fit the expectations, habits, and resources of TTOs. But why should licensing a technology to a VoD company fail because it's a poor fit with the interests of a given TTO, the one that happens to operate in the university where the invention was discovered? Why should it even be *possible* that a TTO can decide unilaterally that any single invention does not deserve an opportunity for licensing?

There's a long-term value to scientists, universities, and investors of reducing the high rate of failure, and better integrating scientific with commercial efforts: fewer bad ideas consume scarce funds, more important and hard-earned discoveries survive the VoD, and everyone in the system benefits from concentrating on the longer term financial opportunity. We've argued that technology transfer is enhanced when TTOs have the charter and autonomy to be more entrepreneurial, more engaged with the process of enhancing the value of their technologies and connecting them to the investor and clinical markets (see chapters: What if It Doesn't Actually Work?, Building a Better Mousetrap). This may require re-thinking the mission, as well as the metrics, and it may result in fewer companies being formed but with a higher probability of success.

This could increase the conflict already extant between TTOs and the inventors who rightfully expect their intellectual progress to be given a chance at commercialization, and chafe at the authority of TTOs when they decline to patent and license those discoveries. If a TTO does not agree that an invention disclosure warrants a patent application, then any commercial progress on the invention stops. Without an investable, IP-based property in hand, the inventor will not be able to raise money for a start-up, nor will he be willing to pay any patent expenses while the property is still owned by the university and a licensor has not been found. Furthermore, scientists can be reluctant to undertake raising money for an invention before a patent application has been filed, because pitching discloses the novel but unprotected concept to potential competitors. This stalemate can be extremely frustrating and demoralizing for faculty members and is clearly antithetical to the intent of Bayh–Dole.

For these reasons, letting technologies have a back door out of the university and into the VoD is essential, so that the "no-go" from a TTO is not a terminal decision. Most universities have a policy that enables them to assign full rights to an invention to an inventor, but this is far more complicated than one would think, as it presents significant risks to the university and is neither common nor easily done.

We should step back and look at the disclosure and patenting process in more detail. The initial submission to the TTO is the invention disclosure, something of a static document representing the scientific discovery at a single point in time. It's likely that the patent application will extend beyond the disclosure, as writing the patent often reveals novel insights and research, of course, continues in the laboratory. There is value to inventors disclosing as much as possible, since evolution into a deep and comprehensive patent has a better chance of success. But the financial incentives are structured to encourage the opposite: partially disclosing an invention in order to obtain the assignment, and then attempting to fold additional information into the IP afterward.

Why? Because universities don't want to give away something valuable without compensation, and if there's more to the invention than has been disclosed, the university could be doing exactly that. In essence, the inventor here is leveraging his knowledge to obtain assignment of the IP. The university would have recourse to administrative sanction or legal action—at which point the inventor could argue that any so-called improvements were obvious from the start and the TTO simply didn't understand the full scope of the invention, or that subsequent evolution was the product of development activity that did not originate within the university. Once money is at stake, it is easy to imagine everyone digging in, especially if the transferred IP eventually results in an exit or marketed product.

Even if an invention is exactly what is disclosed, technology transfer officers can misjudge and potentially let something go via assignment that eventually makes a lot of money. In anticipation of a negative outcome, TTOs are protective of property rights. At the 2015 AUTM annual meeting, James Elmer, Director of Technology Licensing at St. Jude Children's Research Hospital noted, "we always worry about risk, I'm sitting in a director's chair and I'm thinking, if I release an invention … I did my best assessment, but come on, we have early-stage inventions and you never know exactly where the pot of gold is going to be. If I'm wrong and I give it back, and the institution has no financial interest whatsoever, and it hits big, like a drug, oh my God, I'm not going to be sitting in this seat much longer, I don't think. So that terrifies me, but I see that a lot of institutions go that route" [8].

Assignment is thus more complicated than licensing, and letting go of an invention is not a benign process. It offers virtually nothing to the university except the potential for headaches and embarrassment, it incentivizes investigators to be dishonest about invention disclosures, it strains a relationship that is already fractured by a disagreement over the value of the research, and it further increases the likelihood of a negative outcome.

Consider an alternate path, in which rights to the contents of an invention disclosure are granted to the investigator who, strictly limited by the disclosed claims, can decide independently whether to proceed with the patent application. It could proceed as a version of the Express License we discussed above, but with reduced fees that reflect the obligation of the inventor to initiate the patent process on his own. The key to implementing this proposal would be minimizing the demands it places on a TTO, as any agreement to release IP to an inventor consumes time and effort that could be dedicated to opportunities expected to be more lucrative. Robin Rasor, Managing Director of Licensing at the University of Michigan, suggests, "To me these are a time sink. You've already decided you've done a good job, you've done a report. You've already decided it's something you don't want to spend any time on, and here you are, spending all of this time trying to negotiate something. That's why I'm looking for the golden agreement, the one-pager that I could just hand over, no negotiation. We can't afford to spend this much time, that's our dilemma" [9].

Overall, this wouldn't be a big change to the current processes for packaging an invention for the VoD, except in this case we might see an Angel investor engaged before, rather than after, the patent has been submitted. This approach respects both the initiative of the inventor and the contribution the university made to the discovery, while accepting that TTOs cannot possibly be omniscient appraisers of everything that comes into their offices.

AN OUNCE OF PREVENTION

Our earlier statement that scientists are most likely to recognize what is visionary and novel cannot be extended to mean they are the best judges of what is commercially viable. The rejection of an invention as not suited for commercialization, effectively forcing an academic scientist to take assignment rather than a license and come up with patent costs, disrupts the synergistic partnership that can exist between a TTO and the investigator. It's also likely to lead to bitter feelings. A better understanding between inventors and TTOs starts with transparency, and with the investigators taking responsibility for understanding their prospective market. Scientists know how to collect and analyze data, but are unused to doing so in a commercial context. They would be well advised to satisfy themselves there is a significant commercial opportunity through formal or informal market assessment before they take on the responsibilities of assignment. They will certainly need to do so for investors at some point and will be much more credible fundraisers if they are armed with confidence about the real, addressable market.

Biotech Showcase is one of the best-attended partnering meetings in biotechnology, held down the street from the annual J.P. Morgan Healthcare Conference in San Francisco. It is a speed-dating service for biotech. Meetings are set up using an online search and scheduling engine; they take place in half hour increments at hundreds of booths separated by thin walls and gray curtains. In 2016, representatives of more than 1600 companies participated in 5650 one-to-one investor meetings [10]. These included qualified private and public equity investors, industry analysts, bankers, technology transfer officers, and pharmaceutical and biotechnology industry executives. This was all in addition to platform presentations from 300 biotech companies, ranging from startups to small-to-midsize life science companies, pitching therapeutic candidates, diagnostics, and research tools to almost 600 investors.

At the 2016 Biotech Showcase, we ran into Louise Butt, PhD, a post doctoral fellow who studies RNA interactions at the University of Portsmouth, United Kingdom [11]. She had won an iCure scholarship, which provided £30,000 to travel the world for 3 months and meet with industry thought leaders about her discovery, a platform that enables high throughput screening of RNA interactions.

The iCure program is a direct descendant of the Innovation Corps program that started within the National Science Foundation (NSF) [12]. Both are based on the principles of the "Lean Start-up" conceived by Steve Blank [13], who designed the original program in partnership with the NSF. The principle of the Lean Start-up model is that business planning should be a dynamic interplay between discovery and market intelligence. As precursor to a more detailed business plan, companies fill in a "business model canvas" that asks for their best assessment of key market determinants, such as their value proposition, cost structure, and revenue streams (Fig. 22.1).

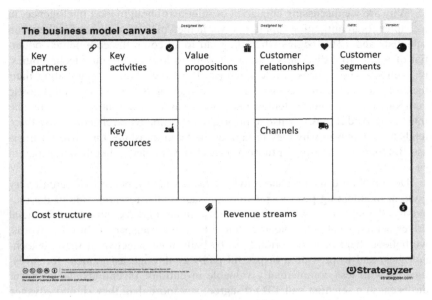

FIGURE 22.1   The business model canvas, adapted from Strategyzer.com.

The idea is for the companies to test these preliminary hypotheses, asking prospective customers and constituents for feedback and guidance. This information is rapidly fed back into the development process, in an iterative process that creates an improved product roadmap and business model.

After receiving her scholarship, Louise filled in the business model canvas and hit the road, meeting almost 100 people in 12 weeks. Her first meetings were at the Biotech Showcase. "That was really eye opening … the first time I spent speaking to actual investors, who literally are in charge of the purse strings [about] which markets are part of the[ir] strategy for the future" [11].

Many of those she spoke to expressed interest, but most thought her technology was too early for investment and offered advice on experiments and applications that would advance her toward commercialization. "…you keep hearing the same type of thing across a number of people…we were starting to see trends." It is perhaps instructive that Louise was a bit surprised to find "real life applications [were] the theme of the conversations."

Since returning to the lab in Portsmouth, she has been sharing her experiences with others through seminars and informal meetings. The advice isn't groundbreaking to anyone involved in early-stage commercial development, but it highlights the difference in academic and commercial worldviews about something as basic as determining what prospective customers (investors) might want. Her advice to other academic scientists: "Have more conversations, go meet them, demonstrate the technology, ask if there is anything they want us to test. Go look people up."

Why are we discussing education of scientists about market intelligence, in a chapter about mitigating supplier power in the VoD? Because conflict between scientists and TTOs begins when they fail to agree on the commercial potential of a scientific discovery. We don't want to lose exceptional technologies, or even very good ones, while scientists learn the ropes of negotiating their technologies out of universities. There's always going to be an opportunistic component to what gets patented and funded, based on whomever is or might be interested. And it makes sense to prioritize big-name researchers because there tends to be a reason why they're famous, and that translates into investor interest. But there's no reason for those motives to be clouded rather than transparent as to purpose.

Despite their usual co-charter to keep faculty happy, many TTOs aren't very good at maintaining positive relationships across the research side of the university. Perhaps there wouldn't be quite so many hurt feelings if the financial driver behind what gets patented were a bit more transparent. In other words, we believe there is an opportunity to be both more selective of the best technologies, and to provide a respectful pathway through assignment for investigators with less commercially valuable inventions. Inventions should never die because a scientist and TTO disagree, any more than they should advance exclusively for internal political reasons that have little to do with the invention itself. Directly immersing scientists in understanding markets, and enabling transparent networking with companies and investors, will help inventors and TTOs have the same conversation and work better together.

We started this chapter with an example of the breakdown in value that can occur when TTOs make decisions about what technologies to transfer and how that will be accomplished. It is not entirely gratuitous to lay this at the feet of the lawyers who are often central business advisors and push back at any simplification of the procedures. As a company founder and an Angel investor, we are certainly in a position to question why so much effort and money has to be consumed by *defensive legal process*. We've both witnessed horror shows of legal impediment:

- An inability to persuade a university's general counsel to bless the most boiler plate of documents, a Confidential Disclosure Agreement. As a result, after four months of wrangling, a technology and a promising relationship with an important source of funding for a university commercialization program were stopped dead in their tracks.
- More recently, we saw months pass by seeking to obtain a Material Transfer and Research Collaboration Agreement to obtain a critical reagent from a VC-funded biotech start-up. The opportunity vanished when the start-up was bought by a Pharma company.

No value was created in either instance, but there was an ultimately useless consumption of time, energy, and billable hours for all parties. When we say that *technology transfer wastes money*, we also mean that friction over agreements diverts time and money that could otherwise be used to advance licensed technologies and build the companies that support them.

The inventions universities spawn are trapped by supplier power, where they suffer from poor decision making, lost opportunity, and excessive expense. The waste we've been describing isn't because people in tech transfer aren't trying to commercialize great technologies. It's because of systemic mismatch of resources, toward or away from inventions: they're too early or don't have a commercial target; they don't have a prominent enough champion or are deemed a good or bad idea due to university policies and interests; they look like opportunities to make money that have little to do with clinical value; or they are stalled by legal process or misaligned incentives.

The most income from an invention comes when it leads to a drug, device or diagnostic that is approved for clinical use and attracts a large number of paying customers. For this to happen, inventions need to transition from support by the university as a research proposition, to support by investors of an investment thesis, to support by customers of a clinical value proposition. Aligning the selection and advocacy of university inventions with the needs of the marketplace offers tremendous benefits to all parties, because it increases the likelihood that an investment thesis can be funded and progress to the long-term annuity of customer sales. Returning to Porter's discussion of supplier power, he notes that "if a particular industry accounts for a large portion of a supplier group's volume or profit ... suppliers will want to protect the industry through reasonable pricing and assist in activities such as R&D (research and development) and lobbying" [3]. Better collaboration on development with scientists and companies that license their technologies is in the best interest of universities, scientists, investors—and clinical medicine.

REFERENCES

[1] Confidential email dated May 19, 2010.
[2] Confidential email dated September 20, 2010.
[3] Porter ME. On competition: updated and expanded edition. Boston, MA: Harvard Business School Publishing; 2008.
[4] Louis Berneman AUTM 2015 annual meeting venture forum. February 24, 2015. <http://www.softconference.com/AUTM/sessionDetail.asp?SID=371165>; 2015.
[5] Carolina Express Exclusive License Agreement, Version 2.0. <http://research.unc.edu/files/2014/01/CarolinaExpressLicenseAgreement2.02011.pdf>; 2016 [accessed 04.05.16].
[6] Fast D. interview with author SD, February 17, 2016.
[7] Litan R, Mitchell L. A faster path from innovation to market: removing the technology licensing obstacle. Breakthrough Ideas for 2010. Harvard Business Review; 2010. January-February 2010.
[8] Elmer J. AUTM 2015 annual meeting. Releasing IP rights to inventors: alternatives and experiences. February 24, 2015. http://www.softconference.com/AUTM/sessionDetail.asp?SID=371140.

[9] Rasor R. AUTM 2015 annual meeting. Releasing IP rights to inventors: alternatives and experiences 2015 February 24, 2015. http://www.softconference.com/AUTM/sessionDetail. asp?SID=371140.

[10] Biotech Showcase™ 2016 reports record high attendance this year. Press Release, EBD Group. <http://www.ebdgroup.com/bts/media/articles/160127.php>; [accessed 04.05.16].

[11] Butt L, PhD interview with author SD, April 15, 2016.

[12] Webinar iCorps™ at NIH for small businesses. November 12, 2015. <http://sbir.cancer.gov/icorps>; 2015.

[13] Blank S. Why the lean start-up changes everything. Harvard Business Review. May, 2013. <https://strategyzer.com/canvas/>; 2013 [accessed 04.05.16].

Chapter 23

Preventing Speeding by Closing the Road

The Bayh–Dole Act assigns property that may have enormous social and commercial value to not-for-profit institutions, setting them up for an existential struggle between academic purity and financial survival. Performing research sponsored by industry is an enticing remedy for declining income from other funding sources. It supplements faculty income historically underwritten by grants and fills the gap of increasing research expenses complicated by regulatory overreach. Institutions also recognize that industry, not academic laboratories, is necessary to translate discoveries into drugs, and the path to both reputation and royalties. Academia is at once eager to build these relationships and suspicious, even contemptuous, of industry motives. There is a fundamental concern that closer relationships will lead to abandoning academic principles, to universities becoming something they don't want to be.

If Bayh–Dole had granted commercial rights to new biotech IP directly to the spinout companies rather than universities, there would be a host of other problems, but no fretting about how to accommodate both commercial imperatives and academic identity. Universities have a struggling business model these days, yet optics remain important, and their core mission demands limits on being "all-in" for business. This clash between financial imperatives and the academic mission animates processes and restrictions that inhibit technology commercialization and are an important contributor to Translation Gap 3, *Technology transfer wastes money and innovation*. Nowhere is this more evident than in the Conflict of Interest (CoI) regulations that seek to protect the academic ideal from the temptations of the commercial realm.

Current university regulations take their cue from the CoI policies imposed on recipients of National Institutes of Health (NIH) grant funding, and are spelled out in the Federal 2011 Public Health Service (PHS) Regulations [1]. They seek to promote "objectivity in research by establishing standards that provide a reasonable expectation that the design, conduct, and reporting of research performed under PHS contracts will be free from bias resulting from Investigator financial conflicts of interest" [1]. "Financial conflict of interest means a significant financial interest that could directly and significantly

Preserving the Promise. DOI: http://dx.doi.org/10.1016/B978-0-12-809216-3.00023-3

affect the design, conduct, or reporting of PHS-funded research" [2]. In short, if a scientist can make money by committing research fraud, or compromising research due to an unconscious bias, a conflict exists.

The goal of the regulations is to set up a firewall that theoretically will protect the integrity and purity of the science, reduce incentives for fraud, and maximize the safety of subjects involved in clinical research. Like most such regulations, these attempt to avoid a negative consequence by imposing artificial constraints that hamstring the process. In this case, CoI regulations attempt to avert deceptive behavior by separating those doing experiments in an academic environment from any financial motivation to bias the experiments. The Federal regulations are not specific about what constitutes a significant CoI; rather, they specify that organizations need to implement a policy of defining, disclosing, and managing them.

Much has been written about the origins of CoI practices, and we won't repeat these stories or analyses here [3–5]. We don't want to minimize the need for scientists to maintain credibility, to function effectively as proponents of social good, or to earn the support of NIH and charitable funding. We also don't want to discount the danger of falsified data, and we share the discomfiture of the research community that a significant proportion of research cannot be replicated. But we do argue for flexibility in thinking about what is actually a CoI, as it relates to university technologies that underpin companies in the Valley of Death (VoD). Overzealous CoI regulation is a costly burden on the technology transfer process and destructive to the chances of a technology surviving the VoD.

While policies for defining and disclosing CoIs are relatively homogeneous with respect to Federal compliance, the exact definitions of what CoIs are allowable, and how they will be addressed, are left to the discretion of universities and vary widely. If there is a common theme, it is to prevent the potential financial windfall attendant on commercializing a technology from influencing the scientific conduct of an investigator. As stated by the Harvard Medical School *Policy on Conflicts of Interest and Commitment:*

> *Research must be protected from bias to ensure that the results of the Research are valid and can be relied on in the development of medical therapies and in furtherance of scientific knowledge. Concerns about the ultimate impact of financial conflicts on end-users of the Research and research integrity exist in all Research.* [6]

Such CoI policies imply that any form of financial benefit could lead to malfeasance or error, but they also seek to achieve a higher purpose, preventing the impression that anything untoward might be happening in order to preserve confidence in the probity of the institution.

In practice, CoI generally relates to preventing a company from sponsoring research in the scientific founder's laboratory and/or limiting the amount of equity a founder can hold in a company that has licensed his or her technology. Harvard also explicitly addresses these issues. Their I(b) Research Support Rule precludes faculty who have "an Equity Financial Interest in a Business" from receiving sponsored research support from that business, and their I(d) External Activity Rule extends this proscription to apply to faculty who serve in any fiduciary role in a company.

Under these and similar policies at other universities, if faculty own a significant part of or play an instrumental role in running a company, they are not able to receive funding from the company to do research in their laboratory. If a scientist wants to own shares in a company developing his invention, or wants to contribute in a leadership role to the success of the company, he is not able to obtain any research funding or engage in a sponsored research agreement with the company.

This is a recipe for wasted value because, whatever choice the scientist makes, CoI policies prevent him from becoming fully engaged as an advocate for the company and its technology. Perhaps this is less of a problem for a company further along on the VoD journey, where venture capital (VC) funding enables the hiring of effective surrogates. But even in that case, CoI policies promote needless duplication of effort. At a minimum, they separate the fledgling technology from its most knowledgeable and committed caregiver. It's not a great leap to appreciate how this might influence the chances of success, and from a practical perspective make it difficult to properly incentivize inventors.

Investors want founders incentivized. As Atlas Venture's Bruce Booth writes: "Maintaining deep connections with scientific founders is often very important to the successful launch and growth of young biotech companies. Beyond the founding observations that catalyzed their start-ups' creation, the role of scientific founders as top advisors and research collaborators is often of huge value" [7].

None of us has an endless capacity to invent or unlimited time to do so. If a scientist stands to be financially rewarded by owning some of a company that licenses his technology, he will naturally spend more of his time working on it—even more so if the company is funding research in his laboratory. There's also the question of whether the licensed technology is an actualized invention, or if there is more to learn to transform the discovery into a product. It's a question that underlies milestone-based investing, but the import is deeper than that. To a scientist, a discovery is just an instant in a lifetime of inquiry that continues whether he is on the team or not. If the founder is not inventing for you, the company that holds the technology license, he may end up inventing for someone else. Booth wants his investments backed by the full creative engagement of his scientific founders, and that means making sure they have skin in the game.

As a venture firm that helps create new start-ups, we're big believers that equity—a share of ownership in the upside—is the ultimate currency of entrepreneurship. Leveraging that currency enables risk-taking, aligns incentives, creates a clarity of focus, and thus unleashes the creative energies required to tackle the challenges of technology transfer and commercialization. [7]

In his book, *Pharmaphobia: How the Conflict of Interest Myth Undermines American Medical Innovation*, Dr. Thomas P. Stossel echoes these sentiments. "Investors have told me that they would not start companies based on technologies invented by Harvard Medical School faculty because Harvard does not permit its faculty members to hold equity (stock) in companies that sponsor their research" [8]. As a Professor at the Harvard Medical School, Stossel is intimately familiar with the regulations and sees their effects first-hand. "Conflict of Interest regulations have polluted the ability for scientific collaboration at the early stages. Inventors have very little motivation to interact with companies" [9].

Restricting sponsored research can waste a lot of investor money. First, the policy demands that the start-up company perform all of its research in a separate, distinct facility. This might be good for the local real estate community, but it means that precious investor dollars need to buy or replicate infrastructure that already exists, increasing the cost of the research. Second, it prevents the intellectual synergies that can occur if research is conducted within the academic environment, while failing to fully leverage the expertise carried by the inventor and his laboratory.

Preventing sponsored research is also a negative for university finances. Academicians Daniel J. Howard and Frank N. Laird have argued that universities need to accept a "New Normal in Funding," which recognizes limits to growth in the size of the scientific enterprise, and where expectations for the amount and types of support that will be available for university research must adapt to the current reality [10]. Universities need a model, they argue, in which they "recognize that even the most distinguished researchers will experience gaps in funding and require in-house assistance to maintain a research program." They propose greater interactions between universities and industry and, recognizing the cultural misunderstandings that exist, they assert that "leaders in both sectors need to rethink how and why they can take advantage of joint work and the diversity of forms that such collaboration can take." Lowering the barriers to receiving sponsored research funds would help universities keep their laboratories filled and their scientists active, even in the face of diminished funding from public and philanthropic sources.

CoI policies that prevent scientific founders from owning substantial equity in companies that license their technology impose another hidden cost on VoD companies. Other parties, including business advisors, hired CEOs, and investors may receive significant founder's equity (along with options), some of which will vest immediately. If the venture is unsuccessful or the hired management becomes uninterested for whatever reason, they still retain any vested shares, that can no longer be used to incentivize work from other parties. Wouldn't a smarter approach be to let the inventor own more of the company, even if he receives sponsored research support for his laboratory, because his commitment to the success of the company is more likely to be sustained? The founders shares can be gradually distributed or diluted by granting shares and options that engage further management and technical expertise.

Universities, founders, and investors are often obsessed about founders' shares, which can seem substantial at the inception of a company. But when you are tens or hundreds of millions of dollars of diluting capital and 7 or more years from a likely exit (let alone the purported $2.6 billion it takes to get a drug to market), it is evident that founders' shares ultimately comprise only a small fraction of the equity to be granted over the long term. Nevertheless, they are fundamental to the negotiation of ownership for an early stage company.

The idea of setting up sponsored research with the laboratory of a scientist founder is not without its challenges. Uncertainty can arise over whether the university is providing uncompensated value to the company, which could affect its not-for-profit status (Conflict of Support); and over who owns new inventions, how they are assigned, and on what terms (Conflict of IP). We believe that both of these can be prospectively handled by thoughtful agreements that focus on enabling progress rather than defensive posturing. For example, Lewis Geffen, a Boston lawyer specializing in Life Sciences and VC suggests considering "an option to include the founder's improvements or related inventions in the original license, which most TTOs are willing to give," and funding the research through an unrestricted grant to the founder's lab [11].

ALIGNING INCENTIVES

The restriction on sponsored research in a founder's laboratory ignores the very real financial stresses on scientists that already exist, not to mention the fact that most are predisposed to honesty, at least with respect to empiric investigation. Because their compensation depends on them raising "soft money," which means publishing scientific manuscripts and presenting research results in grant proposals, researchers' livelihoods are always at risk if their experiments do not go well and their hypotheses are not supported by the data. Accordingly, the immediate motivation to misbehave is more likely to be the certainty that a researcher's lab will be closed down if his grant support dries up, rather than the small probability that he will become rich if his invention becomes a hugely successful drug. There is no reason, *a priori*, why an investigator would be more inclined to cheat on an experiment if it was supported by his company rather than a noncommercial source. The real variable here is the reputation and integrity of the scientist, not the source of funding, and you can't legislate integrity.

In other words, the incentive to scientific fraud is already present and not solely a consequence of commercial potential. If universities were being honest about reducing CoI to maintain research integrity, they would take real steps to reduce CoI for academics. For example, they could completely dissociate the success or failure of experiments from the job security of scientists. Universities could remove the grant-or-perish threat to scientists' livelihood from the equation, granting a stable amount of funding, irrespective of the scope or value of the research effort, index it to inflation, and guarantee it for the duration of employment!

This is of course ridiculous, and hardly the best stimulus for scientific discovery or entrepreneurism. But it is a logical extension of the type of thinking that guides CoI policies related to company relationships. There's a touch of hypocrisy in claiming purity of intent by refusing support from the investigator's company, while at the same time off-loading salary obligations to external grant funds that the investigators themselves are responsible to maintain.

CoI regulations distance investigators from the fair value of their research. This disincentivizes sloppy or criminal acts that would lead to financial gain, but it also disincentivizes activities on the part of the scientist that would contribute to commercial success. Taking away from the inventor all but a small measure of financial participation disdains one of the most important people in the room. Rather than aligning interests, CoI skews them. Instead of functioning like a speed limit on a highway, allowing normal activity but penalizing outliers and miscreants, *CoI policies stop speeding by closing the road.*

There's a better way to reduce conflict of interest: encourage early collaborations with industry. Industry has a ferocious financial incentive to *not make mistakes*. The oversight and layered cross-checking typical of a Big Pharma R&D (research and development) process recognizes the uncertainty intrinsic to the scientific process and is designed to catch what might go undetected in a less rigorous environment. For this reason, industry collaboration is a powerful disincentive for scientific error and should not be discouraged because of the claim that it may have the opposite effect.

We talked about this with Rajul Kakkar, a serial entrepreneur and intensive care cardiologist in Boston. He made the point that "research in a start-up is so many steps away from clinical approval that any errors or fraud will certainly be discovered long before it has any negative impact on patients. The distance is so large to Food and Drug Administration registration, that if you doctor data in a rodent, that project is dead. CoI in the early stages serves nobody's purpose" [9]. Stossel added that the process "does have a natural stop. There is some point where the biology will fail and the program will end" [9].

Failures of scientific interpretation or outright misrepresentation impact investors, of course, and any investment they make in a start-up is clearly a situation of caveat emptor. But the magnitude of their power as buyers provides leverage, despite the absence of perfect information, and even if it's of the "this doesn't smell right" variety. Any deal they write can be structured to reduce incentives for short-term mistakes in scientific decision making: making payments contingent on verifiable milestones, deferring compensation, expecting founders to sacrifice lifestyle to the interests of the company despite progressive and painful dilution. We haven't met an Angel who wants a chunk of their investment to pay substantial consulting fees or salary to a founder/inventor, especially if he retains his academic job. And it's in the founder's interest to play the long game for options and royalty payments, because Angel money is dearly paid for with interest and equity.

Federal CoI regulations are at least smart enough to avoid specifying exactly what relationships are prohibited. As a result, institutions have a great deal of leeway on how they define and manage potential conflicts of interest. CoI practices aren't at fault for intention so much as execution, and we feel the economic incentives for revising these polices are compelling. The utility of CoI regulations, as with other practices that characterize the tech transfer process, is best when it enhances rather than lessens value creation. CoI is at its worst when it inhibits deals, disavows inventors' interests, and seeks to protect institutional integrity by presupposing scientific misconduct. Change is often frustratingly incremental, and there's a national conversation needed among universities on this topic. The subject should be proactive rather than defensive: not how can we protect ourselves from anything bad ever happening, but rather how we can reduce the barriers to commercialization without compromising academic values.

REFERENCES

[1] US 42 C.F.R. Part 50, Subpart F: Promoting Objectivity in Research. <http://www.ecfr.gov/cgi-bin/text-idx?c=ecfr&SID=9928178542077672148956b1fa023755d&rgn=div5&view=text&node=42:1.0.1.4.23&idno=42#sp42.1.50.f>; [accessed 11.05.16].

[2] US 45 C.F.R. Part 94: Responsible Prospective Contractors (45 C.F.R. Part 94). <http://www.ecfr.gov/cgi-bin/retrieveECFR?gp=&SID=b375e3f846d35819320285a892880bc1&mc=true&n=pt45.1.94&r=PART&ty=HTML>; [accessed 11.05.16].

[3] IOM (Institute of Medicine) Conflict of interest in medical research, education, and practice. Washington, DC: The National Academies Press; 2009.

[4] Murray TH, Johnston J, editors. Trust and integrity in biomedical research: the case of financial conflicts of interest. Baltimore: The Johns Hopkins University Press; 2010.

[5] Shamoo AE, Resnik DB. Responsible conduct of research. New York: Oxford University Press; 2015.

[6] Harvard Medical School. Policy on conflicts of interest and commitment. Harvard Medical School. <https://hms.harvard.edu/about-hms/integrity-academic-medicine/faculty-policies-integrity-science/policy-conflicts-interest>; 2016 [accessed 05.05.16].

[7] Booth B. Moving from academia to successful biotech: optimizing tech transfer. LifeSciVC 2016 April 26, 2016. <https://lifescivc.com/2016/04/biotech-startup-optimization-engaging-academic-tech-transfer/#disqus_thread/>; [accessed 05.05.16].

[8] Stossel TP. Pharmaphobia: how the conflict of interest myth undermines American medical innovation. Lanham, Maryland: Rowman & Littlefield; 2015.230.

[9] Interview with authors SD and SF, January 28, 2016.

[10] Howard DJ, Laird FN. The new normal in funding university science. Issues Sci Technol 2013;30(1)<http://issues.org/30-1/the-new-normal-in-funding-university-science/>; [accessed 08.05.16].

[11] Geffen L. Comment on Booth, B. (2016). Moving from academia to successful biotech: optimizing tech transfer. LifeSciVC 2016 April 26, 2016. <https://lifescivc.com/2016/04/biotech-startup-optimization-engaging-academic-tech-transfer/#disqus_thread/>; [accessed 12.05.16].

Chapter 24

Breaking Old Habits

Dr. S. A. Mani has been working for more than 15 years to unravel the problem of cancer metastasis [1]. He is an Associate Professor and Co-Director of the Metastasis Research Center at the MD Anderson Cancer Center in Houston, Texas, but his path to academic success could not have been expected. Mani grew up in a remote village in Tamil Nadu, India, in a home that did not have electricity until he was in high school and which, even now, does not have running water. His parents were subsistence farmers, growing peanuts and rice, and never achieved an education beyond elementary school. Studying by a kerosene lamp, the young Mani aspired to go to college and become a scientist.

Mani recalls the resistance he encountered in his village. At one point, the grocer called him to his store and said, "I heard that you are going to college. Why do you want to waste your time? You know, you will go to college and get some degree and come back to the village and work in the field anyway." Mani remembers, "Just for him, I wanted to prove him wrong." Following an outstanding record in his university studies in biology, he was admitted to the prestigious Indian Institute of Science in Bangalore, India, where he completed his PhD.

When leading cancer researcher Robert Weinberg visited Bangalore in 1998, Mani approached him and asked for a job. Weinberg saw promise in the young man and offered him a coveted postdoctoral fellowship position in his laboratory at the Whitehead Institute laboratory in Cambridge, MA. Working with Weinberg, Mani helped identify the first human gene known to be involved in the metastatic spread of cancer. He then discovered that the gene was a member of a family of genes that induced metastasis by enabling a cancer cell to behave as a stem cell [2]. He runs an active research program at MD Anderson, and is currently meeting with Angel investors in the Boston area about an idea for a company that builds on his research in cancer metastasis.

When we asked Mani how he thought he could transition from a rural village in India to the forefront of international research into cancer metastasis, he recounted an Indian folk tale that his grandmother used to tell. Adult elephants are restrained by relatively small chains, he said, which they could easily break

Preserving the Promise. DOI: http://dx.doi.org/10.1016/B978-0-12-809216-3.00024-5

if they tried. But they do not, because they have been wearing those same chains since they were calves, at which time they were too weak to break them. "As they get older, they do not challenge their original observation, and they remain fettered by early habits even though they could easily overcome the chains. They accept the limitations of their understanding, and are therefore not able to look beyond. In my village, nobody ever tried to do anything different than what everyone else was doing" [1]. The message is profoundly simple: refuse to be bound by the habits and expectations of those around you.

The Valley of Death (VoD) can be envisioned as an elephant bound by such chains. Its operation is constrained by a score of assumptions about how things are *supposed* to be, which have morphed over time into what feels more like an evolutionary dead end than a path to the future. Good people, acting in concert with historical incentives for their roles in the VoD ecosystem, too often end up subverting the mission of this uniquely important field: to convert a biotechnology discovery into meaningful intervention for patients.

The third Translation Gap, *Technology transfer wastes money and innovation*, results from the financial disincentives that make it difficult for the most innovative technologies to leave universities and garner investor support in the VoD. It also includes the conflicts that make it difficult for companies, universities, and their scientific founders to work together *after* a technology has been licensed. Common practices seem to have been codified in defense of property rights and protection from liability, and have brought too many technology transfer offices (TTOs) to the point where they are more interested in preventing bad things from happening than in realizing the value of scientific discovery. The third Translation Gap degrades the prospects for successful biotechnology commercialization through the nature of license deals and the relationships they engender, and enshrines these practices by pursuing metrics and legal process rather than entrepreneurial success.

We could focus on the importance of fulfilling unmet medical needs, economic development, or realizing the promise of intellectual exploration. But the linchpin issue, as with our example of the British boat captains, is operational culture. Humans being what they are, it is unlikely that many in this ecosphere will change their habits based on lofty principles. On the other hand, what might happen if we align these principles to better achieve financial and medical windfalls? The path to adjusting the incentives that drive the system becomes clearer. Technology transfer could play a more effective role in *paving the way* for private money to advance biotechnology. The property leaving the university and the mechanism for extracting rights need to make sense for Angels as well as for the university. Without their investment, passage through the VoD may be impossible.

The likelihood that an Angel will support a biotech start-up depends on the attractiveness of the proposition as one of many investment options, which in turn depends on the health and returns of the VoD marketplace as a whole. Translation Gaps 1 and 3 affect both the short- and long-term decision making of Angels, modulating the calculus that determines whether they will embrace high risk, innovative technologies—or decide not to invest at all.

When we examine sources of waste in technology transfer, our starting point is how to make scarce private investment dollars more effective in generating scientific progress, setting companies on the way to successive investments at favorable terms. Overall, this means finding the most efficient way to start and run a biotechnology company, one that is healthy enough from the outset to survive in the VoD ecosystem.

As we described in the previous chapter, one of the major challenges facing anyone in tech transfer is institutional compulsion around preventing Conflict of Interest (CoI). We're not advocating for abandonment of this very reasonable premise, but against its common practice. As we described earlier, institutional management of CoI effectively divorces a technology from its most knowledgeable and committed caregiver, by putting at arms length the scientist who created it. CoI and the other two essential conflicts of technology transfer, Conflict of Support (CoS) and Conflict of Intellectual Property (CoIP), impose an unnecessary burden on the process. These consume dollars that could be better allocated, and reduce the likelihood that any given invention will survive the VoD, regardless of its innovation or clinical impact. To summarize the three conflicts:

- *Conflict of Interest* prevents investigators from owning substantial equity in the companies they create and from accepting sponsored research money from those companies
- *Conflict of Support* reflects the concern that universities might inadvertently jeopardize their not-for-profit status if they provide real value to spinout companies
- *Conflict of Intellectual Property* concerns the creation of new IP and universities' fear that they won't capture fair value and/or retain control

Collective adherence to these three conflicts is nothing more than an accumulation of bad habits. They impede the formation and launch of new companies, introduce unnecessary friction, and waste money by getting in the way of spinouts efficiently interacting with academic investigators.

Our focus isn't on calling anyone out, but on improving what is, at times, a profoundly inefficient commercialization process. Issues surrounding universities' not-for-profit status and IP ownership can be addressed as a function of perspective and mission. It shouldn't be controversial to ask some probing questions, such as how we might:

- Reduce the costs of technological advancement, limiting unnecessary overhead and upfront transfer costs, and allocating as much of the money raised as possible to essential tasks
- Enhance the cooperation among what is effectively a virtual team of TTO, entrepreneur, business advisors and investors

- Speed up progress to the clinic, in scientific and financial terms, protecting the precious and finite interval before a patent expires
- Lower the amount of money needed to be raised to keep the venture moving forward
- Reduce the impact of overhead on money in, and therefore valuation, which will in turn drive better multiples and make the system more tolerant to future restrictions in drug reimbursement

Improving the efficiency of technology transfer is demonstrably a catalyst to improve the efficiency of the ecosystem; we present three case histories below. The potential exists for a ripple effect, from the earliest point at which a company takes shape around an investment vehicle. It seems only logical that technologies should emerge from universities ready to support a company in the VoD. We talked in Chapter 11, Unintended Consequences of Applying for a Patent, about a softer landing, but the point isn't that new discoveries should be excused from the rigorous demands of commercialization. Rather, it's that they need to be able to land without a crash. A difficult journey shouldn't be made even more arduous through policies that inhibit rather than stimulate creation of value. We are entirely in favor of the goals of tech transfer, which include finding the best ways for universities and companies to work together and creating both meaning and financial value from university research output. We are also proponents for expanding their vision beyond packaging and licensing IP.

COMPANY BUILDING AS A FOCUS OF TECHNOLOGY TRANSFER

The business model of Oxford University Innovation (OUI), the technology transfer arm of the University of Oxford (first noted in Chapter 13: Building a Better Mousetrap), may not be directly applicable for institutions without the resources or cachet of Oxford. But it is a good example of how a flexible commercialization culture can enhance technology transfer and build long-term innovation. Oxford's technology transfer operations have a track record that is among the most successful of such programs globally. In 2015, OUI received £24.6 million in revenue, of which £13.6 million was distributed to the University of Oxford and its faculty, and assisted in raising £25 million in translational research funding [3]. In 2014, OUI was voted as the Technology Transfer Unit of the year by Global University Venturing [4].

OUI starts with a unique attitude and structure. First and foremost, as characterized by longtime CEO Tom Hockaday, "For us the way it was intended to work—we always took the approach within Oxford that we would work with researchers who want to work with us" [5]. Second, OUI is not a division of the university administration, but a fully owned subsidiary of Oxford University, essentially a for-profit institution with a single shareholder. This gives it substantial operational flexibility as it manages all of the University's IP. (Similar to practice in the United States, IP generated by Oxford faculty are technically owned by the University.)

OUI plays an unusually active role in starting companies. They have a total of 100 staff members, of whom 45 are called "project managers" or "technology transfer managers." Hockaday makes a point about the qualifications for these positions: these managers hold scientific PhDs and have not only domain expertise, but also specific industry experience in sales, marketing, or business development. As Hockaday notes, "they understand the language of business and of science." Because their charter is engagement with Oxford scientists, the project managers are expected to create companies around the vision of those clients. "We would start doing the outline business plan, the sort of slide deck with the academics, [and] really building the team of people who become the company. I refer to this as the 'S&M' of university spinout management—we've got the science and the scientists but we haven't got the money and the management ... So how do you go about building this team and how do you introduce the money, and how do you introduce the management of the money?"

For Oxford, company building often involves engaging the Oxford Angels Network (OAN) [6], which consists of investment professionals and private investors with a connection to Oxford and/or an interest in Oxford-based startups. The relationship is based on engagement and mutual interest. Active since 1999, the OAN is structured in a fairly standard way, but benefits from ongoing relationships. According to Hockaday, "We found that you can organize the network, do the usual thing of preparing the teams to present to a roomful investors, and nurture the relationship and see what happens."

Oxford creates and preserves value through licensing and equity distribution that is oriented to long-term success. Hockaday notes that "We license on ... what you could call soft terms, but I'd rather call them sensible. You're licensing to a start-up which has roughly no money and all the money it's got it's going to spend on developing the IP. We've learned over the years not to take upfront fees."

The University does not restrict the amount of equity that a scientific founder takes in a start-up, but their general principle is that, in the beginning, the University should have equal shareholding. Once investors and management are brought on, it typically settles out to a fairly even distribution of perhaps 30% each to the University, the scientific founder, and the investors, with the remaining 10% going to management. Again, the focus is on mutual interest— or at least consensus: "Now every one of those numbers is up for huge debate and argument ... we used to joke that the trick is to lock them into a room and they couldn't come out until they come up with four numbers that added up to hundred," says Hockaday.

This is a distinct contrast to what we've observed at some TTOs, which limit the equity stake of a scientific founder in a company and impose antidilution protection to preserve the ownership held by the university. The Oxford method protects and holds the value of the IP in the start-up stage, but proactively avoids disincentivizing management or future investors, because everyone's shares are fully dilutable.

This may or may not sound good on paper, especially given traditional practice in the US tech transfer community. The proof, of course, is in the figgy pudding. The biggest endorsement of the OUI model is the enthusiasm of their regional investment community, which initiated the Oxford Sciences Innovation plc fund and has raised over £300 million to invest in University of Oxford spinout companies. The fund has a unique philosophy that blends the scope of venture capital (VC) funds with the concept of "patient capital" to create an investment network and pull-through demand for additional investment opportunities. The emphasis is on building value over the long haul.

The Oxford model represents a sustained effort to positively engage the commercialization community at the earliest stage of technology transfer. Now retired, Hockaday summed up his 16 years of work in technology commercialization at OUI: "We are all owned by the University of Oxford ... I've always felt our 'share price' was what the academics thought of us. A key difference is that we really, really help academics build a team that becomes the company. The mindset is not really of a licensing office in administration, *it's an office trying to help a business get going.*"

BUILDING AN INNOVATION COMMUNITY

The OUI model started with a focus on service to Oxford scientists. In contrast, the Wake Forest Baptist Medical Center envisioned a research, industrial, medical, and residential community with a broad charter to stoke healthcare innovation and entrepreneurship [7]. In collaboration with community and governmental support, they established the Wake Forest Innovation Quarter in Winston-Salem, North Carolina, at the site of a manufacturing complex formerly owned by the R.J. Reynolds tobacco company. The Quarter's first tenants were scientists from the Wake Forest School of Medicine's Department of Physiology and Pharmacology and eight researchers from neighboring Winston-Salem State University.

More than two decades later, the site has been transformed into a 250-acre mixed-use district for innovation and economic development and has attracted $800 million in public and private funding [8]. The centerpiece of the complex is the $100 million Wake Forest Biotech Place, a gleaming, glass brick-enclosed transformation of a building that was once used for maintenance of cigarette-making machinery.

The Innovation Quarter now hosts 4000 people working in 70 companies, including the Wake Forest Institute for Regenerative Medicine, a conference center, and the Wet Lab LaunchPad incubator space. It has over 650 apartments and condominiums nearby and a new hotel will be opening soon. It is also a destination for students interested in healthcare. The Wake Forest Baptist Medical

Center will soon complete a $50 million education building for its medical school, and Wake Forest University is planning new undergraduate programs in Biomedical Sciences and Engineering for up to 350 students, that will be based at a University site within the Innovation Quarter.

Overseeing it all since 2012 is Eric Tomlinson, DSc, PhD, President of the Innovation Quarter and Chief Innovation Officer of the Medical Center [7]. Tomlinson is a serial entrepreneur and CEO, having run Somatix, GeneMedicine, and Altea Therapeutics. His experience in building those companies reflects deep expertise in raising private and public financing and executing technology licensing and commercialization deals. By 2012, Tomlinson had retired and was golfing in Australia (Altea having fallen to the 2008 biotech bust), when he received a call inviting him to Winston-Salem.

Shortly after his arrival, he created a new division, Wake Forest Innovations, to handle the technology transfer operations of the Baptist Medical Center. But he doesn't really see his role within the historical definition of technology transfer. "We blew that up. It is much more about collaboration, a two-way street," says Tomlinson. His group provides assistance with capital formation, incubation and early development of start-up companies, testing technologies with a series of validating "stage gate" and animal proof of concept experiments. But underlying all of that is the question of market opportunity. "It is the market that drives everything we do ... What is the market for [the technology]? Are people willing to invest in that?"

For Tomlinson, as for Hockaday, the key is to connect the ecosystem to opportunity, and that requires an entrepreneurial mindset. He recently completed a $15 million fundraise, through the Baptist Medical Center, which will be used to fund the formation of 25 companies. His philosophy: "Why wouldn't you invest in your own people? Innovative thinking is just second nature throughout the medical center." The money is independently managed by Pappas Ventures, a life sciences VC based in Durham, NC. Pappas doesn't have its own money in the fund, but is in place to manage the deal flow and participate when any of these ventures is ready for a larger capital investment.

The movement in Wake Forest may be unusual because of its scale, level of sustained community support, synergies between educational and financial objectives, particular qualifications of its leader—and an impressive piece of real estate. But it is just one example of a new wave of thinking that is essential to advancing the prospects of biotechnology innovation in the VoD. A first rate university technology transfer operation is expensive on the front end, and unlikely to maximize the value of University inventions unless there is also an ecosystem in place with the *cooperative instinct* to advance those technologies. Tech transfer is not simply a set of procedures to monetize the product of university research labs. It can and should be a source of leadership that engenders confidence, stimulates broad community support, and de-risks technologies to ready them for early-stage private investment.

WHAT IS THE LEAST WE CAN DO?

OUI and the Wake Forest Innovation Quarter are examples of what can be done, but these are unusual initiatives that benefit from long tenure and substantial funding. It's important to ask the question of what can be done with the more limited resources of many TTOs. The objective isn't any different: to overcome the three conflicts we've outlined in tech transfer and maximize existing eco-systems to enhance the investment proposition for Angels, who will inevitably be called upon to support new companies.

Martin (Marty) Lehr is trying to build a synergistic, bare-bones model for academic start-ups [9]. He has a history in VC and academic research and was a Senior Associate for six years at Osage Partners, a VC that specializes in university start-ups, before founding Context Therapeutics in 2015. Context is trying to make a small molecule drug that targets the Sigma1 pathway for treatment of prostate cancer. Sigma1 has long been known to be involved in the perception of pain, but it was recently discovered by Dr. Felix Kim at Drexel to play an important role in protein turnover, which makes it an excellent cancer target [10]. The core innovation is the mechanism around how Sigma1 works in cancer, but it's also know-how, assays to measure activity, and the ability to derivatize compounds.

Because Drexel University had a limited experience with biotechnology technology transfer, Lehr was able to build the structure of his relationship with Drexel from scratch, enabling him to operate within the limitations of a small Angel investment. Context Therapeutics stock is split among the President (Lehr) and scientific founders, in rough correlation to their present value to the company and time commitment, and is fully dilutable. The founders receive no salary or consulting fees, but there's a large stock option pool—25% of the company uncommitted—that can be used to incentivize additional work.

Research in Context Therapeutics is performed through a sponsored research agreement with Drexel University, an "all-in" contract that pays for salaries of two postdoctoral level scientists, supplies, and university overhead. Most of the work within Drexel involves assay creation, and validation of assays that are handed over to contract research firms for the drug discovery work. Lehr has prospectively handled new IP coming from the relationship by building into the university agreement an option for Context to license any IP that's filed, within 6 months of the time of filing the provisional patent application. Optioned improvements that simply expand usefulness will not necessarily incur additive milestone or royalty payments as they are, by definition, improvements on IP that is already licensed—and therefore intrinsic to Context's ability to take the best molecule to the clinic. Plus, as Lehr points out, the company is already paying for the research as well as the filing, prosecution, and maintenance of those patents.

Lehr's model would raise red flags at many universities, but he has anticipated some of the potential objections. First, he compensates the university for its contributions to the success of the company by giving equity as well as royalties, in addition to the overhead costs that he pays as part of the sponsored research agreement. He has also clearly communicated to researchers performing work in the academic lab, funded by Context, that their IP is already committed to a company, and that any royalties they receive—essentially deferred compensation—will be pieces of a pie that cannot grow beyond its fixed size.

Lehr's model is one version of a number of nontraditional agreements, undoubtedly growing but just as surely a small percentage of all tech transfer contracts. We describe it in detail because we think it offers a strong conceptual and practical step forward. We feel that sponsored research to the scientific founder's lab should be a practical option for most academic spinouts. CoI issues can be managed proactively by full disclosure and clear communication with the investors.

As a rule, founders don't stay indefinitely in CEO roles. In *The Founder's Dilemma*, Noam Wasserman notes that by the time ventures are three years old, 50% of founders are no longer the CEO, and that fewer than 25% ultimately lead their companies' IPOs [11]. But he also notes the importance of vision, labors of love, and even overconfidence in the early stages of a company's development: "Attachment, overconfidence and naïveté may be necessary to get new ventures up and running, but these emotions later create problems." So it's in the natural evolution of most start-ups that they eventually cede control to investors and transition control from the founder. There is, in fact, a relationship between higher performance and the introduction of more experienced executive management.

The problem is when tech transfer policies and the deals that accompany them too soon create a distance between a company and the vision behind it, relegating scientist founders to a supporting role. As in the models we've cited, there are alternative approaches by which: (1) universities can benefit from additional funds flowing to their scientists (including reimbursement of overhead costs); (2) the original scientific founder can continue to apply their creative energy to progression of their invention; and (3) public (SBIR/STTR) (Small Business Innovation Research/Small Business Technology Transfer) and private (Angel) investment dollars can be stretched to cover more development and less transactional costs.

We conditionally support universities and founders sharing the majority of equity on a fully dilutable basis, as is the policy for OUI and Context. This preserves value in the hands of those who are most committed to the success of the technology, while leaving it appropriately open to dilution when the company receives new money or work. Most people would agree conceptually that it doesn't make sense to have antidilution provisions to protect the interests of a person or organization who is not providing ongoing value to the company. Investors would argue, of course, that their funding is precisely the source of that ongoing value. It's a question of balance and continuing to access the passion and expertise that gestated the company.

One of this book's authors was able to manage a similar ownership structure with his own company. In the beginning, he owned a majority of the founder's shares. Eight years later, after the company had raised several million dollars from Angels as convertible debt, the founder's share was heavily diluted but the company had achieved a sound technical and financial footing. Early-stage therapeutics companies face 7–10 years of development and potentially hundreds of millions in dollars in additional investment prior to market introduction. Trying to preserve value in the short term by protecting founders' shares makes no sense, but real and substantial participation in the long term is, or should be, a necessary and reasonable proposition for all of the parties.

THE MINIMAL COMMERCIALIZATION UNIT

Improving success in the VoD means optimizing the intersection of intellectual property and finance, while reducing the diversion of resources from anything that does not contribute to value creation. These objectives, the initiatives we've described in this chapter, and prior research on the minimum product requirements for a viable launch lead us to a concept we'll call the *minimal commercialization unit* (MCU) for a biotech start-up. This is an acknowledged adaptation of a term coined by Eric Ries [12]. A succinct definition of his *minimum viable product* concept might be creating the least feature-intensive product that delivers enough value to be desired and purchased by early adopters. If we put that in the context of a VoD investment, we can define the biotech MCU as an investment proposition, collateralized by IP, that can create value for prospective buyers—and do so utilizing a minimum amount of overhead. It creates that value by efficiently converting seed-stage investments into proof of concept experiments. For example, Context Therapeutics keeps expenses to a minimum by incentivizing the founding scientist with equity and leveraging the university infrastructure to perform sponsored research in his lab. In short, the MCU represents the most efficient delivery of biotech innovation into the VoD as a viable investment proposition.

A biotech start-up spends time and resources performing continued scientific experiments, acquiring and protecting IP, developing a nascent organization, and raising money to cover all of the above. The first step is the science of discovery. The second is a frictive process in which everyone, from the universities that proffer the IP to the attorneys who prosecute it, relies on the lubricating power of money. The third is normal and expected overhead, which is minimized in the start-up environment by accessing whatever free advice may be available, utilizing virtual teams, and deferring compensation. The fourth is the time and resource sink of business development, imposed on founders who often have little experience and less interest in devoting themselves to an ongoing fundraising dog-and-pony show.

So what does this have to do with an MCU? Intuitively, if we can minimize the Three Conflicts of tech transfer, we should be able to progress to an MCU more efficiently and with less resource-draining baggage. Our first suggestion for doing so is to stop impeding, for spurious reasons, research being done in the academic laboratory of the founding scientist(s). If we look at CoI, for example, why not reframe the discussion from one of "How do we protect ourselves if an inventor is dishonest?" to "How can we construct an agreement that defines a collaborative research program where CoI is intrinsically *not* in anyone's interest?" If a lab is not doing anything deceptive now, then there's no reason to suppose that additional support from a sponsored research agreement will change that. There is, in fact, every reason to believe that commercial oversight can actually reduce "honest bias" mistakes that come from pursuing an unvalidated path. CoS and CoIP can be similarly managed through specific and proactive definitions of collaboration, rather than proscriptive policy.

A sponsored research agreement in this context would define the field(s) of the collaboration, with the understanding that IP resulting from the collaboration is *jointly owned*. The ownership interest of the university in the joint IP would be prospectively and exclusively assigned to the company sponsoring research in exchange for prenegotiated milestone and royalty payments. The fact that IP created with joint support is transferred for a fee would prevent the company from receiving value from the university without compensation, and thus the basis for worrying about CoS.

It naturally follows that the investigator would not require any additional consulting fees or payments in this arrangement, although sponsored research funds could be used to support a portion of his existing academic compensation.

The conventional wisdom of investment might get in the way, of course. Investors may balk at paying for research in a contract that could potentially incur additional milestone payments or royalties. Stepping back to a broader look, however, such an arrangement actually means more of their money would be dedicated to the scientific progress that validates their investment, increases valuation, and enables them to achieve the next round of funding on an uptick rather than a down round. Furthermore, we only envision this as a short-term arrangement, for the phase of a company's lifetime when elemental scientific experiments are critical and the cash lifeblood to support them most uncertain. The flow-through benefit in reducing overhead is obvious: being able to use a founder's lab allows a company to minimize expenditures for real estate, equipment, and regulatory oversight, and reduces the need to hire new staff into an unstable venture.

The research to be funded would be specific to commercialization, and therefore outside the realm of traditional, nondilutive grant funding. We're thinking here about work that enhances value (and valuation): experiments that extend proof of concept and validate the foundational IP, strengthen or expand the IP portfolio, and prospectively address the technical questions that inevitably arise during investor due diligence.

Universities would need to make the arrangement attractive for early stage companies by keeping the costs reasonable and not imposing unreasonable overhead charges. The rationale for doing so is likely to encounter bureaucratic resistance but is no less clear for that. The work being done under such an agreement enhances the value and financial upside of property in which universities already have a substantial vested interest, and economically de-risks IP which intrinsically faces high odds of failure. Reducing add-on royalties or stacking milestones improves the return on investment calculus for investors as a reduction in the cost of the relationship, while preserving value for the founder, the university, and the investor.

What we're talking about isn't very different from the idea of a proof of concept fund, except that investors establish ownership early, and the concept might therefore be best suited for spinouts from universities that are not able to attract significant grant support. For investors, dedicating more of their funding solely to development activity means quicker and much less expensive failures, and the potential for seed money to fund opportunities otherwise deemed "too early." We imagine a staged process where solid scientific progress feeds on itself, reduces the burden on universities from declining funding, and reduces the frustration of urgent but expensive patent filings.

For this to work, everybody needs to get out of their own way. Investigators have to realize that someone willing to commercialize their work is offering something more valuable than consulting fees to work on their own inventions. Those charged with protecting universities from CoI need to recognize that there's a better way than "defense is the best offense" to assure that investigators, who are by and large honest people, won't be induced by commercial interests to start cheating at science if they're not cheating already. Lawyers can't prevent all bad things from happening by recommending no one get out of bed in the morning.

Getting everyone in alignment, recognizing and acting with an appreciation of each other's interests, means deals won't go away that should have happened. It means clinical value remains in the forefront, instead of short-term financial mandates. And it means technology transfer serves as the catalyst it's meant to be for launching important new biotechnologies.

REFERENCES

[1] Mani SA. Interview with author SD, April 18, 2016.
[2] Goldberg C. Breakthroughs seen in cancer spread and stem cells. New York Times, September 9, 2008. <http://www.nytimes.com/2008/09/09/health/09iht-gene.1.16007554.html?pagewanted=all&_r=0>; 2008 [accessed 18.04.16].
[3] Isis Innovation. Annual Report. <http://www.isis-innovation.com/wp-content/uploads/2014/08/Isis-Annual-Report-2015-30Sep15-.pdf>; 2015.
[4] Global University Venturing. Technology Transfer Unit of the Year: Isis Innovation. <http://www.globaluniversityventuring.com/article.php/4049/technology-transfer-unit-of-the-year-isis-innovation>; 2014 [accessed 23.04.16].
[5] Interview with authors SD and SF April 13, 2016.

[6] Isis Angels Network. <http://isis-innovation.com/about/networks/isis-angels-network/>; 2016 [accessed 25.04.16].

[7] Wake Forest Innovation Quarter. <http://www.innovationquarter.com/>; 2016 [accessed 25.04.16].

[8] Tomlinson, Eric. Interview with author SD, April 22, 2016.

[9] Lehr M. Interview with author SD, February 1, 2016.

[10] Kim FJ, Schrock JM, Spino CM, Marino JC, Pasternak GW. Inhibition of tumor cell growth by sigmal ligand mediated translational repression. Biochem Biophys Res Commun 2012;426:177–82.

[11] Wasserman N. The founder's dilemma, anticipating and avoiding the pitfalls that can sink a startup. Princeton, NJ: Princeton University Press; 2011.

[12] Ries N. The lean startup: how today's entrepreneurs use continuous innovation to create radically successful businesses. New York, NY: Crown Business Publishing; 2011.

Epilogue

Chapter 25

Epilogue: Why We Do This

Andrew is an African American in his mid-30s. He looks healthy and comfortable, although he's sitting in an infusion chair at the hospital with an intravenous medication flowing into his arm. The story that brought him here began in 2011, when he noticed a change in his eyesight.

"I was a barber and I started losing my sight in my left eye. It was a dot and I thought it was my glasses or something in my eye, and then I started getting headaches, and I never had headaches in my life" [1]. He went to the emergency room, where he was found to be in a hypertensive crisis with a systolic blood pressure over 200 mm Hg. "They got a CAT scan and said that my brain had swollen and was pressing against the optic nerve. That's why I was losing my sight." His kidneys were also showing signs of damage. The doctors got Andrew's blood pressure under reasonably good control with antihypertensive medication, but he began to develop flu-like symptoms and his headaches returned. "So, about a month later, I found myself back at the hospital. That's when they told me 'your kidneys have failed and we're going to take you down to dialysis right now.'"

Andrew had a condition called atypical hemolytic uremic syndrome (HUS), but because the anemia and low platelet counts characteristic of full-blown HUS were not yet present, his physicians were unable to diagnose the true cause of his high blood pressure and kidney failure. He continued his dialysis treatments for 2 years, until a kidney became available from a living donor and he received a transplant.

Everything seemed to be going pretty well after an early rejection episode was brought under control. But, almost a year after the transplant, "all of a sudden my creatinine [a measure of kidney function] went from 3 to 9. They said 'something is wrong but we don't know what it is. Your blood platelets are dropping, your hemoglobin is not right'—all these words that I had to have them explain to me."

His doctors made a provisional diagnosis of atypical HUS and instituted plasma exchange, but that had no effect. "They told me there were giving me this eculizumab and would see what it would to do. And they said, 'that's the last step, if this doesn't work, then.... '" The eculizumab did work. Andrew's blood counts stabilized, then recovered, and his hypertension became easier to control with medications. That was almost 10 months ago. He is now eligible to receive another kidney transplant.

We asked him if the donor knew that the kidney failed. "Yeah, we're in contact. She felt more sympathetic for me. She's a nice girl. I finally met her at the banquet for the donors and the recipients. I asked her, what made her donate a kidney? She said she was in Kuwait, in the military, and she came across something on the internet that said donate. So when she got back she just donated. She didn't care who it went to, she just wanted to donate. So that's really amazing. It takes a lot for someone to do that."

Andrew's life has settled into a rhythm. He does hemodialysis at home and is back to work, but only part time. "I don't work as much as I would like to work. A lot of times I'm at the doctor, or I'm tired. I don't have the energy that I used to have." He appreciates the time he has with family, "I want to see my children grow up, to see my grandchildren grow up," and he reflects on the spiritual meaning of his illness and recovery. "God is in control of all things. He's got me where he wants to have me, his plan is the ultimate plan, and I put my sole reliance on him."

Three months after this interview, Andrew's physician reviewed Andrew's order for eculizumab with one of the authors, before dropping it off in the hospital infusion unit. Laughing, he said "He doesn't even see me in clinic any more. I'm old news to him. I fixed him!"[1] [2].

Andrew's story captures the conflict and promise of the modern process that converts academic discoveries into therapeutics. We first discussed eculizumab in Chapter 5, Biotechnology and the Future of Pharma, as one of a crop of new biotech drugs that hit the market with stratospheric prices. Eculizumab is a true child of academia, based on discoveries made by Dr. Leonard Bell when he was working as a cardiologist at the Yale School of Medicine in the 1990s [3]. Incentivized by an orphan drug designation and the potential for virtually unlimited pricing, Bell's vision became a blockbuster drug and his company, Alexion, achieved a 2016 market capitalization of over $35 billion [4].

The investment thesis of a blockbuster drug for a small number of patients depends on astronomical pricing and assumes that enough patients will be insulated from the costs by their insurance plans. This works for companies financially, but it diverts development attention from larger problems with less profit potential. Serious public health issues, such as the rapid increase in multi-drug resistant bacterial diseases, are deprioritized in favor of short-term business opportunities among orphan populations (<200,000 patients).

The high risk and massive expense of biotech drug development virtually demand a spectacular payday for those drugs that make it to the clinic. Consequently, the modern drug development paradigm and focus on specialty drugs is extremely vulnerable to the possible advent of drug pricing controls.

---

1. At the time of this writing, Andrew has received a second kidney transplant and is doing well.

Such changes seem inevitable despite the industry's heavy investment in lobbying; it is not sustainable for the insurers, Medicaid or Medicare to spend billions in category after category, on a few thousand patients per drug. To preserve investor ROI we need to reduce the expense of early stage biotech, minimizing overhead costs and aligning financial incentives towards long term goals.

Big Pharma has already sought cost efficiencies by outsourcing much of today's discovery to smaller companies, but there's no way for all the worthwhile innovations to get funded until they become viable acquisition targets for the industry. So improving the process of getting new drugs through the Valley of Death (VoD) becomes essential. This calls not only for optimizing development, but also for improving the desirability of the investment model for early-stage investors and spending less money on inventions that can never make it to the clinic. In the aggregate, reducing system costs means less amortization of development failures (because they won't progress), and therefore a reduced "all-in" cost for the drugs that make it to the finish line. If it costs less to get a drug to market, it may be possible to profitably do so at something less than the current dizzying level of new drug pricing.

Andrew's story also reminds us of what is at stake here. When we define a patient population in a business plan or in an investor pitch slide deck, we're thinking about potential "customers." When we review the patient population that participated in a clinical study, we're thinking about "cases" and "outcomes." We're too prone to forget that these "populations" are groups of *individuals* with a single commonality, their disease, but otherwise singular with respect to their experience, meaning, and connections to other people. When we talk about creating a cure, the context is much greater than a transaction. What we create with biotechnology will become part of these individuals' stories of healing or loss, their hope or regret. We who do this for a living—administer to patients, research new pathways, analyze the value of unmet need, invest in new healthcare solutions—do so because we want to be part of that story.

There's an intrinsic distinction between healthcare and everything else, no matter how innovative or aspirational or apparently enriching those other technology opportunities may be. The difference is this: the product of what we do, whether scientific creation or a role in commercialization, has the potential to have a life-or-death impact. There's a reason people get involved in healthcare and never want to do anything else, It comes down to standing at that boundary in time, before which there was only illness and after which there was a cure, or at least a better quality of life, and being able to say "I helped to make that happen."

The choices we make in the healthcare VoD need to be about more than what's going to make a heap of money. They're about what belongs there, and what we can realistically push through, because at the end of the day those choices determine who will be have a chance at a better life—or a better chance of life. In this way, biotechnology is a sacred trust. It begins with the Mother's Day race that opened this book, shines a light on a secret of nature, is packaged into IP that supports an investment thesis, and is realized in the laboratory. If all goes well, the biotech/healthcare VoD is the commercial and scientific odyssey that enables a discovery to reach a patient.

Dr. Gary Pisano, a Professor of Business Administration at the Harvard Business School, has argued that organizational innovation is necessary to realize the full potential of biotechnology innovation [5]. He cites the work of the influential economist Dr. Alfred Chandler, who showed how the advances of mechanization and the creation of railroads enabled industry to pursue mass production—but observed that mass production only became economically viable through the creation of novel methods of organization, finance and management. Pisano distinguishes science-based companies, like biotech or pharma, from other product- or technology-based companies because (1) their business model depends on continuous, real-time creation of new knowledge and (2) they have a long lead time between discovery and the marketplace. During this time, such companies are continually challenged by the potential failure of their scientific programs. "Science-based businesses need to be able to manage and reward long term risky investments, integrating across bodies of knowledge, and learning cumulatively over time," he writes.

These burdens dovetail with the need for science-based companies, and especially the early-stage companies trying to navigate their way through the VoD, to simultaneously juggle the ongoing threats of scientific and financial uncertainty. As Pisano explains, "The science-based businesses of biotech are a novel organizational form. Unlike the corporate labs of decades past, they face the winds of market forces without the buffer of rich revenue streams and dominant market positions. And ... they face prolonged periods of risky investment in research." These factors place unusual burdens on biotech, which aren't effectively addressed by classic organizational structures.

The business model for biotech VoD companies is unusual in other ways. The foundational basis for a biotech is its singular intellectual property, but it is a property that has unproven safety or efficacy, and unclear clinical implications. By contrast, a technology company might depend on an equally unique microprocessor design, but the path to market is a function of technical and manufacturing challenges, not a question of what happens when you put the new design inside a human.

Moreover, due to deep cuts in Big Pharma's internal R&D spending, the biotechnology industry depends more than ever on IP that originates within university laboratories ... and therefore must undergo a technology transfer process in order to begin commercial development. By granting ownership of these discoveries to universities, the Bayh-Dole Act requires that they participate in explicitly commercial activities to transfer these into the commercial realm, a task for which they were not organizationally designed. Thus, the source of the raw material of biotech development and investing, the molecular discoveries that get packaged into IP and licensed to companies, is a not-for-profit entity that usually loses money on its technology transfer activities. It should be obvious that any business in which a supplier spends more money than it earns on a sale is inefficient, and maybe not even sustainable. Nonetheless, we rely on technology transfer offices (TTOs) to launch the IP that drives the biotechnology industry. They will do better if they operate in a way that increases the profitability of their commercialization function. Overcoming the inefficiencies created by university ownership of biotechnology will require new organizational models within academia, and in its interactions with companies and the VoD ecosystem as a whole.

Organizational innovation is also needed to address the fact that most biotechnology start-ups are funded in their early stages by Angel investors, who buy an interest in a financial instrument, an investment collateralized by the scientific IP obtained from a university. This funding mechanism leads to differentiation of technologies primarily on the basis of whether they can support an investment thesis, rather than on their technological distinction or potential clinical utility. Investor due diligence is supportive of, but not necessarily aligned with, the level of innovation or impact of a technology, because Angels need to select those companies that have the best chance of providing a favorable return on investment.

For their part, start-ups need to recognize the distinction between mission and strategy. From the standpoint of investors in the VoD, fledgling companies are financial opportunities supported by scientific plans, and those plans must support a milestone-based investment paradigm with the wherewithal to survive many rounds of investment. The VoD business model for biotech, almost by definition, involves starting a drug discovery process without a validated drug candidate and without sufficient funds to complete the process. Scientific novelty alone is not a guarantee of commercial viability. Even the presence of an important unmet medical need is insufficient evidence of investability.

These four distinctive factors put together—the risk of scientific inquiry the pivotal role of academia in commercialization, the reality that Angels are funding financial propositions based on exploitable science, and the disconnect between innovation and investability—are the sources for what we have coined *The Translation Gap*. The Translation Gap encompasses obstacles to commercialization that originated when the opportunity of Bayh–Dole collided with this simple reality of investment: the number of companies in the VoD far outnumbers the capacity of investors or industry to support them. Any new venture requiring capital, and biotech in particular, is therefore subject to the vagaries of constituent priorities and must run a financial gauntlet that may be only tangentially connected to the quality of the science or the medical need. Operational innovation can help overcome the Translation Gap, improve the commercialization prospects for the best of academic discoveries, and improve the ROI for investors.

Translation Gap 1, *Universities don't make what companies need*, highlights the disconnect between the metrics for success of academic research, the priorities of tech transfer offices, and the practical constraints that enable support of an investment thesis in the VoD. Patenting university technologies that have no realistic chance of commercial success is not good for universities, inventors, or the drug development ecosystem. It's a long road to convert an innovative discovery into a drug, and there's low predictability at the outset. And there's no question it's a struggle to balance our attraction to the new with our desire to do something that actually makes a difference. What is clear is that no one wants to waste time, money, and effort. Alternate models of evaluation and financial support, prior to patenting, have been demonstrated to be effective. The common feature of these initiatives is greater collaboration and risk sharing among universities, public agencies, and the commercial ecosystem.

Translation Gap 2, *Good innovation is not always a good investment*, describes the tension between Angel investors' need to achieve a financial return and society's need for innovative technologies that satisfy unmet medical needs. For Angel investors, supporting biotechnology is entirely discretionary, and their financial interests largely arbitrate which technologies will advance to commercial development. The decision of Angels to invest follows a due diligence process that ultimately asks whether a company can reach an exit. More than anything else, doing so means surviving a series of financial transactions over many years, collateralized by a high-risk scientific proposition and underpinned by the hope/expectation of being acquired.

Angel decision making is also affected by cognitive patterns that affect risk-reward decisions and is influenced by macroeconomic factors that impact risk tolerance. The anticipated ability of a healthcare investment to have a substantial exit, and the psychological factors that affect behavior, have only an indirect connection to innovation per se or clinical impact. The focus, rather, is the investment proposition. Investment terms are (naturally enough) structured to favor the interests of investors over those of company founders, and, whether formally structured as "equity" or "debt," add to the development burden of any high-risk company in the VoD. Investor interests are short- rather than long-term, and may not be aligned with promotion of the most important technologies or with sustained viability.

Translation Gap 3, *Technology transfer wastes money and innovation* describes the expense and loss of value that occur when technologies leave universities and are licensed or assigned to companies in the VoD. License terms consume investor money through upfront payments before real value has been created. University Conflict of Interest policies stand in the way of incentivizing scientific founders. Self-imposed internal roadblocks inhibit the intellectual and financial synergies that could result, for example, from companies sponsoring research in the scientific founders' laboratories.

We applied Porter's Five Forces to characterize the key power imbalances that contribute to dysfunction in the VoD and reinforce the persistence of the Translation Gap. We took as our starting point the observation that the primary business in the VoD is the production and selling of financial instruments by start-up companies. *Rivalry among existing competitors* and *the threat of new entrants* are so high that the vast majority of companies entering the VoD will find themselves in fierce competition for a finite pool of investment dollars. While they won't be able to survive to an exit on Angel funding alone, it's clear that enormous power in the VoD resides with the Angel investors. These are the *buyers* who determine which VoD start-ups will receive funding and on what terms.

The second major locus of power in the VoD is with the universities; these are the *suppliers* from whom new companies source IP, the underlying collateral for investment. Because they have a monopoly on the technologies their faculty produce and do not rely on any particular license for their economic survival, and because they are not fundamentally dependent on income from IP, their ability to set the terms for licensing—or to refuse to license a technology altogether (for any reason)—is virtually absolute.

The Five Forces not only help explain the dynamics of the issue, but provide guidance for realigning incentives and operational practices. The objective, of course, is to generate better outcomes. Although our overriding goal is to improve the translation of university technologies into therapeutics, we have written this book from an equally foundational objective of improving the success of early-stage biotechnology investments. Without the goodwill and continued infusion of dollars from the Angel investment community, the vast majority of academic biotech spinout companies would not have a chance for success. If Angel investors find financial success in biotech, pharma, and medical device investments, if their portfolio companies survive and create novel drugs with their licensed technologies, their appetite for these inherently high-risk ventures will increase. Founders, university TTOs, investors, clinicians, and most of all, patients, will continue to reap benefits from this extraordinary field of scientific discovery.

Angels have no obligation to invest in any startup, and their ability to walk away is the source of the power and influence they wield over startups that need their money. They are the nexus of decisions about what will be supported, and naturally prefer investments where at least some of the risk has been taken out. Public and philanthropic initiatives that de-risk the financial instruments in the VoD are thus enablers of early private investment, and can encourage the flow of money toward important unmet medical needs.

There are a lot of ways for Angels to exert their influence: for example, by encouraging universities to focus on certain types of patents, to make licensing terms more sensible, and to enable closer relationships between companies and the academic institutions that spawned them. This has to be better than digging in for another point of interest on a convertible note or liquidation preference on an equity investment. In short, it would be a shame if Angels didn't use their enormous buyer power, not only to drive their particular technology interests, but to improve the functioning of the VoD ecosystem.

The plight of university TTOs is understandable. They've been saddled with an unfunded mandate by Bayh–Dole and the outsized expectations that entails, while being forced to operate within the defensive financial and legal constraints of the university. A more productive perspective on the part of university administrators might begin with a reappraisal of the value of risk, a reassessment of the types of interactions with industry whose benefits outweigh the risks, and a recasting of what it means to contribute to the entrepreneurial ecosystem—adding value to their technologies beyond negotiating licenses.

It is inevitable that conflicts will arise when universities try to reconcile the commercial practices of technology licensing and commercialization with their academic precepts. It doesn't have to be a disconnect, however. Why shouldn't TTOs affirm by action the academic principles of their parent institutions, such as the objective collection and analysis of data, data sharing, peer review, and collaboration? Why shouldn't technology licensing practices be focused on creating long-term value, instead of having a transactional focus? Why should they resemble a used car sale, with high-pressure negotiations designed to extract the maximum price before the buyer has had a good chance to take more than a quick test drive?

In his book, *Better, A Surgeon's Notes on Performance*, Atul Gawande, MD, shows how assumptions about the quality of our performance are subject to attribution bias, and should be challenged and improved by objective data analysis [6]. He exhorts us to "Count something. If you count something ... you will learn something interesting." In the field of human health, metrics should count for something; they should reflect outcomes that make a difference. To get to the right ones, we need to determine which measures will move us in the right direction. The scientific process creates discoveries that can change the lives of patients; we should apply the same process to guide those discoveries through the VoD.

Angels too need to reflect on what they really want. Frankly, if the objective is simply and solely ROI, then despite the enormous rewards of a biotech home run, the risk:reward ratio is probably a lot better in other areas than early-stage medicine. Healthcare investors almost have to be in it for something more than ROI, but it's nevertheless stunning how little formal information is available about the results of Angel investments in the VoD. We've presented some of the data that's gathered by organizations like the Center for Venture Research at UNH and the Angel Capital Association. There's a need for more: objective, accurate, anonymous data that explores the how, why, and where of early-stage healthcare investing.

Angel investing will always be an educated bet based on probabilities. If we stop to think about it, though, it's all a bit irrational and therefore can't be just about the financial return. How many people would invest in a mutual fund if they could not estimate, based on past performance of that fund, how much of their money they'd be likely to gain or lose? These investments have no history other than the inferred value of the IP and history of the entrepreneur. We're all for betting on both the jockey and the horse. But we're also convinced, as we hope we've made clear over the course of this work, that there's considerable room to improve a system that has for too long been taken at face value *because that's the way it has always operated.* The failure rate of new companies matters, particularly in medicine, because the result of a one-size-fits-all investment paradigm means that, down the road, someone doesn't survive. And that shouldn't be acceptable to founders, universities, investors, or society.

REFERENCES

[1] "Andrew" is a pseudonym. Interview with author SD, February 4, 2016.

[2] Discussion with author SD, May 12, 2016.

[3] Herper M. How a $440,000 drug is turning Alexion into biotech's new innovation powerhouse. Forbes 2012. September 5, 2012. <http://www.forbes.com/sites/matthewherper/2012/09/05/how-a-440000-drug-is-turning-alexion-into-biotechs-new-innovation-powerhouse/#58a92b1256c7>.

[4] <http://finance.yahoo.com/q?s=ALXN>; [accessed 15.05.16].

[5] Pisano GP. The evolution of science-based business: innovating how we innovate. Ind Corp Change 2016;19(2):465–82.

[6] Gawande A. Better: a surgeon's notes on performance. New York, NY: Metropolitan Books; 2007.

Index

Printed in the United States
By Bookmasters